AF596700

UNIVERSITY
OF
JOHANNESBURG

Linguistics for legal interpretation

Terrence R Carney

UJ Press

Linguistics for legal interpretation

Published by UJ Press
University of Johannesburg
Library
Auckland Park Kingsway Campus
PO Box 524
Auckland Park
2006
https://ujonlinepress.uj.ac.za/

First published 2023

https://doi.org/10.36615/9781776438891

978-1-7764388-8-4 (Paperback)
978-1-7764388-9-1 (PDF)
978-1-7764446-0-1 (EPUB)
978-1-7764446-1-8 (XML)

This publication had been submitted to a rigorous double-blind peer-review process prior to publication and all recommendations by the reviewers were considered and implemented before publication.

Copy editor: Luke Perkins
Cover design: Hester Roets, UJ Graphic Design Studio
Typeset in 10/13pt Merriweather Light

Contents

Law cases contain real language used by real people who present real language problems to solve. Legal battles over language almost beg for a linguistic analysis that bridges the sometimes abstract world of the classroom to the everyday reality of life.

Roger W Shuy, 2008

1. Introduction

1.1. A book about linguistics for legal interpretation

During a trip to India many years ago, I would frequent local markets looking for whatever. Most of the markets would consist of makeshift tables displaying goods of all kinds. Some sellers would only have a tablecloth spread out on the dirt with a number of items for sale. Whenever I walked by these floor displays, the sellers would call out to me as they point to the tablecloth, saying 'Come into my shop; come, come and look. Looking is free.' The fact that each of these sellers would refer to their tablecloths as *shops*, fascinated me. When is a shop a shop? The *Oxford South African Concise Dictionary* defines the word *shop* as a building (or part thereof) where goods or services are sold (DUSAE, 2010:1094). Does this imply that a shop must always be a built structure? Must it contain walls of some kind and a roof? Must a shop have doors and windows? When should we use the word *kiosk*? What about a *market stall*? Definitions of *kiosk* and *stall* also indicate a booth or compartment of sorts, an upright structure. Where does this leave the Indian blanket with items? And what about me? What was I doing at that market? If I were buying anything from one of these Indian merchants, what does that make me? A shopper? What is good for the goose is surely good for the gander! If I were shopping, I could possibly argue that I was buying items from different shops.

We do not have to look as far as India to find odd yet typical examples of ways that we lexicalise concepts in our daily lives. Most houses in South Africa have at least two doors: one in front and a back or side door. Growing up, I learnt that the back door was synonymous with *kitchen door*. This was especially true when the house had more than two doors. When people referred to the back door, they implied the kitchen door. This distinction seems to remain, in my culture at least, even when the kitchen door is very often at the front of the house. Culturally speaking, definitions of *shop* or *back door* might not pose much trouble. However, when people fight over words on legal grounds, semantic interpretations may become problematic quite quickly. A piece of cloth on the floor might not technically qualify as a shop and a back door at the front of a house is possibly an oxymoron. Yet, deciding what words mean within a set context might not always be that easy.

In *ABC Mining v CSARS*, Justice Windell had to decide whether certain tax deductions qualified as incidental costs.[1] The taxpayer in this case, ABC Mining, bought prospecting rights from another company and then proceeded to claim the expenditure incurred as a deduction in terms of section 15(*b*) of the Income Tax Act.[2] This section allows deductions derived from mining operations incurred on prospecting operations or any costs considered incidental to the operation. Because ABC Mining did not conduct any prospecting themselves, they could not deduct expenditure for prospecting.[3] However, they argued that the acquisition of prospecting rights was necessary for prospecting to take place and consequently for the mine to earn an income, which made the costs incidental.[4] The South African Revenue Service (SARS) disallowed the deduction.[5]

It is understandable that SARS denied a deduction for prospecting operations where no prospecting took place. But why does SARS not allow the purchase of prospecting rights as incidental costs? The word *incidental* occurs 34 times across the ruling's 37 pages – obviously, it must be important. The Income Tax Act does not define *Incidental costs*, which means the court must decide what the words mean within context. This makes matters tricky. How can we determine what this word means? Well, we can consult dictionaries; they are always a good place to start. When we consult various English dictionaries, we see one of the senses of *incidental* is *occurring by chance*. In other words, if something is incidental it is neither a regular occurrence nor part of a calculated plan. Another way that we can explore the meaning of *incidental* is by looking at its synonyms and opposites, in this instance the words *extra* (synonym) and *essential* (opposite). We can tell a lot about the meaning of words when we study their relations. Through its synonym, we can see that incidental costs are extra costs – something we did not necessarily budget for. If we talk about *essential costs*, we mean to say that the costs are necessary and that we cannot do without them.

Just by looking at a single synonym and opposite, we can already tell that expenditure on prospecting rights are necessary costs; they are essential to the mining operation. Without the right to prospect, there can be no prospecting and subsequently no mining. These costs can never be incidental, because prospecting is not something that happens by chance or as an extra. In fact, it is the first step in a mining operation.

1 *ABC Mining (Pty) Ltd v Commissioner for the South African Revenue Service* (IT24606) [2021] ZATC (25 February 2021), para 2.
2 Income Tax Act 58 of 1962, s 15(*b*).
3 *ABC Mining*, para 12.
4 *ABC Mining*, para 61.
5 *ABC Mining*, para 14, A–E.

By using simple semantic tools, we were able to understand *incidental* rather quickly.

This brings me to the purpose of this book: the provision of a linguistic toolbox. The well-known forensic linguist, Roger Shuy (1990:302), said, 'I simply reached into the toolbox that my field has given me and selected the necessary tools for the problem to be resolved'. By *toolbox*, he refers to a linguistic skillset comprising of phonetics and phonology, morphology, syntax, semantics, pragmatics and the various theories and techniques that underlie them (Shuy, 1990:302; Shuy, 2020:446). According to him (Shuy, 1986:295; Shuy, 2008:5), legal scholars and practitioners are not always aware of or familiar with linguistics and how it can help them resolve legal disputes, especially those embedded in language challenges. The reason for this is simply that a lawyer and presiding officer's expertise is law and not linguistics (Shuy, 2008:3). Through my research, I have noticed how frequently legal practitioners and presiding officers rely on dictionaries and precedent cases to help them solve word problems (and there is nothing wrong with that). However, through this book I wish to introduce you to many more language tools that could help you understand and interpret contested words better. The aim of this book is not to criticise the existing modus operandi or theories of statutory interpretation; instead, I would like to contribute towards the efforts in interpreting statutes by illustrating the different semantic and pragmatic tools that apply to meaning making.

In addition, I want to make the reader aware of the sociolinguistic factors that influence and help shape the language problems that courts often have to deal with. Language issues can make legal cases both fascinating and difficult. Linguistic interpretation is sometimes problematic due to the law's need for precision and clear boundaries on the one hand and language's fuzziness and evasiveness on the other. Solving linguistic issues as part of the statutory interpretation effort relies partly on the realisation that language is connected to speakers. Speakers constantly create, negotiate, recall and adjust meaning. It is seldom possible to approach linguistic interpretation as a surgeon would, clinically and with gloves. Many factors play a role during meaning making, and they can snowball towards a much larger and more complex context than might be obvious from the start. It would be beneficial to be cognisant of the various factors that could affect the way a (legal) speaker receives, understands and uses a word or a phrase.

1.2. Focus and scope of book

The goal of this book is to provide readers with the basic semantic and pragmatic tools to help them unlock meaning contested in court cases. Furthermore, its purpose is to help readers understand these tools. Understanding what they are and how statutory interpreters might use them, could potentially empower the interpreter to depend less feverishly on dictionaries and attempt analysing words (and language) using linguistic principles instead.

Words do not exist in a vacuum; they relate to other words and to the speakers who use them. It is not possible to divorce language from speakers. When speakers use words, they do so within a much greater context that includes things like interrelated concepts, body language and ideation that differs between speakers and communities. Dealing with the meaning of words is rarely just about a definition. Consequently, the chapters of this book explore what meaning is, how words are related, what non-verbal cues may contribute to communication, how speakers use language, and what dictionaries and language corpora may add to the understanding of words. More specifically, Chapter 2 introduces readers to key terminology and explains the different kinds of meaning. Knowing that we can distinguish between more than one type of meaning helps us to understand why the concept of meaning is so difficult to grasp and describe. Chapter 3 focuses on several word relations. Words are related and this relatedness can help an investigator understand the meaning of contested words in the same way that a doctor might understand your ailment if he or she enquires about your family's medical history. Chapter 4 explores non-verbal communication. How we say things really does contribute to the meaning of what we say. Non-verbal behaviour like body language and tone of voice as well as text stylistics are very important in determining the meaning of spoken and written texts, yet courts often overlook its value. Chapter 5 explores a variety of aspects regarding language use. These aspects link directly with pragmatic meaning, sometimes known as speaker meaning. Speaker meaning plays a role not only during legal proceedings like cross-examination, but also contributes to the meaning making process in several legal texts. Keep in mind that acts, contracts and wills are all spoken texts transferred to written form. Just because a disputed text appears in written form, does not necessarily eliminate its spoken characteristics and pragmatic value. The last two chapters focus on two important resources: dictionaries and corpora. Because dictionaries remain important tools for statutory interpretation, Chapter 6 provides an overview on what dictionaries are and how they should be used. Chapter 7 does the same with corpora. It explains what corpora are, how they function and how one can do basic searches. It also explains how to build your own corpus, something that legal practices or the judiciary could consider doing.

Even though the remaining linguistic tools like phonetics, phonology, morphology and syntax contribute a lot to legal interpretation too, they are deserving of their own book. As a result, this book aims at introducing semantics, pragmatics, and sociolinguistic principles as a starting point.

1.3. Who this book is meant for

The primary target readers are presiding officers and legal practitioners preparing heads of argument. The focus is statutory interpretation, though constitutional interpreters and interpreters of contracts might also gain from this text. Furthermore, I wrote the book specifically for those who must clarify lexical semantic and pragmatic meaning contested in case law, but who have no official training in linguistics or language studies. More precisely, the book aims at providing a resource for those who attempt forensic lexicological investigations in order to resolve legal disputes.

Users of this contribution essentially work within the Roman Dutch and Common Law systems and they will likely be familiar with the Southern African standards of statutory interpretation, which include interpretation theories like textualism, purposivism and the guidelines set by Appellate Justice Wallis's precedent case, *Natal Joint Municipal Pension Fund v Endumeni Municipality* (*Endumeni*).[6]

1.4. Who this book is not meant for

I did not write this book for scholars and students of language studies or linguistics. More importantly, readers of this book should not use it as a guide to improve their legal or academic writing skills. This is not an academic literacy textbook or English for Law Students guide.

The focus of this book is not the different theories behind statutory interpretation and the concept of ordinary meaning in particular. The book presents its content within the parameters of the existing debates of both the interpretation of statutes (as currently set in South Africa) and ordinary meaning as legal fiction.

6 *Natal Joint Municipal Pension Fund v Endumeni Municipality* 2012 (4) SA 593 (SCA).

This book is also not a study of legal language or topics within the much broader discipline of language and law.

1.5. Citation

I will refer primarily to South African cases and statutes throughout this book. Where foreign legislation or case law present interesting and relevant examples, those will be included. The goal is always to illustrate the use of a semantic or pragmatic device and not to criticise any of the judgements. It is possible that parliament might since have amended some of these statutes and that some of the cases have lost their validity. References to statutes and cases are for illustrative purposes only.

Legislation and case law are cited by means of a footnote system, whereas academic references will follow the shortened Harvard system.

1.6. Writing and typographic conventions

I will use the pronouns *we* and *our* throughout the rest of the book to refer to readers and myself collectively. After all, I am a speaker like everyone else and the various aspects highlighted in this book applies to me in equal measure. Therefore, the collective *we* does not refer to more than one author, but to you and me. Where necessary, I will use the pronouns *I* and *me* for distinction.

Words in boldface identify terminology. The subsection where the boldfaced word first appears will briefly explain what the word means. If you remain uncertain, please consult the glossary at the end of this book. Boldface is also used in Chapters 6 and 7 to highlight lemmas and node words.

Where a word represents two respective terms in linguistics and law, I will clarify that distinction in a footnote.

I will use a common linguistic convention throughout this book to indicate when language output is ungrammatical or incorrect: an asterisk in front of the 'wrong' bit. For example,

> John is sick. → *John sick is.

The use of an asterisk within corpus linguistic practices signifies a wildcard (see Chapter 7).

Lastly, cursive font is used when a word is being discussed or stressed.

1.7. Acknowledgements

I was able to write and publish this book because I received research and development leave as well as funding. I want to thank the College of Human Sciences at the University of South Africa as well as my department, the Department of Afrikaans and Theory of Literature, for giving me the time and money to make this book possible.

I received ethical clearance to conduct this research: reference number 2021-CHS-90163184.

2. Understanding Meaning

Ultimately, statutory interpretation is about meaning making. The interpreter attempts to infer the meaning expressed by a statute and tries to determine how it applies to the situation or condition they are dealing with. The statute (and its addenda) is the primary source of meaning. When the statute is unclear, vague or ambiguous, the interpreter must look elsewhere for clarity. Interpreters often have to answer the question: 'But what does X mean?' Linguistically speaking, meaning is a hard nut to crack. Meaning can be very elusive, especially because the word *meaning* can mean so many different things itself (Lyons 1979:1–5). Even though it is difficult to define *meaning*, this chapter will provide an overview of the different types of meaning applicable to the interpretation of statutes. This chapter will also assist you in understanding the chapters that follow.

2.1. Basic terminology

We usually define the term *semantics* as the study of meaning. It is a daunting and somewhat unrealistic way of looking at meaning. Often, we use the word *semantics* to speak about the meaning of words by themselves and in the context of phrases and sentences. When we refer to the *meaning of words*, we do so informally because *word* is quite a difficult term to describe, mostly because we fail to capture what words are (Murphy 2012:11–14). Besides, when we study words and their meaning, we do much more. To enable us to study words, we need to use the appropriate instruments to avoid confusion. Therefore, in this section we start by introducing a small set of terminology that we will be using throughout the book:

2.1.1 Lexicon

Almost like a dictionary, a **lexicon** is a collection of words and related information. On the one hand, a lexicon contains a speaker's vocabulary (the lexis) as well as the rules that govern language use (like grammar and pragmatic principles). On the other hand, a lexicon extends to include the lexis of a speaker's wider language community. As Murphy (2012:3–5) points out, the two lexicons are interrelated because we need to share a common understanding of what words and expressions mean in order to communicate successfully. The lexicon does not contain words and associated rules only. Our lexicons also contain knowledge about the world in general. So, when we recall a specific word, we simultaneously recall information associated with what the word represents (Murphy 2012:38).

Think of the word *dog*. Not only do we think of a dog's physical appearance and behaviour, but we also recall its interaction with humans: friendship, work, both ethical and unethical ownership, sport and so on.

Lexicons are organic, which means that they gain and lose content throughout a speaker's life.

2.1.2 Lexeme

Simply put, we call the items in the lexicon that carry semantic meaning **lexemes**. A lexeme is a lexical unit that connects a set of words through inflection. For instance, *eat*, *eats*, *ate*, *eaten* and *eating* are all forms of the same lexeme: eat. Lexemes can also contain a series of words such as idioms or frequently co-occurring word units: *black coffee*, *have your cake and eat it*, *like father like son*. Lexemes are mostly non-compositional (Murphy 2012:6). In other words, we do not have to combine a set of parts to create meaning. A word like *eat* makes sense by itself. A lexeme communicates a single concept, regardless of the inflection or the number of words it contains. Its dictionary equivalent is the headword (also known as a *lemma*); the word being defined.

Generally, when we speak of *words*, we mostly mean *lexemes* or *lexical items*.

2.1.3 Lexical item

A **lexical item** is a single unit that forms the basic element within a lexicon. They include simple words, parts of words (like morphemes), phrases, collocations, idioms, discourse markers and so on. Let us take the word *eating*. It consists of two lexical items: the simple verb *eat* and a suffix *-ing*. The suffix tells us something about the verb; the action is continuous. The lexical item *set free* in legal context means that someone was let go, probably from some kind of detention or imprisonment.

2.1.4 Lexical word

When we use the term **lexical word**, we mean a word that carries semantic content, as opposed to **grammar words**, which are function words and carry less semantic value. Lexical words are typically categorised as nouns, verbs, adjectives and adverbs. As such, they belong to an open class, which means that we can constantly add new words and we can add to or extend the meaning of existing words. Lexical words are conceptual in nature.

2.1.5 Concept

As speakers of language, we have abstract notions of the various objects (natural or fabricated) in our world, like vehicles, fruit and mammals. They include cognitive or emotional ideas of abstraction like knowledge, happiness, and equality. To describe these mental representations of the world, we often use the term **concept**. We can view concepts as abstract mental images of these objects. We acquire and create concepts to know and understand our surroundings (which include fictional or imaginary worlds too (Cruse 2015:53)). This means that our collection of concepts can expand or shrink as we gain new knowledge and forget existing information. Some concepts are unique to each individual and others are common to a group. Speakers could also use concepts that are difficult to describe whereas others easily correspond to known words (Saeed 2009:33).

We use words (lexemes!) to give form to concepts. When we do this, we **lexicalise** the concept.

2.1.6 Sense

We know by now that words may have more than one meaning and they can be related to other words conceptually. In general, **sense** represents one of the meanings of a lexeme. A word's various meanings may all point toward the same concept (see *polysemy* in chapter 3), or they could refer to a wider set of qualities that a lexeme might represent conceptually (see *hyponymy* in chapter 3). When we talk about a word's *meaning*, we mostly mean its *sense*. Sense is the conceptual representation expressed by the lexeme (Saeed 2009:58; Cruse 2015:46). Let us look at the following examples:

2.1 John needs a new sole for his left shoe.

2.2 John eats sole every Friday.

2.3 John is a pescetarian.

The word *sole* has two different senses; 2.1 refers to the undersurface of a shoe while 2.2 refers to a type of fish. Historically, they are related, because the fish was named for the shoe. Where does it leave 2.3? The word *pescetarian* is unrelated to 2.1, but it is connected to *sole* in 2.2. The sense of *pescetarian* is related to the concepts *vegetarianism*, *lifestyle* and even *religion*.

2.1.7 Expression

According to Lyons (1979:23), we require a term that serves to describe the linguistic units used to identify whatever it is we are talking about. Similarly, we need a term for the linguistic units used to describe the properties of the things we refer to. The word for this is **expression**. An expression may be written, spoken or signed and they can consist of single lexemes or more complex linguistic units like discourses. Expressions are not bound by context and they do not necessarily represent actual language output. Instead of labelling *pure filth* as *words*, we can refer to *pure filth* as an expression with a conventional interpretation.

2.1.8 Utterance

An **utterance** is a real piece of language, usually spoken but often also captured in writing.[1] Speakers produce utterances on specific occasions to express a particular communicational intent (Cruse 2015:25). It is important to note that utterances are context bound – speakers situate their utterances in time and place. They can be of any length – single words, phrases or sentences – and if spoken, they can include other types of linguistic information like tone and body language. Written utterances may convey linguistic information such as stylistic choices.

Utterances are important for semantic meaning making, especially where pragmatics is concerned.

2.1.9 Sentence

A **sentence** is a composition of different lexical items that express a complete thought. For it to qualify as a sentence, it must contain a verb as a minimum criterion. Sentences usually contain subjects that undergo the action or state of events. A sentence can be simple in structure or it can have one or more clauses that describe either the subject or the verb. Speakers may construct sentences as statements, questions, commands, exclamations, requests or for phatic purposes.

2.1.10 Phrase

We can view a phrase in two ways: as a syntactic phrase or a common phrase. A syntactic phrase is a group of words that act together as a grammatical unit. We typically divide them into Noun Phrases, Verb Phrases, Adjective Phrases and Prepositional Phrases. At the core of each syntactic phrase is a headword (noun, verb, adjective or preposition). These kinds of phrases can tell us about the semantic meaning

1 Utterances are discussed in more detail in Chapter 5, section 5.6.1.

communicated through sentences. An example of a Noun Phrase is *The big cat*.

Common phrases are either incomplete sentences lacking a verb (*scones with jam and cream*) or multiword units that express idiomatic meaning (*fly by night*).

Let us now turn to different kinds of meaning.

2.2. Word meaning

2.2.1 Lexical words

As we have seen in the previous section, lexical words are also known as content words because they carry and transfer information. They label and describe objects and actions, both abstract and concrete. As such, they are essential to convey ideas.

Usually, when we talk about the meaning of words, we busy ourselves with **lexical semantics**. We can split the focus of lexical semantics into two aspects: (1) the meaning of every word in a given language, and (2) the interrelation between words (Saeed 2009:53). Words do not exist in isolation; instead, they interlink in different ways. Imagine words as part of a network. This network is not only directly associated with the words in a constructed sentence or utterance, but is also connected to words that go unmentioned. Consider the following example (Saeed 2009:53):

2.4 John eats every morning.

Studying this sentence, we know what the subject is doing and how often the activity occurs. We combine the words *eat* and *every morning* to express another idea: breakfast. The words *every morning* further imply routine. The proper noun *John* tells us that the subject is probably male. The words *breakfast* and *routine* form part of the meaning of *every morning*, just as *male* contributes to the meaning of *John*.

Each item in 2.4 is a lexical word and all of them bear conceptual information. When someone says the name *John* aloud, most speakers will call a mental representation of a John to mind. This representation will likely differ for each speaker. Though most of us might think of a man when we hear the name *John*, some speakers might think of pets with the same name or of family and friends called *John*. In other words, some mental representations might be vague while others could be quite specific. Just as the concept of personhood is lexicalised, so too are the concepts of habit, time and frequency by way of *every* and *morning*.

When we busy ourselves with word meaning, we are essentially studying the meaning mostly associated with that word by its speakers. If someone says the word *apple*, you will not recall the concept *national elections*; instead, you will likely think of a fruit borne by apple trees and everything else you know about apples (their shape, colour, smell, use, and connotations). It is likely that another speaker could imagine a different type of apple to the one you or I might have in mind. However, the word *apple* represents both my concept and that of the other speaker. This variation in concept is not necessarily a problem, because there are many factors that work together to ensure that we understand the word to mean the same thing at a specific time. These factors include context, communal background information, shared experiences and our encyclopaedic knowledge of the world we live in.

Even though a concept is usually lexicalised through a single word at a time,[2] a lexical item can also consist of a number of words. Typical examples include metaphors, idioms and other **multiword units**, like syntactic phrases and collocations. They may contain multiple words, but they work together to express one concept. For instance, *the apple doesn't fall far from the tree*. This multi-word unit expresses a single concept, that of a likeness between children and their parents. Because this lexical item expresses one concept, we consider it a single word. The implication? When we have to determine the meaning of a multi-word unit, we must read it as one word and not divide the unit into individual items. Dividing the unit into smaller items and studying each item separately could seriously impact the interpretation of that lexical item.

When we speak of lexical words, we refer to words that have the capacity to extend their meaning to include more than one concept, either related or unrelated. Word classes that typically qualify as lexical words are nouns, verbs, adjectives and adverbs. As the example below will demonstrate, words like *original* and *selected* can mean more than one thing. Lexical words also belong to an open class, meaning that we can continuously add new words to this class and we can assign new meanings to existing words.

Let us now turn to a case about the word *inferior*. Both Stellenbosch Wine Trust and the Oude Meester Group had a wine called *Paarl Perlé*. As a solution to ongoing litigation, the two parties entered into an agreement of settlement. Notably, clause 7 of the agreement prevented both parties from using words or phrases that would suggest the other product was

2 This is not entirely true – a concept can be lexicalised simultaneously by an array of synonyms. But we will get to that in the next chapter.

inferior.[3] Clause 8 further prevented labelling from confusing the public as to which Perlé belongs to which company. In January 1972, a subsidiary of Stellenbosch Wine Trust started advertising a wine indicated as 'selected Paarl Perlé'. The advertisement stated that this product 'tastes better' and that it was the 'original Paarl Perlé'. The product was not be sold at 'standard Paarl Perlé prices'. Lastly, the neck label of the bottle read 'The Champagne of Paarl Perlés'.[4] This led to the case *Stellenbosch Wine Trust Ltd v Oude Meester Group Ltd*,[5] in which the court had to decide whether Stellenbosch Wine Trust and its subsidiaries had breached the settlement agreement by suggesting that the Oude Meester Group's Perlé was inferior. In order to fully understand the lexical meaning of *inferior* within this context, the lexical items *selected*, *tastes better*, *standard Paarl Perlé* and *the Champagne of Paarl Perlés* must be considered as well. An investigation into these words includes scrutiny of these items' extended conceptual networks too.

In this instance, two different companies used the same lexical items (in this case, proper nouns as trademarks) but wanted the public to recall two different concepts when they read the words (and their associated wording). From this case, it is also clear that an investigation into meaning engages lexical items both as single words (*inferior*, *selected*) and as multi-word units (*tastes better, standard Paarl Parlé, the Champagne of Perlés*). The multiplicity of meanings and consequently, interpretation, will become more obvious as we move on.

2.2.2 Grammatical words

In the previous section, we referred to lexical words as open class words, because we can expand existing meanings and we can create new lexical words. There is also a closed class containing words that chiefly have grammatical function. We consider this class closed, because speakers do not add new words to the category.[6] Grammar words include pronouns,

3 *Stellenbosch Wine Trust Ltd v Oude Meester Group Ltd* 1974 (1) SA 729 (A), at 733.

4 *Stellenbosch Wine Trust*, at 734.

5 *Stellenbosch Wine Trust Ltd v Oude Meester Group Ltd* 1974 (1) SA 729 (A).

6 This is especially noticeable in English (at least) where the non-binary and transgender communities have adopted the pronouns *them* and *they* in an attempt to escape gender conformity imposed by the existing binary male/female pronouns. Introducing a new grammatical word is not impossible, but might not be easily accepted by the larger language community. Swedish activists introduced a generic pronoun in the 1960's for the same purpose. It initially met with a lot of resistance, but has since been accepted by the Swedish language academy and society (Yeung 2020; Bradley 2020; Sendén, Renström & Lindqvist 2021).

propositions, conjunctions and discourse markers, modal verbs and determiners. They too can communicate semantic and pragmatic meaning (for instance, through deixis), but their meaning is much more restricted, less detailed, and contains reduced reference capacity. However, we should not underestimate their semantic richness. The richness increases once we consider grammatical words in terms of their grammatical function, especially in sentences (Murphy 2012:15).

For example, a preposition can communicate important information. Consider the following sentences:

2.5 I'm having soup for dinner.

2.6 I'm having soup before dinner.

The difference between the two sentences focuses entirely on the two prepositions, *for* and *before*. The difference between the two communicates an important distinction: soup as the main course (2.5) and soup as a starter (2.6). The preposition in 2.5 also implies that soup will be the only item; it is not a three-course meal.

In *South African Airways (Pty) Ltd v Aviation Union of South Africa*,[7] the Supreme Court of Appeal dealt with the transfer of contract of employment between parties, also known as first and second-generation outsourcing. This type of transfer is regulated by section 197 of the Labour Relations Act and defines *transfer* as 'the transfer of a business by one employer (the old employer) to another employer (the new employer) as a going concern'.[8] One of the concerns was the use of the preposition *by* instead of *from*.[9] If section 197(1)*(b)* were to be read as the transfer of a business *from* one employer to another, then the definition changes. The word *by* identifies an agent and indicates how an action should take place. The word *from* indicates direction and time and fails to identify the agent. As the legislation stands, *by* identifies the old employer as the agent of transfer, whereas *from* might alleviate the old employer from its required actions.[10]

More success has been had with the honorifics *Ms* and *Mx* (which some consider to be pronouns).

7 *South African Airways (Pty) Ltd v Aviation Union of South Africa* 2011 (3) SA 148 (SCA),

8 Labour Relations Act 66 of 1995, section 197(1)*(b)*.

9 Another example includes *Lueven Metals (Pty) Ltd v CSARS* (31356/2021) [2022] ZAGPPHC 325 (19 May 2022). Here the relative pronoun which plays a noteworthy role. See Chapter 7, section 7.5.3 for a brief discussion.

10 *South African Airways (Pty) Ltd v Aviation Union of South Africa*, para 31.

Clearly, although grammar words do not usually express conceptual information, they still communicate valuable information and may also contribute towards the lexicalisation effort.

2.3. Sentence meaning

Often, when people hear the term *semantics*, they think only of lexical semantics – the study of word meaning. Through lexical semantics, we try to make sense of the meaning assigned to words and we try to understand how they relate to one another as well as to the concepts of the world beyond language (the so-called 'real' world). However, sentences also carry semantic meaning. The difference between word and sentence meaning lies in the productivity of producing sentences (and utterances) and the way in which speakers do this.

Speakers do not string words together willy-nilly. Rather, we tend to group words together in very specific components. We use words to form phrases, clauses and sentences and these too express semantic value. Sometimes speakers forget that when they isolate a word to explore its meaning, that word belongs to an already existing syntactic unit, which operates to communicate meaning.

We construct meaning through sentences through the ways we combine and arrange words within a sequence and according to the grammatical rules that govern word order. Sometimes, if we change the word order, we can change semantic meaning within a sentence without changing the words of the sentence. Consider the following three examples:

2.7 John eats breakfast on Mondays only.

2.8 On Mondays, John eats breakfast only.

2.9 Only John eats breakfast on Mondays.

Each of the three example sentences expresses a different semantic value: John eats breakfast one day of the week (and foregoes it the rest of the week); John fasts most of Monday (but follows his usual meal plan the remainder of the week); no one else eats breakfast on Mondays but John. At this point, it should be clear that words and word components have specific functions and roles within a sentence. Some words identify the agents (expressed by nouns and noun phrases), some words express activities or states (verbs and verb phrases), while other words modify the words they precede or provide essential and contextual information necessary to understand the output as a whole (adjectives, adverbs, and a host of grammar words).[11]

If we use the Paarl Perlé examples once again, we see that they too function as noun phrases and communicate semantic value as units. See figure 2.1 below.

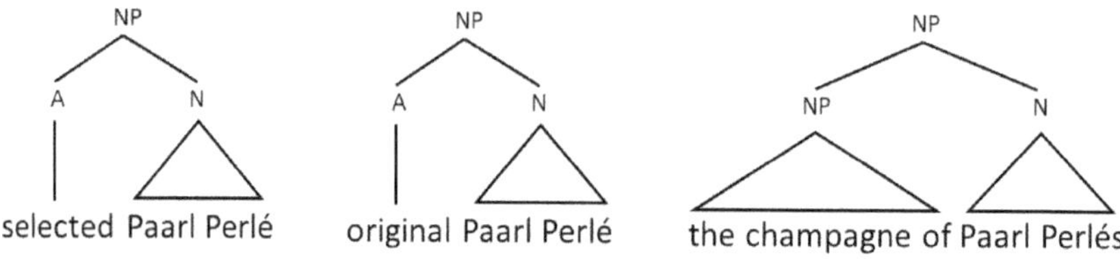

Figure 2.1: Paarl Perlé

Modifiers within noun phrases always work in favour of the noun. Even though we can gauge the modifiers in front of the (proper) noun *Paarl Perlé* independently, the qualities of the modifiers must never be divorced from the noun. In the first example, the noun phrase clearly states that someone (the public, the producer, wine critics) specifically chose this Paarl Perlé. The noun phrase by itself also implies that it is part of a curated collection and reflects a certain quality. The second example makes it clear that this is the first Paarl Perlé. The noun phrase suggests that there are more than one and that the rest are copies (which further suggests they can never rival the genuine product). The third example crowns this particular Paarl Perlé as something delicate and costly, a Perlé of fine quality. The fact that *Perlés* is plural communicates a similar message to the second example – there is more than one such product, but this one is the finest of them all. Clearly, the noun phrases succeed in establishing a superior-inferior binary, to the Oude Meester Group's displeasure.

Syntactic investigations also help us to clear up ambiguity or vagueness. Consider the following well-known example:

2.10 John shoots the man with the gun.

11 Sentences are also vehicles for propositional content, expressing potential truth conditions about specific agents and actions. See the sections on *entailment* and *presupposition* in Chapter 3.

The ambiguity lies in the noun phrase *the gun*. Who is holding it? John, or the man being shot by John? To help us visualise the ambiguity, let us look at figure 2.2 below.

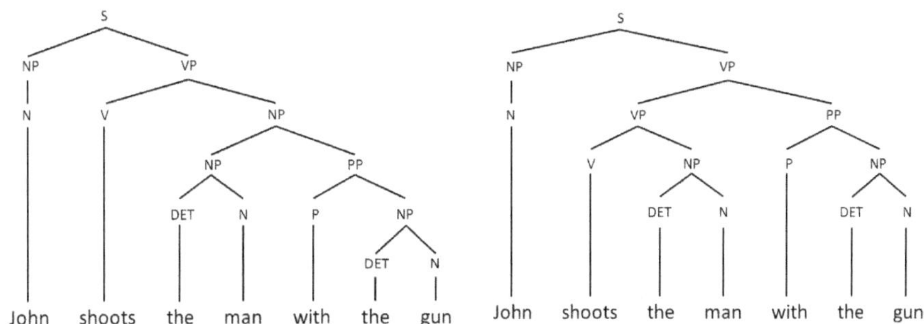

Figure 2.2: Tree diagram of *John shoots the man with the gun*

From the tree diagram, we can see a clear distinction:

2.11 John shoots [the man with the gun]. (John shoots a man holding a gun).

2.12 John shoots the man [with the gun]. (John shoots someone by using a gun).

In example 2.11, the verb *shoots* takes the noun phrase *the man with the gun* as a complement (necessary information to understand the phrase). The noun phrase should be read as one unit and as such it tells us a lot about the action taking place, the shooting. This noun phrase also clearly signals that there are two weapons present (though only one of them is definitely a gun). The noun phrase *the gun* is one of the distinguishing features of the man being shot by John. If we leave out any references to the gun, important information would go missing.

In example 2.12, the main verb phrase splits into two syntactic phrases, that is, another verb phrase and a prepositional phrase. Here the verb *shoots* takes only the noun phrase *the man* as a complement. Unlike the example in 2.11, the prepositional phrase forms contextual information (an adjunct), which we can leave out without altering the meaning of the sentence: John shoots the man. Reference to the gun is not essential here.

Sentences not only communicate semantic information by means of the components within them. Sentence type and function also communicate information, as well as the relations between sentences. Knowing that a specific sentence or utterance is an exclamation or imperative tells us a lot about the content a speaker tries to communicate.[12] Also, when speakers write or talk, they do not compose a few simple sentences and then retire for the rest of the day. In fact, speakers constantly string sentences together to produce compound and complex sentences. Long and complex sentences are typical of legal language. Knowing how independent and subordinate clauses relate to one another is quite important. In the case, *Universal Church of the Kingdom of God v Myeni*,[13] the Labour Appeal Court (LAC) decided that Mr Myeni was not an employee of the Universal Church of the Kingdom of God, because there was no official contract of employment between the two parties despite a task description and having received payslips reflecting UIF and tax deductions. At the heart of the matter was the following sentence taken from section 200A of the Labour Relations Act:[14]

> Until the contrary is proven, a person, who works for or renders services to any other person, is presumed, regardless of the form of the contract, to be an employee, if any one or more of the following factors are present: [...].

This definition of 'employee' is indeed a long and complex sentence. Cited here, it consists of a main clause and five dependent clauses. When broken down, the sentence looks like this:

2.13 A person is an employee [factual statement]
a. who works for (any other person) [relative clause]
b. or (who) renders services to any other person [relative clause]
c. regardless of the form of the contract [adnominal adjunct]
d. if the following factors are present [conditional adverbial clause]
e. until the contrary is proven [adverbial clause of time]

Before we continue, a reminder that a complex sentence consists of an independent clause (the main sentence) and one or more dependent clauses (related subordinate sentences). A dependent clause cannot stand on its own and always depends on the independent clause. Furthermore, dependent clauses function in relation to the independent clause. For

12 This will become more relevant when the focus shifts to *speech acts* in Chapter 5.
13 *Universal Church of the Kingdom of God v Myeni* (DA 3/14) 2015 ZALAC 31 (28 July 2015); see also Carney (2022).
14 Labour Relations Act 66 of 1995.

instance, adverbial clauses describe the action taking place in the main sentence, describing aspects of time, place and manner. Relative clauses modify a noun or noun phrase (the subject or object) in the main sentence. The sub-clauses all work together to support the information (either by extension or restriction) in the main clause.

The LAC focused solely on adverbial phrase (c). To them, it meant that a contract is a prerequisite for section 200A to apply (Germishuys 2016:364). This is an odd conclusion to come to. If we join the main clause with dependent clause (c), it leaves us with the following:

2.14 A person is an employee regardless of the form of the contract.

A suitable substitute for the discourse marker *regardless*, is *no matter what.* John is an employee no matter the form of the contract. Yet, this dependent clause must be read together with the others, because they describe who an employer is, and they set the conditions for employment. When we analyse this sentence, we see that the main clause is a factual statement. It tells us something about employees. The noun phrase *a person* is modified by the relative clauses (a) and (b), embedded within the main clause: thus, an employee is someone who works and renders services. The status of *employee* further depends on the conditions expressed in clause (d) and the time constraint present in clause (e). The status of *employee* is altered when none of the factors is present, or when new evidence emerges that redefines the term *employee.* Another important aspect worth mentioning is that clause (c) is an adjunct. As we saw earlier, adjuncts are phrases that provide additional information. As a rule, adjuncts can be deleted without affecting the semantic inference of the sentence (look at example 2.12 once more) (Ruigendijk, De Belder and Schippers 2021:204-205; 214-215; Parrott 2016: 301-302). This means clause (c) is unnecessary:

> an employee is an individual who works or renders services for someone else if the listed conditions / criteria are present, until the contrary is proven.

The description of *employee* does not suffer when the reference to a contract is deleted; in fact, it remains the same.[15] It is therefore strange that a court would isolate a clause from the rest of its grammatical

15 If the deletion of clause (c) is legally impossible and reference must be made to a contract in some shape or form, then the formulation (the legislative drafting) is to blame. The description of *employee* is poorly formulated and raises enough syntactic questions to cast necessary doubt about the semantic meaning being conveyed.

context without much regard, especially when interpretation theories and standards such as *Endumeni* clearly state that interpreters must pay attention to the syntax of a language.[16]

Nevertheless, meaning communicated by sentences (and phrases and clauses) play an important role, even when courts consider lexical items like individual words within context. This will become clearer as we progress through the remaining chapters.

2.4. Reference and denotative meaning

When we study the meaning of lexical words, it often comes down to reference, sense and denotation. Cruse (2015:381) describes it best:

> One of the most basic things that we do when we communicate through language is to pick out entities in the world and ascribe properties to them, or indicate relations between them. Reference is concerned with designating entities in the world by linguistic means.

Remember that we live in a world, either real or imaginary. We use language to describe the concepts of our world. Words become bridges between language and the world; they allow us to identify items and events and to make statements about them (Saeed 2009:12; Lyons 1979:177). When the subsidiary of Stellenbosch Wine Trust makes a statement that their product would not be sold at 'standard Paarl Perlé prices', it is saying something about specific entities in the world: Paarl Perlé wine and prices. We call this linguistic mechanism that attaches language to world entities **reference**, because the speaker (or author) is using particular words to **refer** to something outside of language. When a speaker says *my mother is now retired*, he or she is using the words *my mother* to refer to something that exists in the world. The noun phrase *my mother* is the **referent** of my utterance, the thing (person) the speaker is referring to.

While we use referencing to describe a speaker's action of identifying items in the world through language, **denotation** expresses the relationship between the actual language output and the world (persons, things, places, properties, processes and activities external to the language system (Lyons 1979:207)). Put differently, denotative meaning represents a word's literal meaning, and more importantly, the denotation of a word is the set of its possible referents. This means that

16 *Natal Joint Municipal Pension Fund v Endumeni Municipality* 2012 (4) SA 593 (SCA), para 18.

when a word denotes, it recalls the properties of a set of things it can refer to (Kaplan 2020:6-7; Cruse 2015:382; Murphy 2012:35). For example, the word *mother* denotes all women who raise and nurture children to adulthood, whether biological, adoptive, communal or social mothers. The noun phrase *Paarl Perlé prices* denotes the fixed amount Paarl Perlé wines are sold for. Reference and denotation both bridge the gap between language and the things beyond language, but reference represents the active selection of words to express a certain meaning, whereas denotation expresses the established meaning of those words. The proper noun *Perlé* refers to wine produced in South Africa and denotes a lightly sparkling wine that is usually carbonated before bottling.

There is an important distinction between reference and denotation. Referencing is context sensitive, but denotation is not. A speaker can mean something entirely different by his or her chosen referent depending on the circumstances of the utterance. If we take part in a conversation about parents and we say *my mother is now retired*, the word *mother* still denotes a woman who raised and nurtured us. This is the literal meaning of *mother*. Now imagine that John and Steve are hosting a party. It is getting late and John decides to go to bed, leaving Steve with the last two stragglers. Steve says to them *my mother is now retired*. The denotation of *mother* remains the same but extends to include other properties like *nagging*, *controlling* and *overbearing*. This becomes even more striking if John and Steve were romantic partners.

The class of words that does most of the referring is nouns and noun phrases.[17] This is because nouns name items, both concrete and abstract. Using the example of *my mother* once again, the referent refers to a tangible person (my living and breathing mother (or partner)). Yet, not all nouns and noun phrases have referencing power in an utterance. Nouns and noun phrases that have generic interpretations have no reference. Compare the next two sentences:

2.15 My mother will retire soon.

2.16 Someone's mother will retire soon.

17 Other words like pronouns and verbs have referring power as well. Löbner (2002:28–29) uses the sentence *My dog has ripped my blue dress* to illustrate this. Although *my* forms part of the noun phrase *my dog*, it refers to the speaker specifically. The verb phrase *has ripped* not only indicates the action, but also refers to the time of the event. As a proposition, the sentence refers as a unit; it refers to a specific incident involving particular actors. If the proposition were false (if it were a lie), the sentence and its content words no longer refer to anything, because the proposition does not exist in the real world.

In 2.15, the noun phrase *my mother* refers to someone specific, the speaker's physical mother. However, the noun phrase *someone's mother* in 2.16 is generic and does not refer to a specific person in the natural world. Sometimes the referent in an utterance can be quite ambiguous. Saeed (2009:26) uses the example of a person entering a bar looking for a missing woman. When he says *I'm looking for a woman*, the noun phrase *a woman* refers to someone specific for the investigator (the missing person) but remains generic for the barman (any woman).

2.5. Connotative meaning

The meaning of words manifests, extends, and changes through the way that we use them, as well as the manner by which we use the items described by them. We do not always use words strictly according to their denotations, but add a number of associations too. We call these associations *connotations*. Connotations vary between personal and cultural associations, and they are mostly emotive and stylistic (Bosman and Pienaar 2014:254; Löbner 2003:48-49). Let us look at the following examples (Murphy 2012:33):

2.17 Welcome to my new abode.

2.18 Welcome to my new house.

2.19 Welcome to my new pondokkie.[18]

The words *abode*, *house* and *pondokkie* all denote a set of the same things – a dwelling – however they have very distinct associations. The word *house* represents Standard English and as such, a reader or listener would probably imagine a stock standard house. *Abode* is a more formal word and could therefore imply a more expensive or fancy house. The last word, *pondokkie*, indicates a very basic structure; a slum dwelling. Not only is there a clear stylistic difference between the three words, but *abode* and *pondokkie* are used emotively as well: *abode* implies that it is the speaker's respected home, whereas *pondokkie* indicates that the house is small and basic, but loved.[19] Of course, the speaker can use both *abode* and *pondokkie* ironically. In the case of *pondokkie* the speaker's house might be quite impressive and by referring to it as insignificant, the speaker is actually

18 The word *pondok* (/pɔndɔk/) denotes a shelter made of scraps of material like wood or corrugated iron in South African vernacular. It has a similar meaning in Bahasa. It is used here in its diminutive form.

19 Afrikaans nouns are often placed in the diminutive to indicate endearment or sarcasm.

stressing the point that the house is indeed splendid. The opposite can be true for *abode*; the word might refer to a very ordinary house.

It is important to note that connotation is not an integral part of a word's denotation. In other words, the association that a speaker or speech community recalls when they use a certain word, usually remains separate from that word's definition. This is clearly visible in the use of the word *pondokkie* in example 2.19. A pondok is a shanty, a crudely built dwelling; however, that is not what the speaker is saying in 2.19. He or she is not welcoming guests to his/her shack. Instead, the speaker is communicating certain characteristics the speaker and his/her community associates with pondok-like structures.

Emotive connotation was present in the defamation case *Jonker v Davis*,[20] in which Appellative Justice Bresler had to confirm whether the Afrikaans word *krot* defamed the plaintiff's good name. The defendant published the following in the presence of others:

> You must remember that I am the son of a rich man and that I have been well educated. I will not stand for a boy like you, who grew up in a 'krot' and obtained a little education from your father, sending me such an insulting letter.[21]

Appellate Justice Bresler correctly stated that the word *krot* (slum dwelling) connoted squalor and a lack of breeding and anyone growing up in a slum is thought to be indecent.[22] One of the tests in a case like this would be what a reasonable person would think or understand when they came across a word like *krot*. What associative meaning would a speaker (or community) assign to a word such as this? The word denotes negative characteristics and for this reason the connotations associated with the word's conventional definition would most likely be negative too. When your mother claims that your sister is *slumming it* with her new boyfriend, the association is not necessarily that they are living together in squalor (even though that could be the case), but rather that she is stooping in station and is mixing with 'the wrong crowd'.

2.6. Social meaning

Usually, we can infer a lot about a speaker and the situation in which a conversation is taking place by paying attention to the words that speaker has chosen to express him/herself with. We refer to this as social

20 *Jonker v Davis* 1953 (2) SA 726 (GW).
21 *Jonker v Davis*, at 726. For the original Afrikaans text, see page 727.
22 *Jonker v Davis*, at 726–727.

meaning.[23] Because social meaning expresses affect (a speaker's feelings and attitudes toward the thing they are discussing (Murphy 2012:33)), it intertwines with connotative meaning. Both speaker and listener might associate certain characteristics with the chosen denotations. We typically use negative words with negative connotations to express negative ideation; or positive words with positive associations to communicate positive thinking. Let us look at the following two examples:

2.20 John will never buy a new car; he's a stingy man.

2.21 John will never buy a new car; he's a frugal man.

The word *stingy* is a negative description of someone who does not want to part with his or her money. We often view stingy individuals as cheap, uncharitable, rigid and selfish people; someone who comes across as joyless. *Frugal* on the other hand is a bit more positive. It also describes someone who prefers to save money, but we see that person rather as economical, cautious and sensible. Using a word like *stingy* as opposed to *sensible* tells us something about the social situation of the expression. The speaker of 2.20 is criticising John for being tight-fisted. The speaker is either lamenting or gossiping. The speaker of 2.21 might be gossiping too, but we also get a sense that he or she is saying that John would prefer to spend his money on more important matters. It is a less critical appraisal of John. These are, of course, assumptions about the speaker. Once again, the words themselves denote the same set of things: *saving money*. The additional meaning attributed to these words are connotative in order to construct a social (expressive) meaning about the speaker and the situation.

This is visible in the *Jonker v Davis* case. The defendant used a very strong word (*krot*) to debase the plaintiff and to create an obvious power relation between the two. The defendant deliberately used a negative word with many negative connotations to express something about himself and the social standing of the plaintiff. The defendant wanted people to view the plaintiff as dirty, poor, uneducated and unable to take care of himself. In other words, this is not someone society should take seriously. However, the choice of words and the utterance as a whole also tells us something about the speaker. We can tell that the speaker is arrogant and feels himself superior; a slum dweller will not tell him what to do.

Even though social meaning is subjective, it contributes a lot to the meaning of words within context. This will become increasingly clear

23 Many semanticists use the words 'expressive meaning' instead. See amongst others Löbner (2003:47–48) and Lyons (1979:50–52).

once interpreters start considering word relations and pragmatic factors as well.

2.7. Conventional meaning and arbitrariness

As mentioned before, speakers do not function in isolation. As members of one or more speech communities, we assign the same or similar meanings to words. This happens through frequency of use. If members of a community start using an existing word in a new way, the usage spreads through the community, and the new meaning gets used repeatedly, this new meaning becomes a standard adage to the meaning of the word. We refer to this as *conventionality*: speakers agree on a new meaning and it becomes common knowledge among most. Whenever an outsider enters a community with the intention of staying, they must acquire the conventional meanings of words too. Otherwise, miscommunication would be inevitable.

Conventional meaning can be very exclusive to one specific sub-culture, or it can span the globe. For instance, international speakers of English agree that the word *tree* refers to perennial plants with long stems, branches and very strong root systems. However, speakers of English might not all agree on what the words *fresh fish* mean. To some *fresh fish* refers to fish caught seconds before eating it, whereas others might interpret *fresh fish* as fish caught sometime that day. We can juxtapose *fresh fish* with *frozen boxed fish*, meaning that the fish is not older than a few days.

The meaning assigned to words is arbitrary, however. This means that there is no natural or logical relationship between the form of a word and its meaning. The speech community decides what words mean and then conventionalises that meaning. If there were a more natural relation between form and meaning, we would use the same words across language families. In other words, we would all be using the word *tree*. Instead, speakers of different languages use various unrelated words to signify the same concept: *boom*, *muri*, *umuthi*, *setlhare*.

From our *tree* example, it is clear that conventional meaning can correspond with the denotation of a word. However, the conventional meaning can be an extension of the existing denotation, or it can be a secondary meaning. Many South Africans will undoubtedly recognise the following utterance:

2.22 *Quickly borrow me your ID.[24]

The utterance in 2.22 is ungrammatical for at least two obvious reasons:

1. *me* is the objective case for *I* and incorrectly mirrors the expression *lend me*; the correct expression is *may I borrow*;
2. the speaker is correctly asking for permission, but the ID in question is not an item one lends to another.

Grammar aside, the mistake has been entrenched in various South African English vernaculars and it simply functions as a request to see or briefly use the identification document.

Another example of this is the case *Wells v Atoll Media (Pty) Ltd* in which Justice Davis had to interpret the words *pure filth*.[25] The facts of the case revolve around a photo of a 12-year-old girl published in *Zigzag*, an established surfing magazine in South Africa. The photo, published without consent, was bearing the word *filth*, while other captions described the people in the photographs as *pure filth*.[26] The court had to establish whether this amounted to defamation, whether the magazine used the words *pure filth* deliberately in its denotative sense. The magazine claimed that they used the word in the way surfers understood the word. One of the arguments correctly put forward during the proceedings, was the fact that the magazine represented a very specific community with their own vocabulary. Readers familiar with the magazine and the surfing culture would know to depart from the denotation of *filth* and instead infer its conventional meaning, which implies something of good quality (mostly referring to waves or women).[27]

There is no logical relation between the word *filth* and its secondary meaning *good quality*. The relationship is entirely arbitrary. However, the fact that the word does have a secondary meaning given to it by a specific community is something to acknowledge and to take into consideration when interpreting. It might be obvious by now that conventional meaning (as well as connotative and social meaning) can have serious implications for the principle of ordinary meaning.

24 This phenomenon is not unique to South Africa. Similar examples are prevalent in the Midwest of the United States.

25 *Wells v Atoll Media (Pty) Ltd* [2010] 4 All SA 548 (WCC) (9 November 2009).

26 *Wells v Atoll Media*, at paras 3 to 6.

27 *Wells v Atoll Media*, at paras 14; 24, 25, 29.

2.8. Ordinary meaning

At this point, we turn our attention to a very important concept within statutory interpretation – ordinary meaning. It is worth mentioning that *ordinary meaning* is a legal construct and does not exist in linguistics in the same way. For a linguist to claim that meaning can be ordinary would almost certainly be contentious, and we can see why just by reviewing the preceding subsections.

Hutton (2014:2; Hutton 2020:90) views ordinary meaning as a legal fiction similar to the legal personality of companies. We can add the fictions of the reasonable person and the biological link between parents and their adoptive children. Understanding ordinary meaning as a legal fiction helps us to realise that (1) linguistic interpretation is ultimately necessary to push the legal process forward, but (2) meaning making could easily be questioned or challenged (and often is). Believing that it is a legal fiction might help us understand the function and purpose of ordinary meaning within the interpretation of law, but it remains somewhat of an unstable tool to work with, at least in its current form. Hutton (2020:79) adds:

> An implicit claim to neutrality, stability and communality makes ordinary language an intuitively attractive reference point in legal argumentation. But the category suffers from a corresponding sociological and sociolinguistic deficit. Put simply, it has intuitive plausibility and utility, but lacks empirical content.

If we accept that ordinary meaning is representative of the language spoken by ordinary people – you and I – then we must agree on certain aspects. Firstly, we must understand ordinary meaning in relation to terms of art and specific legal definitions. It is common practice for legislative drafters to extend a word's definition to serve the law. A clear example is the definition of *deal in* in the Drugs and Drug Trafficking Act.[28] The definition of *deal in* includes the transportation, cultivation, and manufacture of drugs. This is an extension of the denotation, which recalls buying and selling. If the police caught you manufacturing any type of drug, even if it were for personal use, they could arrest you for dealing in drugs despite no transaction taking place.[29] A term of art is a word with

28 Drugs and Drug Trafficking Act 140 of 1992; section 1.

29 *S v Mbatha* 2012 (2) SACR 302 (N). The Constitutional Court confirmed a judgment by Davis J allowing the use and cultivation of cannabis for personal use and instructed parliament to amend the Drugs and Drug Trafficking Act to reflect the allowance. The Cannabis for Private

technical meaning. It is given a very specific denotation to serve a very specific goal. An example of a term of art would be the word *intentional*. Within a legal context, *intentional* implies a knowledge of wrongdoing. A person who intends committing a crime does so knowing what the result would be and still wishes to continue.

Using terms of art and extending legislative definitions to cast the net as wide as possible usually serve the legal process and the justice system well. Yet it is impossible to include every word related to an act as a definition. So, many words contested in court are interpreted according to their ordinary meaning. Ordinary meaning, then, is neither terminology nor extensions of existing words. Some scholars describe it as the plain and grammatical meaning of words. However, as Du Plessis (1986:104) points out, one of the assumptions of ordinary meaning is that

> statutes are written in 'popular language', and that their 'ordinary meaning' is therefore also their 'popular meaning'. 'Lay people' would most probably be rather sceptical – and even cynical – to learn that statutory language is supposed, in principle at least, to be 'ordinary' language.

In fact, laws are written in statutory language akin to legal language (Du Plessis 1986:104). This means that ordinary language is something entirely different to legislative language. For many, ordinary meaning is equal to a dictionary definition (Carney and Bergh 2014:40-46: Hutton 2014:44-46), because dictionary definitions represent the denotation of words as understood by the 'reasonable person'. Hutton (2020:84) describes one possible benefit of using dictionaries as tools of ordinary meaning:

> More fundamentally, the general dictionary serves the ideology of one legal system, one language. If legal doctrine requires that there exist available facts about ordinary language external to law, then a standard dictionary is not only an interpretive tool but serves to bolster this central ideology.

Though this approach to ordinary meaning is problematic (controversial even) on many levels, we must understand the concept to contrast with jargon and terminology. It is the meaning assigned to words that do not

Purposes Bill B19 of 2020 is currently undergoing revision. See *Minister of Justice and Constitutional Development v Prince; National Director of Public Prosecutions v Rubin; National Director of Public Prosecutions v Acton* [2018] ZACC 30.

reflect any kind of technicality. Bell and Engle (1995:32) say that a user of ordinary meaning 'is able to rely on an immediate understanding of the purpose behind the use of the words without engaging in any further research'. This means that a judge does not assign meaning to words divorced from their immediate context, but rather adopts a meaning that is appropriate to the situation (Bell and Engle 1995:32).

Solan (2010:11) makes an interesting distinction between plain and ordinary meaning. He sees them as two different instruments. To him, a presiding officer will employ the *plain meaning* when the language of a text is unambiguous; when there is no doubt as to what an expression means. When a text offers more than one interpretation possibility and one of the inferences is more typical than the other, the presiding officer will employ *ordinary meaning* as a device.

Presiding officers and legal scholars sometimes use the words *grammatical meaning* and *ordinary meaning* interchangeably to indicate the same thing. However, as we have seen at the very start, grammatical meaning is not the same as lexical meaning. Grammatical meaning expresses meaning constructed through composition of the different building blocks (of which some are lexical words and others are grammar words). Lexical words also gain meaning through pragmatic conditions, which sometimes flout the rules of grammar. Instead of using these terms interchangeably, it would be better to accept that grammatical meaning is one of the criteria for ordinary meaning.

An important guiding force for Southern Africans is Appellate Justice Wallis' standard set in *Endumeni*.[30] He says that the interpreter must view language 'in light of the ordinary rules of grammar and syntax', as well as the context of the utterance or expression.[31] Furthermore, when words have more than one possible meaning, grammar, syntax and context must provide the necessary guidance.[32] According to Carney (2020:277), this approach leaves little room for pragmatic meaning and restricts linguistic interpretation to the contested text itself. Yet, Appellate Justice Wallis' maxim for linguistic interpretation alludes to what Bell and Engle referred to as 'immediate understanding'. Another word for this is *conventional* meaning; that common-sense meaning that speakers assign to the words they use frequently. This includes secondary meaning (recall Solan's understanding of *ordinary meaning*), when the text seems ambiguous or vague. Importantly, Appellate Justice Wallis

30 *Natal Joint Municipal Pension Fund v Endumeni Municipality* 2012 (4) SA 593 (SCA).
31 *Endumeni*, paras 18, 25.
32 *Endumeni*, paras 18, 25.

states that an interpretation must not lead to 'impractical, unbusinesslike or oppressive consequences'.[33] For instance, an interpretation should not prevent the effectiveness of existing enterprises and structures. Narrow interpretations purely in favour of the obvious ordinary meaning of the text could hamper successful business models, ultimately preventing optimal functioning. The practical outcome of a judgement should therefore be a serious consideration and therefore becomes one of the characteristics of the ordinary meaning instrument.

Often, the ordinary meaning of a word is obvious when considered against the facts of the case. In *S v Makhubela*,[34] the accused was arrested for driving a vehicle without a valid licence in terms of section 57(1) of the Road Traffic Act.[35] Even though the accused pleaded guilty, it transpired that the car he was driving was no longer working. Men were pushing the car along the side of the road and he was steering it.[36] The question is whether Mr Makhubela was actually driving (or steering?). The court indicated that to earn a licence, a potential driver must be able to operate a car (to start it, put it in motion and keep it on course).[37] The court found that because the car in question was not in a mechanically working condition, it did not view Mr Makhubela as a driver. What Mr Makhubela was doing, did not require the technical skill expected of a licence.[38]

In *Purveyors South Africa Mine Services (Pty) Ltd v Commissioner for the South African Revenue Services*,[39] the Supreme Court of Appeal (SCA) decided a company did not meet the requirements for the Voluntary Disclosure Programme as set out in section 227 of the Tax Administration Act.[40] Central to the issue was the meaning of both *voluntary* and *disclosure*. For both, the SCA and the court *a quo* interpreted these words according to their ordinary meanings. Concerning *disclosure*, the court decided it denotes the reveal of information to others; it meant that information becomes common knowledge to others.[41] Similarly, the court *a quo* claimed that *disclosure* implied new information; if the South African Revenue Service (SARS) was already in possession of the information, no

33 *Endumeni*, para 26.
34 *S v Makhubela* 1981 (4) SA 210 (B).
35 Road Traffic Act 7 of 1973.
36 *S v Makhubela*, at 210.
37 *S v Makhubela*, at 211.
38 *S v Makhubela*, at 211.
39 *Purveyors South Africa Mine Services (Pty) Ltd v Commissioner for the South African Revenue Services* (135/2021) [2021] ZASCA 170 (7 December 2021).
40 Tax Administration Act 28 of 2011.
41 *Purveyors* 2021, para 19.

disclosure has taken place (because there is nothing new to disclose).[42] An investigation by Van Zyl and Carney (2021:106) showed that information does not need to be new or secret to qualify for disclosure. However, the courts chose the primary ordinary meaning that they felt came the closest to the purpose of the Voluntary Disclosure Programme. For SARS, information must be wholly new in every way before the Voluntary Disclosure Programme can succeed. Apparently, SARS views *disclosure* more as a term than an ordinary word. The word *disclosure* is undefined in the Tax Administration Act, which means it would serve SARS well to define it and make explicit what semantic features they associate with it.

Another way of looking at ordinary meaning is as several senses. Lee and Mouritsen (2018:800-801) use a continuum to illustrate the broad range of senses that represent judges' notion of ordinary meaning (see figure 2.3). The far left of the continuum represents the linguistically permissible idea, one that a court will measure against the possibility that other people have used a word in that particular way before. However, it remains uncommon in conventional situations. At the far right, the continuum symbolises plain meaning in the same sense as Solan does. It characterises the most obvious meaning, which is considered more pertinent than a meaning that occurs frequently. When meaning is plain, it is evident enough that it becomes nearly exclusive. Depending on the nature of the interpretation obstacle and the relevant context, ordinary meaning moves up and down the spectrum.

POSSIBLE → COMMON → MOST FREQUENT → EXCLUSIVE

Figure 2.3: Continuum representing the notion of ordinary meaning

The continuum does not capture a fifth sense of ordinary meaning, namely prototypical meaning (Lee and Mouritsen 2018:801-802). A prototype is considered the best example within its category and as such it is a strong association with the term in its context. The word *building* conjures images of a multistorey structure made of brick, steel and cement. This would be its strongest association. The word does not typically characterise a single storey log cabin. (See Chapter 3 for a discussion of *categorisation.*)

42 *Purveyors South Africa Mine Service (Pty) Ltd v Commissioner for the South African Revenue Service* (611689/2019) [202] ZAGPPHC 409 (25 August 2020), paras 13, 14.3.

Clearly, as a legal concept *ordinary meaning* has many facets and it is these facets that sometimes make it an unstable tool. Nevertheless, it is also the space where language and law meet intimately to either determine or establish meaning, which is also what makes statutory interpretation so fascinating and exciting.

2.9. Ambiguity and vagueness

Poscher (2012:128) reminds us that few topics in the theory of language are so closely related to legal interpretation as the phenomena *ambiguity* and *vagueness*. He says that courts at appellate and supreme levels usually spend less time 'disentangling the facts of cases' and focus more intently on the 'indeterminacies of the law' (Poscher 2012:128). That is because words do not always provide clear-cut meanings. It is because words are either ambiguous or vague that people tend to fight over meaning.

Löbner (2003:53) mentions that we often think a word (and therefore an expression or utterance) is limited to a single meaning; and of course this is not true. Nearly all lexical words have more than one meaning (as well as the potential to have many more). It therefore stands to reason that a variety of interpretation possibilities exist, depending on the context of the expression or utterance. Lyons (1979:38) refers to a communication channel between X and Y. When the message is clear, the communication travels through the channel between X and Y, reaching the end in the same manner it went out. The signal remains the same for both X and Y. However, when a signal encodes two or more messages, the receiver (Y) could receive any one of these, leading to uncertainty and / or misunderstanding. When we can interpret a word, expression or utterance in more than one way, we refer to this as **ambiguity**. Let us look at the following two examples:

2.23 I saw John at the bank.

2.24 John spoke to the chair for at least 20 minutes.

In sentence 2.23, the word *bank* is ambiguous due to its homonymy. It can refer to a financial institution or the land alongside a river. Without sufficient context, we will never know whether the speaker saw John at United Bank for business or whether John was out swimming in the Gariep. The utterance can easily mean both. In 2.24, we can assume that John was speaking to the moderator at a conference or maybe to a professor heading a certain discipline. There is also the possibility that John suffers from a mental disorder and spoke to his kitchen chair. All three inferences are possible. Sufficient context and complement compounding can help us clarify the ambiguity (Hutton 2014:10). For example (Poscher 2012:129; Kaplan 2020:183):

2.25 I saw John at the bank. He was speaking to a teller.

2.26 I saw John at the riverbank.

We find a well-known incident of ambiguity in the now famous American case *Smith v US*.[43] Mr Smith tried to buy cocaine with the hopes of reselling. He had with him a valuable firearm and proceeded to sell the gun for drugs instead of money. To Mr Smith's dismay, his buyers were undercover police.[44] Upon finding him guilty, Mr Smith received an additional five years to his sentence because the law states:

> [...] any person who, during and in relation to any crime of violence or drug trafficking crime [...] uses or carries a firearm [...] shall, in addition to the punishment provided for such crime of violence or drug trafficking crime, be sentenced to a term of imprisonment of not less than 5 years.[45]

Mr Smith appealed against the additional five years because, he argued, the code referred to the use of a firearm as a weapon and he used the firearm as a barter item instead.[46] The words *uses or carries a firearm* are ambiguous. In his dissenting opinion, Justice Scalia agreed with the plaintiff and argued that if one said they used a gun, they meant to use it according to its purpose (shooting, or threatening to shoot) (Kaplan 2020:184-185; Solan 1995:1074-1076). Employing a gun as currency is not a typical usage. The words *uses or carries a firearm* in the context of the entire statute denotes that a firearm is used as a weapon during the drug trade to compel people.

Where ambiguity refers to multiple interpretation possibilities for a single word (or expression and utterance), **vagueness** refers to a single interpretation prospect that is fuzzy at the edges, allowing a bit more interpretation flexibility (Löbner 2003:62). Context may help us to resolve ambiguity, but it will not necessarily offer us much clarity where vagueness is concerned. Vague words often contain generality; the implication is that a word's meaning can both include or exclude a set of criteria. It is therefore best to view vagueness as a continuum (Löbner 2003:63; Murphy 2012:91-93). For instance, when we say that John is

43 *Smith v US* 508 US 223 (1993).
44 *Smith*, at 225–226.
45 18 US Code Nr 924 (c)(1).
46 *Smith*, at 227.

tall without providing the exact measurements, the word 'tall' is vague. Guessing, we might say that John is between 1.75-1.85 meters tall. But how tall must someone be to qualify as *tall*? To some, 1.75 might be an average height and to others it might be extremely tall. The same applies to the word *child*. As a society, we could see a seventeen-year-old as a young adult, yet a parent would probably view his or her seventeen-year-old as just one of their children (meaning *offspring* and *juvenile*). The meaning of a vague word like *tall* or *child* varies along a continuum. In the case of height, we have *short* at one end and *extremely tall* at the other. Somewhere between the two, the word *tall* moves back and forth, depending on perspective. The same applies to *child*. See figure 2.4 below. The borders between *child* and *young adult* are vague. A young adult could be anyone between the ages of sixteen and twenty-five.

BABY → CHILD → YOUNG ADULT → ADULT

Figure 2.4: An example of a continuum for *life stages*.

For an interesting example of vague words, we look at two German cases that dealt with the same issue but resulted in two different outcomes. Both cases were under review by the high regional court of Bamberg and Nürnberg respectively. The cases hinged on the word *ashes*, more precisely what qualifies as ash remains and what does not (Christensen and Kübbeler 2011:1-3).

When a human body is cremated, any gold from the teeth stay behind. Sometimes workers at the crematorium take the gold unlawfully. The Bamberg court dealt with three workers of a crematorium, who would rifle through the ash remains after each cremation and collect any gold left behind with the sole purpose of selling it and dividing the money between the three of them.[47] Within a year and a half, the workers collected more than 12 kg of gold and sold most of it for more than 50 000 euros.[48] The question was whether the accused were guilty of violating a dead human body, seeing as there was no body left to violate.[49]

The court stated that the dead human body enjoys the right to protection and this right carries over to the ash remains of the deceased. As such, the body is protected before the cremation process and that

47 OLG Bamberg NJW 2008, paras 6–8.
48 OLG Bamberg NJW 2008, paras 9–10.
49 OLG Bamberg NJW 2008, para 12.

protection continues once the remains have been processed. Whatever formed part of the person when living remains his or hers after death.[50] Violating the ashes then qualifies as a disrespectful disturbance of the deceased;[51] unlawfully taking possession of someone else's body parts.

The case reviewed by the court in Nürnberg dealt with two oven managers at a city mortuary and a number of assistants.[52] Over a period of about two years, they collected the dental gold found in the ash remains and sold it to jewellers for a profit.[53] They too were arrested for violating a dead body. The Nürnberg court also confirmed that what is part of the body remains part of the ash.[54] This guarantees that the ash remains of each urn remains unmixed.[55] However, according to the interpretation of the Nürnberg court, whatever is not destroyed by the cremation process (like dental gold and any other type of prosthesis), does not form part of the ash remains.[56] Referring to the Bamberg case, the Nürnberg court viewed their extended denotation of *ash* as a mistake, which to Nürnberg was a deviation of the ordinary meaning of the word.[57] As a result, the accused in Nürnberg could not be charged for violating a corpse, because the gold found in the ash no longer forms part of the body.[58] The body enjoys legal protection because it is recognisable as an individual. This is no longer the case when a body is cremated. When a cremation furnace's waste bin collects the gold pieces from different bodies, it is too difficult to determine which gold piece formed part of which individual.[59]

From the difference in interpretation, it is noticeable that the word *ash* is vague, because it is not entirely clear what is included and what is not. One court considers the gold as ash remains while the other views the gold as objects left over together with the ash remains. On the one hand, if a body is cremated in a coffin, the coffin material (like wood, nails, handles) do not form part of the ash remains of the human body. Also, any of these items that do not burn to ash and that can easily be identified and picked out might not qualify as ash. On the other hand, the same applies to the bones of a cremated body – bones are seldom burnt to fine ash. Consequently, the crematorium uses a grinder to grind bigger pieces to

50 OLG Bamberg NJW 2008, paras 33–36.
51 OLG Bamberg NJW 2008, para 37.
52 OLG Nürnberg NJW 2010, para 10.
53 OLG Nürnberg NJW 2010, para 10.
54 OLG Nürnberg NJW 2010, para 18.
55 OLG Nürnberg NJW 2010, para 21.
56 OLG Nürnberg NJW 2010, para 33.
57 OLG Nürnberg NJW 2010, para 37.
58 OLG Nürnberg NJW 2010, para 34.
59 OLG Nürnberg NJW 2010, para 35.

powder to fit the urn. Do the bigger pieces that need grinding still qualify as ash? What came to light in these two cases is that crematorium workers must remove any prosthesis that survive the crematorium oven (like pacemakers or hip replacements) and discard them because they will not fit the urn. Yet, the workers must leave the gold.

Some words may be simultaneously ambiguous and vague. This is particularly visible in the case *Herselman v Geleba*, which concerns hate speech. Mr Geleba was busy sweeping the hallway when he scratched an office door with his broom. Mr Herselman witnessed the incident and cried 'don't act like a baboon; you're damaging the building'.[60] Mr Herselman denied that he referred to Mr Geleba directly as a baboon, and instead held that he was asking Mr Geleba to stop acting stupid.[61] The utterance 'stop acting like a baboon' is ambiguous, because 'to act like a baboon' can mean different things:

1. to behave like an animal;
2. to behave foolishly;
3. to behave destructively.

The utterance can be vague as well, because what exactly does it mean to act like a baboon? Does it mean someone has to take on the physical characteristics and behaviour of baboons (crouching, flashing teeth, grunting)? Or should the listener only heed the connotation of lower intelligence and a lack of common sense?

Of course, the question of whether hate speech was present strongly depended on the historic misuse of the word *baboon* as a racial slur. Consequently, it was not difficult for the court to determine whether *baboon* had any hurtful or harmful connotations. As a potential racial slur, 'don't act like a baboon' seemingly offered enough unambiguous evidence to decide in Mr Geleba's favour.

2.10. Conclusion

In this chapter, we looked at the fundamentals of meaning, namely concepts, words, lexemes, expressions, and utterances. We realised that speakers use words to give form to mental representations archived in their lexicons. We distinguished between word and sentence meaning and we explored different aspects of meaning like reference and denotation. Referring is something that speakers do, and denoting is something that words, expressions and utterances do. Reference is context dependent;

60 *Herselman v Geleba* (231/2009) [2011] ZAECGHC 108 (1 September 2011), paras 2(i)(*i*)–(*iii*) and 2(j).

61 *Herselman v Geleba*, para 2(k)(bb).

denotation remains the same regardless of context. We also saw that meaning is often something that a society determines through convention. Based on various factors like experience and encyclopaedic knowledge, both individuals and groups tend to associate many things with words and these associations may change according to the situation. In this chapter, we also learnt that ordinary meaning is a vital legal fiction necessary for meaning making, and that two of the biggest challenges for the ordinary meaning principle are ambiguity and vagueness.

With the necessary background, we can now move to the next aspect of meaning: the relation between words.

3. Understanding Word Relations

In chapter 2, we referred to a speaker's lexicon (that huge and growing collection of concepts, words, and language data) and we equated it to a network of sorts. Indeed, it is helpful to think of the lexicon as a network that interrelates lexical items and concepts in different ways. The relation between words and concepts plays a vital role in constructing their meaning. We can tell a lot about words and concepts by looking at the other words and concepts that relate to them. These relations take on different forms and rely on various language factors like similarity, opposition, co-occurrence, hierarchy and so on.

Let us briefly consider the noun *die*. It has at least three different senses:

1. a small cube used in different games (the plural is *dice*);
2. an instrument used to cast metal equipment;
3. a square of silicon with circuitry used in computer technology.

The three denotations are quite different; subsequently, we can describe them as homographs, because they look the same (die-die-die) but denote different things. If we add the word *dye*, we speak of homophones, because the words sound the same (die-dye), but still denote different things. So far, these words relate in terms of form and sound, but not in meaning. However, when we zoom in on the die used to play games, we can recall other lexical items like *board games* and *gambling*, *chance* and *fortune telling*. Other words include *casting*, *throwing*, *playing*, *wagering* and even *dicey*. These senses are all related to our first instance of *die*, even if they do not mean exactly the same thing. Looking at these words, we can see a semantic field taking shape related to other concepts like *unpredictability*, *leisure*, *addiction*, *money*, *social interaction* and *sport*.

Remember, words are containers of various meanings and they never exist in isolation.

3.1. Semantic features

One of the simplest ways to study a word's relations is by looking at its general features. Many semanticists believe that a word's conceptual meaning is built up of smaller components. By studying these smaller components, we might be able to reduce complex meaning to recognisable semantic building blocks (Murphy 2012:44-49; Bauer 2012:21; Shuy 1986:299). Words that contain the same or similar features are semantically related to some extent. In other words, **semantic features** (also called *semantic primitives*) help us to understand the meaning of lexemes and provide us with interpretation possibilities.

A classic example of semantic features is the word *man*. What do we know about the concept *man*? We know the word implies that he is male, that he is an adult and that he is human. We represent the information semantically as follows:

3.1 man [MALE] [ADULT] [HUMAN]

However, when we think about the lexeme *man*, we also know which features do not fit: a man is not an animal, he is not a child and he is not a rock. In order to include these features, we use a binary code with plus and minus symbols to indicate the features that apply and those that do not:

3.2 man [+MALE] [+ADULT] [+HUMAN] [-INANIMATE]

3.3 man [+MALE] [-JUVENILE] [-ANIMAL] [+CONCRETE]

The features listed above are the conventional features assigned to the lexeme *man*. But what can we tell from the following features?

3.4 man [+MALE] [+JUVENILE] [+ANIMAL] [+INANIMATE]

The example in 3.4 provides us with a lot of information. At a quick glance, it seems that we are dealing with connotation or social meaning of some kind. We can infer that men are boys who behave like animals that probably have no emotions. These features also tell us that this is not a standard denotation, because a lexeme cannot simultaneously comply with both binaries. A man cannot be animate and inanimate or human and animal at the same time – the law of opposition prevents it (see *antonymy*, this chapter). A better way to analyse immature or emotionless men would be like this:

3.5 man [+MALE] [+ADULT] [+HUMAN] [-IMMATURE]

3.6 man [+MALE] [+ADULT] [+HUMAN] [-EMOTIONS]

A few things should be obvious by now. The first is that semantic features are economical, which means that we identify as few features as possible (depending on our analytic need). Ordinarily, four features are enough. Secondly, each feature binds the concept to the lexical network and each contains its own set of features. For instance, *adult* may contain the features [+LIVING CREATURE], [+MATURITY], [-INANIMATE], and so on.

In the matter of *The Road Accident Fund v Mbele*,[1] the Supreme Court of Appeal had to decide whether a reach stacker was a motor vehicle. Ms Mbele's partner worked at a terminal in Cape Town harbour and was killed when the operator of the reach stacker collided with him. Consequently, Ms Mbele claimed against the Road Accident Fund (RAF) for a loss of support.[2] The RAF denied the claim, because according to them, a reach stacker was not a motor vehicle as defined in section 1 of the Road Accident Fund Act.[3]

The Act defines *motor vehicle* as:

> any vehicle designed or adapted for propulsion or haulage on a road by means of fuel, gas or electricity, including a trailer, a caravan, an agricultural or any other implement designed or adapted to be drawn by such motor vehicle.[4]

The court proceeded to isolate the features of *motor vehicle*: fuel, gas or electricity must propel it, its design must make propulsion possible and propulsion must take place on a road.[5] We can translate the information to the following metalanguage:

3.7 motor vehicle [+BUILT TO MOVE FORWARD]
[+MOVEMENT DEPENDS ON ENERGY SOURCE]
[+DESIGNED FOR USE ON ROAD]

If we look at the features of a reach stacker, then we are left with the following components:[6]

3.8 reach stacker [+BUILT TO MOVE FORWARD]
[+MOVEMENT DEPENDS ON ENERGY SOURCE]
[+DESIGNED FOR USE ON ROAD]
[+INDUSTRIAL]

1 *The Road Accident Fund v Mbele* 2020 (6) SA 118 (SCA), para 1.
2 *The Road Accident Fund v Mbele*, paras 1–3.
3 *The Road Accident Fund v Mbele*, para 3; Act 56 of 1996.
4 The Road Accident Fund Act 56 of 1996, section 1(xi); *The Road Accident Fund v Mbele*, para 5.
5 *The Road Accident Fund v Mbele*, para 5.
6 *The Road Accident Fund v Mbele*, paras 6–9.

By looking at the semantic features, we can see that a reach stacker shares most of the semantic components of a motor vehicle. It has an engine that uses diesel fuel to propel it forward on a set of wheels. Though it is an industrial machine, a reach stacker has a number of specifications that makes driving on a road possible. It is therefore difficult to argue that a reach stacker is anything different.

For experimental reasons, let us also consider the features of a remote-control car.

3.9 Remote-control car [+BUILT TO MOVE FORWARD]
[+MOVEMENT DEPENDS ON ENERGY SOURCE]
[-DESIGNED FOR USE ON ROAD]
[+TOY]

Similar to *motor vehicle* and *reach stacker*, a remote-control car is a vehicle that propels itself forward by means of electricity. It is built for forward propulsion and requires a driver or operator to control the movement. It is probably not made to drive on an open road along with other types of motor vehicles like cars, buses, and trucks. Yet, nothing in its design prevents it from being used on a road. To complicate matters, the court indicated that the word 'road' is not necessarily limited to a public road.[7] Does this mean that a remote-control car qualifies as a motor vehicle too? Not entirely.

The semantic feature that might need the most scrutiny is [DESIGNED FOR USE ON ROAD], because 'road' is vague. Does it denote 'public road' or 'restricted road'? Besides, the reach stacker in question was registered for use on public roads and had a registration number.[8] The same cannot be said for the remote-control car. The latter's design will not allow registration for use on public roads. The features of 'public road' looks something like this:

3.10 public road [+ROAD] [+PUBLIC] [+URBAN AREA] [-RESTRICTED]

A public road is a thoroughfare used by everyday people for a variety of reasons. It is typically found in and outside of urban spaces (including highways and national roads) and no part thereof is restricted for a select group or for a specific purpose (like the military, or for safety reasons).

7 *The Road Accident Fund v Mbele*, para 9.
8 *The Road Accident Fund v Mbele*, para 8.

Though the use of 'road' in the definition of 'motor vehicle' does not denote 'public road' in any clear way, reference to a trailer, a caravan and implements such as agricultural vehicles implies that 'road' does not restrict the greater public in any obvious manner. A remote-control car, however, is almost certainly intended for use in private and restricted spaces based on its design and purpose.

Semantic features can help us work out which criteria are at the core of contested meanings.

3.2. Synonymy

Synonyms allow us to tap into the broader lexical network of words. Because they have many semantic features in common, we can tell a lot by considering words similar to the one we are scrutinising. Let us imagine that John is in need of food. We can choose from a wide range of words to describe his need: John is hungry, peckish, starved, ravenous, famished or craving. Because all of these words relate to the concept of eating, we can substitute some of them to an extent but there will always be a nuanced difference in meaning. For instance, if John were ravenous, he is extremely hungry. If he were only peckish, it means that he is not hungry as such but wants something to tide him over until lunch or supper. If John were craving something, it means that he had a strong desire for something specific regardless of hunger.

We can use the same set of words metaphorically to describe a different situation: John is starved for attention. He craves it. If John were an attention-obsessed person, we might even say that he was ravenous for it. However, we cannot say that John is peckish, famished or malnourished for attention. As speakers, we know intuitively when certain words are more appropriate. We know when to say that John kicked the bucket, and when to refer to his passing.

Speakers often view synonyms as two or more words that have the same meaning. Unfortunately, this is a misconception because very few words have the honour of denoting in exactly the same way. Instead, **synonymy** is about semantic similarities in which the similarities are more important than the differences between them. We can distinguish at least two main types of synonymy: absolute and near synonyms.

Absolute synonyms are words that are entirely substitutable in every context without affecting their denotation. There are various reasons why some words have almost identical meanings. They could have different origins or they may even belong to different varieties of the same language. Some words are euphemisms for more taboo lexemes (Saeed 2009:65). Consider the following three examples:

3.11 Harmonica; mouth organ
John played a tune on his harmonica.
John played a tune on his mouth organ.

3.12 Boy; laaitie
John took his boy to the game.
John took his laaitie to the game.

3.13 Toilet; lavatory; water closet
John had to use the toilet urgently.
John had to use the lavatory urgently.
John had to use the water closet urgently.

In 3.11, *mouth organ* is simply a description of what a harmonica is and has since become a compound noun as allowable substitute. There is no difference in meaning between the two sentences in 3.11. The sentences in 3.12 share the same meaning as well. Both *boy* and *laaitie* denote a boy or young adult male in South African English. We could add *lad* to this class too. Another example includes *speed cop* and *traffic officer*. The sentences in 3.13 also express the same meaning, though *lavatory* is more formal than the other two.

If the context changes, the meaning of the synonyms may also change, suspending the absoluteness of their similarities. The words *insect* and *bug* are absolute synonyms; however, once the context changes, the relation between the two changes too. For example:

3.14 John keeps pestering me; he's a real bug.

The word *bug* no longer refers to an insect in 3.14; instead, it refers to an annoyance or hindrance.

Near synonyms are words that have similar features, of which the similarities are salient. The differences between near synonyms are usually minor or backgrounded (Cruse 2015:145). Most synonyms fall into this category. Words like *pretty*, *beautiful* and *handsome* are not exactly the same, but all imply *good-looking*. As we have noticed at the beginning, near synonyms remain different words with different denotations, and cannot substitute that easily without altering the meaning in some way.

3.15 John's daughter is pretty.

3.16 John's daughter is beautiful.

3.17 John's daughter is handsome.

The word *pretty* refers to delicate features whereas *beautiful* implies pleasing features. *Handsome* refers to well proportioned, strong and somewhat masculine features. The relation between the three words is obvious, but the denotation is different for each example sentence. John's daughter is delicate in 3.15, but attractive in 3.17. It is also possible for John's daughter to be beautiful but not pretty. As with our *hungry* example, we can use the same set of words to describe non-human and non-living objects. We can talk of a beautiful painting and a handsome sum of money. But it would be odd to speak of a handsome car and a beautiful disciplinary hearing.

Additionally, synonyms reveal something about stylistic and emotive word choices. Consider the following examples:

3.18 John was wasted last night.

3.19 John was drunk last night.

3.20 John was inebriated last night.

All three of these sentences imply 'drank too much'; however, 3.18 is an informal conversational word choice whereas *drunk* is standard language and *inebriated* formal.

Some words might look like near synonyms but are in fact not synonyms at all. This is not always easy to determine. Cruse (1015:145) says that when words like *pretty* and *handsome* are used in a traditional gendered sense, they no longer qualify as synonyms. The handsome young man does not have the same features as a pretty young woman (or so it goes) and therefore share no similarities. Another example is *rob* and *steal*. Both imply 'to take without permission or right', but there is a fundamental difference between the two: to rob is to take with force or threat of force, and to steal is to take without the victim knowing. They will still share a proximity in the lexical network and the semantic distance between synonyms (absolute, near and pseudo), will depend on the relevant context.

In the case *S v Mavungu*,[9] the court had to decide whether a caravan qualified as a building in order for housebreaking and trespassing to take place. Mr Mavungu entered a caravan without permission and slept there for the night. He was found the next morning and arrested in terms of the

9 *S v Mavungu* 2009 (1) SACR 425 (T).

Criminal Procedure Act.[10] The court *a quo* raised the question of whether Mr Mavungu also trespassed in terms of section 1(1) of the Trespass Act.[11] The latter states that a person is guilty of trespassing if he or she enters land or a building (or part of a building) unlawfully.[12] The court felt the words *caravan* and *building* necessitated further scrutiny. Was a caravan a *premises*, *house*, *building* or *structure*?[13] If not, can the accused be guilty of trespassing (or housebreaking)?

Before we attempt a componential analysis by identifying each word's semantic features, we must consider their synonyms. When we look up *caravan*, *house* and *building* in a thesaurus we see (amongst others) the following options:

3.21 Caravan: camper van, mobile home, house trailer, home trailer, holidaymaker.

3.22 House: residence, accommodation, home, dwelling, building, apartment, shack, abode, crash pad.

3.23 Building: construction, edifice, architecture, house, home, monument, skyscraper, habitation.

It is significant that the word *home* repeats as synonym for all three lexemes, and items like *house* and *habitation* reflect as well. All three words are clearly associated with places meant for living or staying. We find the same sense when we consider *premises*. The words *digs*, *pad*, *joint*, *flat*, *house*, *home* and *property* are all synonyms. A caravan might not be built structurally the same as a house (or block of flats), but it still consists of [+DOORS], [+WINDOWS], [+WALLS] and a [+ROOF]. This means a caravan has a lot in common with *house* and *building* and there is no reason why we cannot view a caravan in the same light. Another quality most of these synonyms share, is the fact that we can distinguish between an [+INSIDE] and an [-OUTSIDE]. A person has to enter through a porthole after which they will be inside. A caravan, a house and a building are therefore all [+ENCLOSURES] of some kind. Entering any of the three without permission should be equally unlawful.

10 *S v Mavungu*, paras 1–13; section 262(2) of the Criminal Procedure Act 51 of 1977.

11 Trespass Act 6 of 1959; *S v Mavungu*, para 22.

12 Trespass Act 6 of 1959, section 1(1)(*a*) and (*b*); *S v Mavungu*, para 29.

13 *S v Mavungu*, paras 31–41.

3.3. Antonymy

If synonyms are about the similarities shared between words, then antonyms are words that display significant semantic distance. A typical example of this would seem to be the words *hot* and *cold*. However, this is not true. Antonyms are words that actually share many similarities. In fact, for words to be opposites they must share a number of features. Yes, hot and cold are at opposite ends of a scale, but that scale represents one concept, temperature. Temperature is gradable, which means that some temperatures are high while others are low. Words like *hot* and *cold* tend to appear in frequently co-occurring pairs. When we recall the one lexical item, we can easily reach for its opposite too, because opposites are binary. Since they are binary, the two items are mostly incompatible and as such, they cannot express both values simultaneously (Löbner 2003:124). This ties with the maxim of contradiction, which states that something cannot be true and false at the same time (Löbner 2003:82). Furthermore, we can tell a lot about what something is by considering what it is not.

Semantically speaking, what we have described so far falls under *opposites*. We can distinguish different types of opposites, but we will limit it to three broad categories: complementaries, antonyms and converses (Cruse 2015:153-161).

Complementary opposites represent two extremes of a domain that we can equate to an either-or relationship. This means that if an item falls within one compartment it cannot fall into the other as well. John is either dead or alive; he is either sick or well; he is either someone's aunt or uncle. John can never satisfy both conditions at the same time. Complementary opposites extend to adjective pairs that differ based on negating prefixes. For example, John is either married or unmarried; his suggested solution is either possible or impossible; he either obeys or disobeys the rules. Once again, John cannot be single and married simultaneously.

Antonyms represent gradable adjectives that we can view in terms of a continuum (Löbner 2003:124). In other words, we use adjectives and adverbs to describe aspects like size, height and strength. We can adjust these values according to a scale: John is small but Mzwandile is big; John is short, but Mzwandile is tall; John is strong, but Mzwandile is weak. The lexical items are at opposite ends of the scale and could represent extreme values (instead of neutral, in-between values). Since antonyms are gradable, we can use modes of comparison to indicate the relevant degree. John is smaller than Mzwandile (but bigger than Vitesh); John is shorter than Mzwandile (but taller than Vitesh); John is stronger than Mzwandile (but weaker than Vitesh). We can express gradability through a range of modifiers as well (Cruse 2015:156). For instance, we can say that John is *very* short or *extremely* tall. John's mood might be *quite* low, or his temper might be *seriously* out of control.

Converses represent a different kind of opposite, because lexical items express a relationship that we do not find between complementary opposites and antonyms. With converses, one item always implies the other. If we say *mother*, then surely there must be a son or daughter (or both). If we say *doctor*, then there must also be a patient. If John is selling something, then there must (hopefully) be a buyer. We can use both items to describe the same situation. Consider the following:

3.24 John's house is below the N1 highway.

3.25 The N1 highway is above John's house.

The words *above* and *below* describe the same situation (the location of the house), but they are also implied opposites of one another; the presence of the one recalls the presence (or absence) of the other.

Can semantic opposites help us understand whether someone is a legitimate employee, despite not having an actual contract of employment? Remember Mr Myeni, who sued his employer, the Universal Church of the Kingdom of God?[14] The opposite of *employee* is simply *employer*, which might not seem like much. Let us have a closer look. According to the conditions listed in section 200A of the Labour Relations Act, an employee's work must be controlled or directed by another person and said employee must be economically dependent on the person who he or she works for.[15] Services are rendered to that one person only and must be for an average of 40 hours per month and for more than 3 months.[16] The conditions in section 200A(1) clearly describe both employee and employer. *Employee-employer* is a converse set, which means that a relationship is implied between the two lexical items. If there is an employer, there must be an employee as well. If the Universal Church of the Kingdom of God benefited from Mr Myeni's services or labour, if they controlled his labour activity, if they paid him money for work done over more than 40 hours per month for longer than 3 months, then it should be hard to prove that no relationship existed between the two.[17]

14 *Universal Church of the Kingdom of God v Myeni* (DA 3/14) 2015 ZALAC 31 (28 July 2015).

15 Labour Relations Act 66 of 1995, section 200A(1)(*a*) and (*e*)

16 Labour Relations Act 66 of 1995, section 200A(1)(*d*) and (*g*).

17 There are other conditions too, like the provision of tools of the trade, and participation in the organization; sections 200A(1)(*c*) and (*f*), of the Labour Relations Act 66 of 1995.

We can study the opposite of *employed* as well. If someone is unemployed (a complementary opposite), he or she is jobless and receives no money for any labour. Free labour is charity work. To be unemployed also means that you are unrestricted (which contrasts with the conditions of employment – being controlled by an employer). The opposite of having 'one employer' is to have various employers, which already says something about working hours spent at one place. If a person is not *economically dependent* on an employer, then he or she is obviously *economically independent* or *partially dependent* on someone for money. The opposite of 'provided with tools of the trade' is to bring your own tools in order to get a job done. By considering opposites, we can differentiate between what clearly seems to be *employee* and *independent contractor*. It is doubtful that Mr Myeni was an independent contractor.

3.4. Homonymy

Homonymy is in many respects something that occurs by chance and offer us yet another good example of the arbitrariness of language. The fact that some words look and sound the same happened accidentally. There is no semantic link between homonyms, but their similarity of form often leads to confusion. To better understand polysemy (in the next section), it is helpful to spend a brief moment on homonymy.

We can differentiate between strong and weak forms of homonymy (Bosman and Pienaar, 2014:270–271). Strong **homonyms** are words that look and sound the same. Think of the nouns *bat* and *match*. *Bat* can refer either to a flying mammal or to a piece of sports equipment used in cricket and baseball. *Match* describes both a sports game between two opponents and a tool used to start a fire. Weak homonyms can be divided between homographs and homophones. **Homophones** are words that sound the same, but look different. Examples include *compliment* x *complement*, *bare* x *bear*, *not* x *knot*, *soul* x *sole* and *cent* x *scent*. **Homographs** are words that look the same, but sound differently. Look at the following examples:

3.26 Minute
John will call you back in a minute. /mənət/
John explains the work in minute detail. /mainju:t/

3.27 Tears
John wipes the tears from his eyes. /tiəz/
John tears the paper to pieces. /teəz/

3.28 Bow
John ties a bow to the gift. /bəu/

John must bow when he meets the queen. /bau/

Homonyms can lead to some confusion, especially when they look the same as polysemes. Consider the following example:

3.29 John knows where the mole is.

The word *mole* can have two related senses: (1) a burrowing animal that has weak eyesight and (2) a spy who hides within an organisation. References to the spy relate to the mammal, because like the animal, the spy hides underground and burrows for information. But *mole* can also refer to a dark spot on someone's face, and it can refer to a structure that serves as a small harbour of sorts. The lexeme *mole* in 3.29 can refer to any one of these four denotations and is therefore vague. Proper contextualisation is necessary to make sense of the word. The following contextualisation remains vague:

3.30 John knows where the mole is. He thinks he can reach it in time.

3.31 John knows where the mole is, because he's seen it before.

We still do not know if John is trying to get close to the burrowing mammal, the spot on someone's face or the pier. In the following sentences we note the word relation and provide better context:

3.32 John knows where the mole is. He swims there regularly. (Homonym)

3.33 John knows where the mole is. He has notified the detective working the case. (Polyseme)

3.34 John knows where the mole is. There is a small mound of dirt in his backyard. (Polyseme)

3.35 John knows where the mole is. It is just above his eye. (Homonym)

Now that we know what homonyms are and since we have touched on polysemy as well, we can explore polysemy in more detail.

3.5. Polysemy

By now, we have seen a few instances where words have different meanings, yet somehow the meanings are still related. It is an economic tendency of language to reduce a speaker's effort in constantly creating new ways to express him or herself (Löbner 2003:60). Instead, we use the same devices in new contexts. For this reason, there will always be a link between the original usage of a word and its new context.[18] A **polyseme** is therefore a lexeme that contains clearly distinguishable senses that remain connected. A classic example to illustrate this is the word *school.* Let us look at the following instances:

3.36 School starts at 07h00. (school = tuition / classes / learning)

3.37 The school has decided to build a swimming pool. (school = management, parents)

3.38 I finished school two years ago. (school = secondary education)

3.39 The school fared poorly in the hockey match. (school = athletes / hockey team)

3.40 Apparently the school burnt down on Wednesday. (school = buildings / premises)

In each of the five examples, we see that the word *school* refers to distinct concepts, but they still have *educational institute* in common. We understand the different senses of *school* in 3.36 to 3.40 because we know its base value. In the same vein, we also know what a *sperm bank* is, because we understand what a *money bank* is. The words *river mouth* makes sense to us, because we understand what *mouth* refers to. However, because polysemes can represent different but related senses, they can easily lead to confusion (due to ambiguity) or present an opportunity for different probable interpretations.

We saw previously that words such as *baboon* or *monkey* can be polysemous. They can refer to the actual mammal, but they can also refer to people, especially when used metaphorically. Sometimes it is not clear whether a word actually has more than one sense and whether any of the senses may apply to a specific case. The word *search* is such an example. Overall, *search* means 'to look for something'. However, it is not that simple. We can distinguish between different senses, for example:

18 Some polysemes have become fossilised, which means that their sense relation is no longer that obvious, moving them closer to homonymous relations. Today we consider *bank*[1] (financial institution) and *bank*[2] (sand bar) as homonyms, because they denote two unrelated concepts. However, the word *bank* is German in origin and was used to refer to the high bench used by tellers. The same concept was applied to the landform either side of a river, recalling the high benches. They had the base value of height (specifically a high table) in common (Fellbaum 2017:353).

3.41 John searched the book for answers. (search = explore / investigate)

3.42 John searched the woods for the stag. (search = hunt / pursue)

3.43 John searched the literature, but found very little evidence. (search = research / study)

3.44 John searched the room for the murder weapon. (search = seek / uncover)

Though all four instances of 'search' relate to the base value of looking for something, the context may require a specific sense. In *Minister of Safety and Security v Xaba*,[19] the presiding officer had to decide, amongst other things, whether the word *search* could apply to the surgical removal of a bullet in terms of sections 20–23, 27 and 37 of the Criminal Procedure Act.[20] The accused was a suspect in a vehicle hijacking case and the police believed that a bullet lodged in his leg would be sufficient evidence to convict him.[21] They requested a confirmation of a rule *nisi* that will allow the removal of the bullet at an identified hospital.[22] Because the word *search* is undefined by the Act, it must be given its ordinary meaning.[23] However, as can be seen from examples 3.41 to 3.44, this is not necessarily so straightforward. The presiding officer identified the direct context of *search* as sections 20–23, 27 and 37 of the Act that dealt with search and seizure, and determined that 'search' applied to the thoroughly examination of a person's body. In this instance, a police officer would conduct a search to notice any physical characteristics or to find anything concealed (similar to examples 3.41 and 3.44).[24]

Based on the context identified, the court concluded that a search of this kind did not include a medical procedure under general anaesthesia.[25] Yet, if we consider the examples in 3.42 and 3.44 once more, we can also argue that the word *search* includes another sense; that is, to recover something. When you know of something's existence but you are uncertain as to its location, a search could serve to recover the object. Better still, if you know the exact location, but you need to extract and take possession of an object, you also recover it. *Recover* relates directly to the concept of *search and seizure*. As we have seen before, a phrase like *search and seizure* may function as one lexical item and as such, we

19 *Minister of Safety and Security v Xaba* 2004 (1) SACR 149.
20 Criminal Procedure Act 51 of 1977.
21 *Minister of Safety and Security v Xaba*, at 150.
22 *Minister of Safety and Security v Xaba*, at 152.
23 *Minister of Safety and Security v Xaba*, at 158.
24 *Minister of Safety and Security v Xaba*, at 159.
25 *Minister of Safety and Security v Xaba*, at 159.

might gain more by interpreting it as a unit. If the court had done that, the notion of recovering the bullet in terms of the Criminal Procedure Act might have succeeded.

3.6. Categorisation

Speakers process information constantly. We place information into mental compartments, organising items according to frequency of use. Based on frequency, we arrange items from typical examples to less obvious ones. When a South African says he or she will be watching a match on Saturday, rugby, soccer or cricket would probably come to mind because these are the typical and most frequently supported team sports in the country. We might be surprised when that person mentions lacrosse or hurling – both are poor examples of South African team sports and are therefore atypical. The process of organising items according to typicality is known as **categorisation** and it is an important process in meaning making.

Traditionally, in order for a chair to be signified as a chair or a dog to be signified as a dog, they have to conform to the criteria of *chairness* and *dogness*. That means objects need to satisfy the known characteristics of their kind to be classified as such. Let us say a chair has to be made of wood and has to have four legs, a seat and back support. Items that claim to be a chair but lack any of the clearly defined criteria can never qualify as a chair. In other words, a bar stool with one leg and no back support can never be a chair. The same goes for a small ottoman that only has a seat and four legs. We will have to disqualify a sofa with six legs as well, and every chair made of metal, plastic and canvas.

This Aristotelian approach to categorisation has many flaws. To start with, there is little room for kinship terms like stool, sofa, bench, lounger, etc. The internal structure of categories implies that every member of the category has equal status. So, if you hear the word *chair*, all of the different types of chairs will come to mind simultaneously, because you think of all of them in equal measure all the time. The classic approach further suggests that the borders between categories are very clear and solid. A stool is not a type of chair and that is final!

However, work done by scholars like Brent Berlin and Paul Kay (1969), William Labov (1973) and a series of experiments by Eleanor Rosch and her colleagues (1975, 1976, 1978) proved in a number of ways why the classic theory of categorisation is insufficient. They found that borders between categories are fuzzy and that it is not so simple to exclude objects from a category based on a finite set of criteria. Instead, when speakers categorise information, they do so using a grading system.

We place the items we consider to be the best examples of that category at the top of the list. We call these best examples **prototypes**. Words that appear the furthest from the prototype are the least common examples within a category, though they still represent the category to some extent. Items within a category tend to share family resemblances, which means that even if they do not share the exact same criteria they still share family traits. In this case, a bar stool is very different from a six-legged sofa, but they share traits in their overall design and purpose. That said, a sofa would probably be higher up the list (closer to the prototype) and a bar stool lower down the list. Prototypes also reflect frequency of use. In other words, we tend to recall the concepts we use the most often when we think of or hear specific lexical items. When someone starts talking about kitchen appliances, we might think of stoves, fridges, and air fryers first and a soda machine last.

More importantly, we identify levels of categorisation. When speakers categorise information, they organise items on three distinct levels: the superordinate, the basic and the subordinate level. Let us look at each of them.

The superordinate level is the most inclusive category, covering a number of basic-level items. It represents broad classes like *fruit*, *vehicles*, *beverages*, etc. This level seldom shares names with basic category items and there are few defining attributes in common (Cruse 2015:63).

The basic-level category rests in the middle of the three levels and represents the most basic class of items. The basic-level contains the items speakers acquire first when learning a language (both mother tongue and additional language). Basic items are the words we use most frequently and which represent our most common vocabulary. For this reason, when we categorise information, we tend to dip into the basic-level category for lexical items that signify the best examples (the prototypes) of a concept. This is also the category closely related to ordinary meaning.[26] When a court seeks to understand what a word means ordinarily, they want to summon a basic-level item. The basic-level items representing *fruit* are usually *apples*, *oranges* and *bananas*. When we think of *vehicles*, words like *car*, *motorcycle* and *bus* come to mind. It is basic-level items that speakers recognise the easiest and that we are inclined to call by generic names, even if we know a more specific name. For instance, we would rather say *John ate an apple* than *John ate a Golden Delicious*. Everyone speaking the

26 As a potential tool within statutory interpretation, see Solan (1995), Carney and Bergh (2016), Lee and Mouritsen (2018) as well as Carney (2022).

same language will understand *apple*, though many might have to expend cognitive effort to work out what *Golden Delicious* means.

Subordinate levels are the least inclusive class. Items in this category are very specific and tend to communicate less information than basic-level items. As Cruse (2015:63) points out, the names of subordinate level items identify a single property, though the concept may still distinguish more than one property at a time. It is in this category that we find the name *Golden Delicious* and this category is more representative of terminology or jargon.

Knowledge of prototypes can assist in determining what a word's most typical meaning might be, especially where words are undefined by the legislature. However, it is important to note that prototypes are context sensitive and that fuzzy borders could make category membership tricky at times. Context sensitivity extends to culture and language groups, and especially usage. The way that South Africans use and understand concepts and words may differ greatly from other cultures and countries. As a result, a court should be sensitive to the prototypicality of contested words.

If a word has more than one sense that potentially applies to a context (in other words, a polyseme), then prototypicality can be used as a discrimination tool. If we consider the *search* example taken from *Minister of Safety and Security v Xaba* once again, we know it means within the context of *search and seizure* to examine someone's body or to uncover concealed items. It does not refer to hunting or research.

Jowells Transport v South African Road Transportation Services offers an interesting situation too.[27] Jowells Transport had a permit allowing it to transport various items ranging from coal and lime to stock meal, stock licks and calf meal.[28] The applicant's truck was stopped and more than 500 bags of mealie meal[29] were found inside.[30] Authorities believed that the applicant contravened the permit, which only allows it to transport animal feed. To the contrary, the applicant believed that the word *stock meal* meant *ordinary meal*, which entitled him to carry mealie meal as well. According to a language expert's affidavit, the word *stock meal* also denoted 'meal for stockpiling'.[31] It is this understanding that motivated the applicant to transport mealie meal.

27 *Jowells Transport v South African Road Transportation Services* 1986 (2) SA 252 (SWA).
28 *Jowells Transport v South African Road Transportation Services*, at 253.
29 Also known as *maize meal*; Afrikaans: *mieliemeel.*
30 *Jowells Transport v South African Road Transportation Services*, 253.
31 *Jowells Transport v South African Road Transportation Services*, 254.

The first problem is that the word *stock meal* is undefined by the Road Transportation Act.[32] The second issue is that the compound *stock meal* (Afrikaans: *veemeel*) is not included in any dictionary, neither in 1986 nor at the time of writing this book. The presiding officer had to rely on other means to determine its meaning. The Afrikaans equivalent makes it clear that it denotes feed for livestock, and does not refer to stockpiling as well. Where the English word is polysemous, the Afrikaans word is not. Furthermore, the words *stock meal* are used together with *stock licks* and *calf meal*, eliminating any confusion as to whom the feed is meant for.[33] Nevertheless, the court decided to scrutinise the word *stock* on its own.[34] It is true that *stock* in *livestock* is related to the concept of stockpiling; however, the prototypical meaning of *stock* in this context refers to animals and not to a storage cache. The fact that the word *stock* is also used as a modifier for *meal* further suggests that its prototypical denotation is *feed for livestock*. In the same vein, *mealie meal* has a wider interpretation because it has a wider usage (for human and animal consumption). Though, if speakers were to categorise the two items between *feed for animals* and *food for humans*, it is doubtful that people would have trouble deciding. The borders between the two concepts are not that fuzzy. And, even though the two items share family resemblance (both are ground, both are meant as foodstuffs), their main difference is based on the most salient criteria: animals / humans.

We can visualise some of the relations of the lexical item *stock meal* as follows:

Table 3.1: Stock meal

Synonymy	**Homonymy**	**Polysemy**	**Prototype**	**Semantic features**
stock crumbles stock pellets stock grains stock fodder	powder used to make stock	feed easily stored in large quantities feed for animals	foodstuff given to livestock (and game)	[+FOOD] [+ANIMALS] [+EASY STORAGE]

32 Road Transportation Act 74 of 1977.

33 Interestingly, the court did not apply the *eiusdem generis* rule, which would have forced the court to consider the genus of words listed in the transportation permit.

34 *Jowells Transport v South African Road Transportation Services*, at 258-259.

From Table 3.1, it is clear that the prototype represents the best example of the senses associated with the lexical item under scrutiny. We can see from its potential synonyms that the compound noun is better linked to animal feed and that it is removed from foodstuffs for human consumption, as seen from the homonymous relation that denotes broth. Considering the polysemy of *stock meal*, the prototype is much closer to the second sense, although the first sense still applies – farmers usually buy animal feed in bulk and stockpile it for use over weeks or months. The storage capability of stock meal does not necessarily render it edible for humans.

As can be seen, a study of prototypes can reveal salient information about a contested word's ordinary meaning. Another semantic relation that closely resembles prototype categorisation is hyponymy, which we will review next.

3.7. Hyponymy

Hyponymy is known as a relation of inclusion, because one item's extension includes another item as a subset. *Chocolate* is included in *confectionary*, just as *extreme sports* includes *bungee jumping*. We know that *cars* are part of a more general category called *vehicles* and that a *president* is one of many *government officials*.

Similar to prototypes, we call the more general term the superordinate and its subset the hyponym (also known as a subordinate). The word *building* is the superordinate of *house*, its hyponym. Hyponymy creates vertical taxonomies of inclusion. Remember Mr Mavungu, who slept in a caravan and was charged for housebreaking and trespassing?[35] The court considered whether a caravan qualified as a house in order for housebreaking and trespassing to have taken place. We can use a hyponym taxonomy to determine where *caravan* fits in a broader conceptual field like *housing*. See figure 3.1 below.

35 *S v Mavungu* 2009 (1) SACR 425 (T).

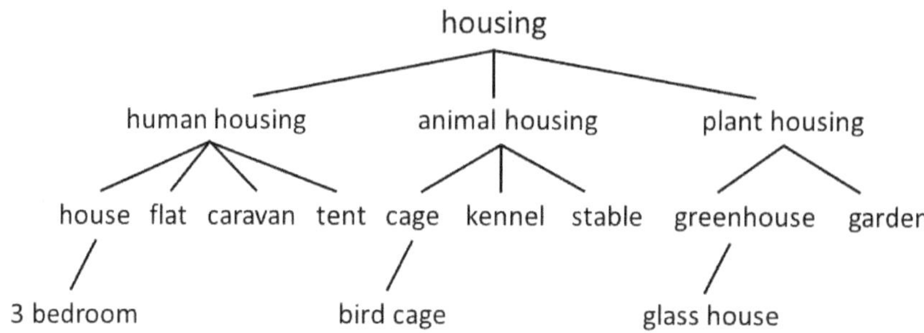

Figure 3.1: Hyponym taxonomy of *housing*

From figure 3.1, we can see that a caravan is a type of housing structure used by humans. A hyponym taxonomy for *building* will look somewhat different. If we accept that a building is a structure with a roof and walls, we can identify hyponyms like *house*, *office block* and *factory*. The word *house* can contain other hyponyms like *two-storey*, *hut*, *shack*, *flat*, *palace* and yes, a *caravan* and a *tent*. Hyponymy helps us understand that words like *house*, *building* and *structure* are inclusive and represent much broader conceptual fields. It is also important to note that most of our vocabulary is structured in this way: larger generic classes inclusive of subsets.

Cruse (2015:135) highlights an aspect of hyponymy that is common in legislative drafting and that is sometimes challenged in court. The relation between superordinates and their hyponyms are often constrained to the extent that we interpret X as inclusive of Y, even when it is unexpected. The pattern is *Xs and other Ys*. He provides the following examples to illustrate this (Cruse 2015:135):

3.45 Dogs and other pets.

3.46 The murder weapon was a bread knife.

In 3.45, *dog* is included in *pets*. It immediately implies that *dog* refers to domestic dogs specifically and that *pets* places dogs on par with budgies, bearded dragons and cats. In 3.46, *bread knife* is a hyponym of *murder weapon*. The latter is the broader category, now inclusive of an item that is maybe not typical of murder weapons. Once again, the context plays an important role in the way we construct and interpret meaning.

The legislative text can provide an important part of the context, as can be seen in *S v Kohler*.[36] Mr Kohler kept a number of peacocks on his premises without the necessary permit, as stipulated by the Heidelberg municipality.[37] The specific ordinance prevents citizens from keeping poultry in their yard without the required permission. The word *poultry* was at issue, which the ordinance describes as:

> any chicken, duck, goose, turkey, guineafowl, partridge, pheasant, pigeon and their chicks or any other bird.[38]

The court felt they had to determine whether peacocks were poultry and qualified as any of the birds listed. To do this, they also felt compelled to apply the *eiusdem generis* rule on the words *any other bird* to restrict a broader interpretation.[39] The presiding officer concluded that peacocks were some kind of pheasant and therefore included in the list, which meant that peacocks were illegal without official permission.[40]

Viewed from a hyponymous perspective, the court was not required to restrict the meaning of *any other bird*. In fact, *any other bird* is used synonymously for *poultry*, which means *poultry* remains the superordinate for the birds listed. This is what Cruse refers to as the *Xs and other Ys*; chickens and any other bird (chickens and any other poultry). Because *poultry* refers to domesticated birds kept for their eggs, meat and feathers, *any other bird* could hardly refer to parrots, budgies or finches in this instance.

For another example, we look to *Jowells Transport v South African Transportation Service* again.[41] Their applicable permit allowed Jowells Transport to carry the following goods:

> Coal, lime, mine props, coke, lucern, hay, chaff, teff, silage, stock meal, stock licks, calf meal, stone, sand, bricks, earthen tiles, ceramic tiles, roofing slates, rough unsawn timber, fertilizers, crude and untreated ores, as well as crude and untreated minerals...

What we see here is not a definition of a generic lexical item; instead, it offers a collection of permissible goods. However, looking at the items

36 *S v Kohler* 1979 (1) SA 861 (T).
37 *S v Kohler*, at 862.
38 *S v Kohler*, at 862.
39 *S v Kohler*, at 863.
40 *S v Kohler*, at 863.
41 *Jowells Transport v South African Road Transportation Services* 1986 (2) SA 252 (SWA).

listed, we can identify potential superordinates like *fodder* (hyponyms: lucern, hay, chaff, teff, silage, stock meal, stock licks, calf meal), *building material* (hyponyms: stone, sand, bricks, earthen tiles, ceramic tiles, roofing slates, rough unsawn timber) and *mined minerals* (hyponyms: coal, lime, crude and untreated ores, crude and untreated minerals). None of these three are inclusive of human food, as claimed by the appellant.[42]

Hyponymy assists in categorising items vertically from broad inclusive terms to examples that are more specific. The hyponyms of each superordinate are key to understanding the superordinate, but also allow us to explore the conceptual field in terms of each hyponym's co-hyponym (its neighbour). Knowing a contested word's semantic family helps to understand the concept overall.

3.8. Meronymy

Meronymy expresses a part-whole relationship between lexical items. Typical examples include *house – roof, book – cover, door – handle.* We recall a concept by means of its parts: *X is part of* Y, Y *has X*; a *hand* has *fingers*, *fingers* are part of a *hand.* We refer to the part as a meronym (for instance, *fingers* is the meronym of *hand*). Similar to hyponymy, a meronymous classification is hierarchical and both express inclusion. We should not confuse the two, though. A hyponym is a subset of a broader concept, whereas a meronym represents a concept through its parts. A *dog* is not part of an *animal* (hyponymy), but a *tail* could be part of a *dog* (meronymy) (Cruse 2015:138).

Meronymy is not as stable as hyponymy, because there are often many borderline cases. In some cases, parts are necessary to their wholes, but other parts might not be. For example, *eyes* are a necessary part of *face*, but *ponytail* is not a necessary part of *head.*

If we consider the case of *S v Mavungu* once more,[43] we could view *caravan* meronymously in order to explore to what extent a *caravan* qualifies as a *house* (to test whether housebreaking and trespassing can take place in a caravan). See figures 3.2 and 3.3 below.

42 A notable exception is teff, which is an important staple food for humans in countries like Ethiopia. However, when we study all the other lexical items in the category *fodder*, it is quite obvious that the permit is meant for the transportation of *animal feed* specifically.

43 *S v Mavungu* 2009 (1) SACR 425 (T).

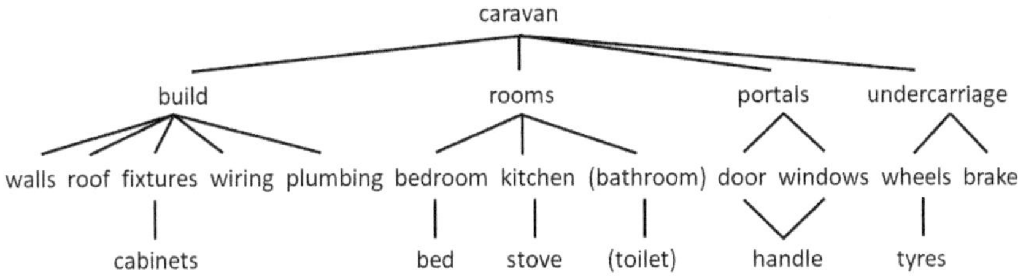

Figure 3.2: Meronymy of *caravan*

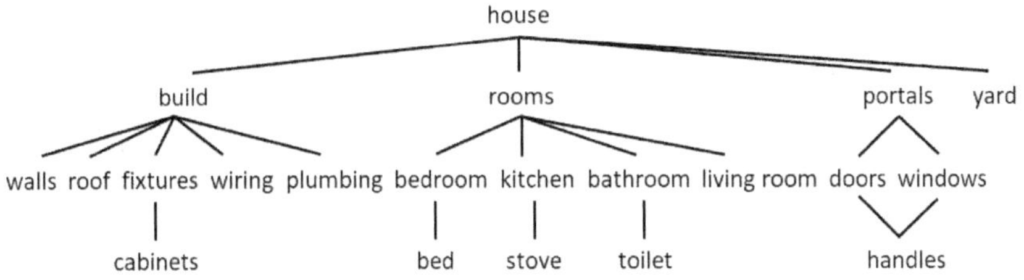

Figure 3.3: Meronymy of *house*

When we view the meronyms of both *caravan* and *house*, we see that they share a great many parts between them. Like *house*, *caravan* has a built structure consisting of a *roof*, *walls*, *fixtures* like *cabinets* as well as *wiring* and *plumbing* (though limited), *rooms* (at least a *bedroom* and *kitchenette*) and *portals* like *doors* and *windows*. Separate *rooms* are not a necessary part of *caravan* and neither is a *bathroom*. *Caravan* does not have a *yard*, but a *yard* is not a necessary part of *house* either. Based on the similarity between the two, there is very little to indicate that a house and a caravan are not comparable. For this reason, we can argue that, based on the many similarities, housebreaking and trespassing can take place in a caravan too.

3.9. Metonymy

Initially, metonyms might look a lot like meronyms, but they are two distinct devices. Where meronyms express part-whole relations between lexical items as part of a classification system, **metonymy** functions as a shorthand when referring (Saeed 2009:85, 198–199). When we employ metonymy, we refer to an object by naming something we associate with it. Look at the following examples:

3.47 The Union Buildings confirmed the official date for next year's national elections.

3.48 John is late for work because he had a flat tyre on the way.

3.49 My car is empty, so I made a quick stop at the service station.

3.50 John had to close down his shop due to a lack of feet.

3.51 What is your number?

In our first example (3.47), *Union Buildings* is a metonym for *government* or even the *presidency*. *Government* and *presidency* are metonyms too, because they represent a particular committee and specific individuals responsible for deciding what the election date must be. In 3.48, the pronoun *he* is a metonym for *car*; it is not possible for John to have a flat tyre, because he was not born with wheels. The word *car* in 3.49 is a metonym for *tank*, because the car itself is filled with a variety of things: engine, seats, the driver; and it is the tank that is empty. This example also employs the part-whole structure: a tank is part of a car. *Feet* in 3.50 is a metonym for *customers* and *your number* in 3.51 refers to the number a telephone company allocates to a SIM card.

In each of these examples, we use the name of one property of something in one domain and use it to name the property of something in a different domain, when both correspond in a certain way (Cruse 2015:258). Identification of a metonym depends on the context. We associate the Union Buildings with government, we associate a phone number with the phone's owner, we associate feet with people and people represent customers. Take note that metonymy does not express connotation; emotive associations are not present here. We substitute one item with another, because both items signify the same referent.

Metonymy can result in polysemy. *Union Buildings* refers to both the actual *building* as well as the *presidency* housed there. Metonymy is also a strong device of figurative language due to its associative nature. Examples 3.48 to 3.50 are illustrations of this. Another includes the expression *touching hearts and minds*. Of course, we are not literally touching someone's heart – that could be deadly.

In *Jacobs v Waks*,[44] the Court of Appeal dealt with decisions by the City Council of Carletonville in 1988 and 1989 respectively that saw the

44 *Jacobs v Waks* 1992 (1) SA 521 (A).

declaration of a number of parks and public spaces for the exclusive use by white people.[45] Preventing black and Indian people to use these spaces led to a business boycott, impoverishing businesses near these spaces (which, ultimately, led to this case).[46] Before this ordinance, no public park or space was restricted; in fact, black and Indian people who worked in Carletonville frequented many of these spaces.[47] One of the issues that the court addressed was the City Council's argument that applicable legislation clearly distinguished between *residents* and *the public*.[48] In support of their decision to declare particular spaces as white-only zones, the City Council of Carletonville argued that certain spaces were meant for *the public* and others for *residents* of Carletonville.[49] In this particular context, the words *residents* and *the public* take on metonymous relation, because the applicants used them to signify specific groups by means of association. In the case of *residents*, the City Council of Carletonville refer to white people specifically. Even though *the public* represent a broad category of people in general, it signifies *everyone else* in this situation (to be precise, the black and Indian workers). Cases involving place, container or collective representation may typically show metonymy. In *Jacobs v Waks*, we see a collective representation. The same applies to cases where political parties are involved. When the Public Prosecutor investigates the Economic Freedom Fighters (EFF) for inciting and instigating a crime like trespassing, we use *EFF* to name the trespassers and the party members who did the instigating.[50] When someone sues the President of South Africa, the president himself is not necessarily an active party in the lawsuit. Instead, we use *President of South Africa* to name something else, like the government or specific divisions within government.

3.10. Field relations and semantic frames

As we have mentioned early on, the vocabulary of a language is an integrated and interrelated system of meaning. Lyons (1979:252) reminds us that the system is in constant flux – words and their meanings come and go and the relationship between words adjusts and changes. When semantic changes take place within a lexicon, they do not affect individual words only, but affect whole structures within the lexicon (Geeraerts 2010:56). The conceptual field holds the conceptual ideation

45 *Jacobs v Waks*, at 527.
46 *Jacobs v Waks*, at 531–532.
47 *Jacobs v Waks*, at 530, 539.
48 *Jacobs v Waks*, at 538.
49 *Jacobs v Waks*, at 539.
50 *Economic Freedom Fighters v Minister of Justice and Constitutional Development* (87638/2016) [2019] ZAGPPHC 253.

of a particular object or entity, for instance a continuum of colour (Lyons 1979:253). Diverse cultures and language speakers view colour differently. Some might discriminate between many different types of blue (indigo, navy, azure, cerulean, admiral), while others might only differentiate between light and dark (Rosch 1973). To express this varying distinction, we use a set of lexemes to cover a certain area of a conceptual field (Lyons 1979:254).

Having reviewed a number of word relation types by now, it must be clear that we call many different concepts to the surface when we use specific words. John Firth famously said 'You shall know a word by the company it keeps' (Geeraerts 2010:59). Because words are linked to other words and because they are connected to various conceptual fields, we never use words in isolation. Consider the concepts *living* and *dying*. *Living* summons many different notions. To live, we must eat, we must work and we may partake in various social functions and rites. It is not simply a matter of breathing. *Living* involves people, systems, bureaucracy, politics, and so on. The same applies to *dying*. In fact, *dying* is not only physically and emotionally taxing, it can also be expensive. *Dying* often involves medical interventions, funeral arrangements, testaments, social and religious visits. Many of these involve people and money. The word *dying* does not refer solely to death; instead, it activates many different ideas and activities. We refer to this approach to meaning making as Charles Fillmore's frame semantics.

Semantic frames involve layers of meaning and the perspectives they allow. It depends quite strongly on the notion that George Lakoff (1987) expressed through his work, which states that our knowledge of language is intimately related to our knowledge of the world, which includes a speaker's experience (Fillmore 2007:238).[51] This knowledge takes the form of cognitive models or frames. To illustrate this, both Lakoff (1987:70-71) and Fillmore (1982) considered the meaning of the word *bachelor*. Certain societies use the word to categorise people in terms of marriage. *Bachelor*, then, denotes an unmarried adult man. The word recalls notions of marital status, marriageable age and says a lot about the individual labelled *bachelor*. The status of *bachelor* is usually positive whereas *spinster* is mostly negative and recalls notions of financial status, missed opportunity and attractiveness (both physical and emotional).

51 This is sometimes expressed by a variety of related terms such as *background knowledge*, *common-sense knowledge*, *socio-cultural knowledge* and *real-world knowledge*. As Evans (2010:17) points out, this knowledge is primarily non-linguistic and constitute a vast body of relation information that is highly detailed and necessary for semantic inference.

Our knowledge of the world helps us to understand that *bachelor* does not apply to unmarried men who are in long-term relationships, nor does it apply to the Roman Catholic pope. We would not refer to Pope Francis as the *bachelor of the century*.

Fillmore (2007:238) defines frames as:

> a system of concepts related in such a way that to understand any of them you have to understand the whole structure in which it fits...

According to Fillmore (1982:60), if we understand what the bigger picture looks like we will comprehend the related lexis as well. At the core of frame semantics is the understanding that we comprehend individual words by understanding the factual relationship between the concepts expressed by their lexical items. In other words, we use a word to frame a much broader conceptual field and call related words to the surface to help us express and understand the concept in general. Frames make it possible to understand the bigger picture without necessarily understanding each individual word (Fillmore 1985:229). This is possible in part because speakers take on a greater encyclopaedic perspective on the scrutinised meaning (Fillmore 1985:233). A well-known example of frames is the *commercial transaction* frame (Fillmore 2007:242; Geeraerts 2010:226). This frame involves words like *buy* and *sell*, which immediately invokes *possession*, *agreement*, and *money exchange*. We know that person A owns something and transfers ownership to person B for money. The exchange brings about an agreement between the two. Simultaneously, we are dealing with aspects of *ownership*, *money economy*, and *commercial contracts* (Geeraerts 2010:226). Someone who buys an item on *credit* also pays *interest*. This calls *debt* and *affordability* to mind.

Frames too are context sensitive, which is clearly visible from the *bachelor* example. Likewise, someone who chooses not to eat meat might be labelled *vegetarian* or *vegan*; however, if a person only eats plant-based food because there is no meat available, we cannot classify that person as *vegetarian* or a *vegan* because he or she did not actively give up meat (Fillmore 2007:246).

We can see the working of semantic frames in *S v Abrahams*.[52] Police stopped the accused and his companion and found a large quantity of ammunition in their car, including six petrol bombs.[53] The police arrested them in terms of section 32 of the Arms and Ammunition Act

52 *S v Abrahams* 2001 (2) SACR 266 (C).
53 *S v Abrahams*, at 267.

for possession of *armaments*.[54] The accused appealed their sentencing on the grounds that their petrol bombs did not qualify as *armaments*, which, according to them implied items of military origin.[55] Even though the court viewed a petrol bomb as an *incendiary device*,[56] it agreed with the accused and did not view the petrol bombs as military ammunition.[57] As a result, their appeal was successful. The Act does not define the word *armament*, but many examples are included: *cannon*, *recoilless gun* or *mortar*, *rocket launcher*, *machine gun*, *projectile* or *rocket*, *grenade*, *missile*, *bomb*, etc.[58] To determine whether a petrol bomb could be *armament*, we can consider the *explosives* frame.

Firstly, there are different types of bombers ranging from the military to commercial bombers who work for mines or road works. It includes everyday people who dabble in fireworks at parties and those who plan criminal activities (like money heists, gang violence or terrorism). The military could use their explosives for warfare or military exercises. Protesters use bombs to destabilise the government or to undermine certain movements. Bombers do not expend their bombs willy-nilly. They have specific targets and those targets imply a particular purpose. Explosives often claim victims as well, some innocent, and they may cause damage to existing structures (which further implies financial losses). The types of explosives may differ based on the target and purpose of the bomber. Bombers like the military may use bombs, grenades, missiles and rockets either to attack another nation or to defend their country. The police might use water cannons or smoke bombs to disperse angry crowds or to deny them access into dangerous settings. Protesters and criminals might do the same, but would use bombs that they make themselves (like petrol bombs). Commercial bombers would use dynamite to clear a patch or open closed-off spaces. So far, we can see that the *purpose* and the *target* play an important role in how we understand *explosives*. It is not simply restricted to their make and the people who use them.

From our real-world knowledge, we understand that a civil engineer will not use a petrol bomb to clear land for road works. In fact, it is difficult to imagine a commercial use for petrol bombs. Yet, we know

54 Arms and Ammunition Act 75 of 1969.

55 *S v Abrahams*, at 268.

56 Section 32(1)(*c*) of the Act prohibits possession of explosives, incendiary devices or parts thereof.

57 *S v Abrahams*, at 268–269. The court *a quo* and the court of appeal saw petrol bombs in their commercial sense; Binns-Ward AJ (at 270) refers to section 28 of the Explosives Act 26 of 1956 that covers the unlawful possession of so-called commercial explosives.

58 See sections 32(1)(*a*) and (*b*).

that people often use petrol bombs in guerrilla warfare (and have done for many years). Its historic association with war places *petrol bomb* much closer to *armament* than *commercial bomb*. A petrol bomb is an incendiary device also known as a Molotov cocktail and has been used by soldiers during various wars like the Spanish Civil War and the Second World War (Helmenstine 2021). In his judgment, Appellate Justice Binns-Ward argued that the legislature did not intend for *armament* to include *petrol bomb*, mostly because it was not a typical *military explosive*.[59] But, the legislature probably also did not have *petrol bomb* in mind when they referred to *explosives of commercial nature* in the Explosives Act. The classification of *petrol bomb* will never suffice without framing its *user*, its *target* and its *purpose* against its *history* as an incendiary device. Meaning making engages more than a standard dictionary definition.

3.11. Collocations

Collocations are words that frequently co-occur, so much so that we often consider them fixed expressions that we can easily rely on. Because of the co-occurring pattern, one word usually evokes the next. Common examples include: *pen and paper*, *black coffee*, *heated argument*, *dark chocolate*, *cushy job*, *pick a fight*. Semantically speaking, we do not have to say *black coffee* or *dark chocolate*. Instead, we can say *dark coffee* or even *milkfree coffee*; we can refer to *black* or *cacao-rich chocolate*. We do not have to say *cushy job*; instead, we could use *comfortable* or *convenient job*. Yet, speakers have conventionalised these co-occurring patterns to make them rather predictable. When we hear the word *table*, we will probably think of *chair* next and when South Africans hear *pap*, they will undoubtedly think of *wors*, *mogodu* or *sheba*. Al three words frequently co-occur with *pap*.

You will remember that the court had to decide the meaning of *stock meal* in *Jowells Transport v South African Road Transportation Services*.[60] The word was undefined by both legislation and dictionaries. The words *stock meal* is a compound noun, but it is also a good example of collocation. The modifying word, *stock*, frequently co-occurs with other words as well, like *stock farming*, *stock fencing*, *stock licks* and *stock feed*. By considering words with similar collocate composition, we can infer more about the meaning of our contested word, *stock meal*, realising that it could not denote *common meal* for human consumption as well. As a modifier in a collocation, the denotation is clearly that of *animal feed*.

59 *S v Abrahams*, at 269.

60 *Jowells Transport v South African Road Transportation Services* 1986 (2) SA 252 (SWA).

Collocations have an important semantic function in corpus linguistic searches, which we will revisit later in Chapter 7.

3.12. Entailment

Entailment expresses a semantic relation between sentences. It is often described as *If P, then Q* conditions, which means that the truth (or falsity) of Q logically follows from the truth (or falsity) of P. In other words, if we know P, then we will also know Q. More specifically, entailment expresses truth relations. For P to entail Q, both must be true (or false). Let us look at the following example.

3.52 (p) John is an adult man.
(q) John is a human.
3.53 (p) John killed the mosquito.
(q) The mosquito is dead.

If someone tells us 3.52 (p), we automatically know 3.52 (q), even when it is not said. The fact that we identify John as an adult male implies that he is human too. This particular relationship is hyponymous (many hyponyms are entailments), because *adult male* is contained within *human*, the one implies the inclusion of the other.

We see another truth condition in 3.53. If John killed the mosquito (p), it must be dead (q). We know this based on our knowledge of the English language and the real world: there is an obvious semantic link between *kill* and *dead.* The relationship expressed in 3.53 is therefore lexical, because of the relation between *kill* and *dead.*

Saeed (2009:99) summarises the definition of truth entailment as follows:

> A sentence **p** entails a sentence **q** when the truth of the first (**p**) guarantees the truth of the second (**q**), and the falsity of the second (**q**) guarantees the falsity of the first (**p**).

Because entailment expresses truth conditions, it forms part of logic. We can use logic to test whether speakers' inferences of statements or utterances are indeed true or logical. Consider the following examples:

3.54 (p) John ate a slice of pizza.
(q) John is dead.
3.55 (p) John killed the mosquito.

(q) The mosquito is alive.

3.56 (p) John's car is blue.

(q) John's car is yellow.

Because there is no logical link between *slice of pizza* and *dead*, no entailment exists between P and Q in 3.54. Eating pizza does not automatically lead to death (hopefully). Perhaps if we used *choked on* instead of *ate*, P could entail Q, because choking could lead to death, though not necessarily. The relation between P and Q would still be conditional. In 3.55, we see a contradiction. The mosquito cannot be both dead and alive. This means that P is true, but Q is false. Lastly, we see what Cruse (2015:29) calls a contrary proposition. Contrary pairs may not be simultaneously true, but they can both be false. Note that the relational direction is always from P to Q. In 3.56, *John's car is blue* entails that John's car cannot be yellow. However, the fact that the car is not yellow does not imply that the car is blue, because it might actually be red or green.

An important aspect of entailment is the fact that it is context-independent. This means that the truth condition can only be determined based on the constituents of the relevant sentence. For instance, our inference of 3.54 is based on the two sentences presented here. If we knew that John ate his slice of pizza alone in his kitchen and started choking uncontrollably with no one to help him, and he died, we need to see all of this presented in 3.54.

We can illustrate entailment some more at the hand of *Ryan v Petrus*.[61] Mrs Ryan brought a case of defamation and injuria against Mr Petrus because of a confrontation they had. The plaintiff was having an extramarital affair with the father of Mr Petrus. At some point, he attacked her verbally, saying:[62]

> You bitch. You are a fornicator. You fornicate with my dad and you and my dad make a fool of my mother. [...] you are a whore.[63]

61 *Ryan v Petrus* 2010 (1) SACR 274 (ECG).

62 *Ryan v Petrus*, at 277.

63 The original text is Afrikaans: 'Jou teef. Jy is 'n naaier. Jy naai saam met my pa en jy en my pa maak van my ma 'n poes. [...] jy is 'n hoer.' Note that the words *naaier* and *poes* have connotative meaning and therefore have different referential value to their denotations, as seen in the translation. The translation can reflect the informal, vulgar tone of the Afrikaans text too: 'You bitch. You are a slut. You fuck my dad and you and my dad make a pussy of my mother. [...] you are a whore.' As a side note, also pay attention to the fact that the court did not include any stylistic devices in their transcription. Looking at the words, we can assume that the words were said with venom, but there are no stresses

The court tried to determine how the words in the utterance contributed to injuria and how it affected her dignity as a (self-proclaimed) devout Catholic. To be clear, the truth of whether Mrs Ryan is a whore or an adulterer is not at issue here, but rather the way in which Mr Petrus expressed the matter.[64] Nevertheless, let us take a look at the truth condition present. We will see that there is no logical link between the words employed by Mr Petrus, which means that we must look at them connotatively (which supports claims of injuria).

3.57 (p) You are a bitch.
(q) You are a fornicator.
3.58 (p) You fornicate with my father.
(q) You are a whore.
3.59 (p) You are a fornicator.
(q) You are a whore.
3.60 (p) You fornicate with my father.
(q) You make a fool of my mother.

Because the word *bitch* has become a common insult for both women and men, it no longer has the same degrading connotation of *vicious dog* or *bitch in heat*. Instead, it takes on polysemous senses. Its semantic link to *fornicator* is therefore no longer very obvious, making an entailment between P and Q in 3.57 less logical. Someone can be a *bitch* (or *mean*) without necessarily being an *adulterer*. The word *whore* prototypically signifies *sex worker*, followed by someone who has many sexual partners. We can view *fornicator* as a synonym, but *fornicator* prototypically signifies a person who has sex with someone they are not married to. Due to this nuanced difference, P does not entail Q in 3.58 or 3.59. Someone can have many unmarried partners and be labelled a *whore* because of this; however, none of those many partners are necessarily married. Being a *whore* is therefore not the same as being a *fornicator*.

Lastly, the semantic relation between *fornicate* and *making a fool* is not precise enough for P to entail Q. What we have in 3.60 is an assumption. *Adultery* has many connotations of which some are emotional, summoning feelings like *embarrassment* and *humiliation*. We can say that there is a semantic connotative link between *fornicate* and *make a fool*, because we

or exclamations to support this. We will address this issue again; see *text stylistics* in Chapter 4.

64 *Ryan v Petrus*, at 283.

assume the one leads to the other. When we start assuming, we work with presupposition, which is a relation within entailment.

3.13. Presupposition

Speakers design their linguistic messages based on large-scale assumptions about what the listener already knows. We call what a speaker assumes is true or commonly known by a listener **presupposition** (Yule 2020:155; Cruse 2015:42). Like entailment, we infer something about Q based on what is stated in P. An important difference between the two lies with context. As we have mentioned before, entailment does not consider context at all; it only works with the facts present in the propositions provided. Presupposition, however, engages the communicative act and takes note of a speaker's viewpoint. Before we continue, let us study the following examples:

3.61 (p) John takes his dog to the park.
(q) John has a dog.

3.62 (p) The King of Eswatini turned 56 on Monday.
(q) Eswatini has a king.

3.63 (p) John used to work in Pretoria.
(q) John no longer works in Pretoria.

3.64 (p) John drank a glass of wine.
(q) John drank a liquid.

In each of these examples, P presupposes Q; we assume Q is true based on P. What we see from the examples above is the proposition that certain entities exist or that certain events or states either continue or ceases to take place. We can test whether presupposition is present by means of negation. If we state that John does not take his dog to the park (see 3.61), the presupposition that John owns a dog persists. Saeed (2009:103) summarises presupposition as follows:

- If p is true, then q is true.
- If p is false, then q is still true.
- If q is true, then p could be either true or false.

If it is true that the king of Eswatini celebrated his 56th birthday on Monday, it is also true that Eswatini has a king. If the king of Eswatini did not turn 56 on Monday, the preposition that Eswatini has a king remains true. If it is true that Eswatini has a king, then he may or may not have turned 56 on Monday.

We mentioned that presupposition is sensitive to context. We see this in what is known as *presupposition failure* and *defeasibility*. Consider the following example:

> 3.65 The prime minister's wife heads the Committee for Women and Children.

This sentence presupposes at least three things: (1) there is a prime minister, (2) he is married to a woman, and (3) she is the head of a committee. A problem arises when there exists no referent for the nominal in the sentence. For instance, if 3.65 referred to a government official in South Africa, we know that there is no such thing as a prime minister. If *prime minister* referred to Leo Varadkar, the head of government of Ireland, we know that he is not married to a woman because he has a male partner. If there is no committee dedicated to women and children, then the wife cannot be its head. The mismatch between the real-world context and the facts conveyed in the sentence brings about presupposition failure, because the statement itself is neither true nor false, leaving us with nothing meaningful.

We can block or cancel presupposition when it clashes with what we know about the world. We refer to this as *defeasibility*. Consider the following example taken from Huang (2013:69):

> 3.66 (p) John died before he finished his PhD.
> (q) John finished his PhD.

We know that it is impossible to do anything after death; as a result, P cannot presuppose Q. We must therefore cancel it. In the same vein, we can cancel the presuppositions in 3.65, because – depending on the context – we know the information to be inaccurate. In order for us to cancel a presupposition, we depend on context.

In the instance of *Ryan v Petrus*, Mr Petrus made a statement saying that his father's adultery was making a fool of his mother:[65]

> 3.67 (p) You fornicate with my father.
> (q) You make a fool of my mother.

If we use the pattern for presupposition, we see the following:

> 3.68 If p is true, then q is true: If you fornicate with my father, then you make a fool of my mother.

65 *Ryan v Petrus*, at 277.

3.69 If p is false, then q is still true: If you do not fornicate with my father, then you still make a fool of my mother.

3.70 If q is true, then p could be either true or false: If you made a fool of my mother, you either fornicated with my father or did not.

What we see in 3.68, is the assumption that adultery by one party could lead to a feeling of shame and ridicule by the other. However, we also see in 3.69 that to claim feelings of shame when no adultery has taken place is much more subjective and depends on a lot more context (which is absent). What are the other causes for shame? If we accept 3.70, we must believe that Mrs Petrus looks foolish whether or not her husband engages in an extramarital relationship with Mrs Ryan. Based on this analysis, the presupposition in 3.67 fails without the necessary context.

3.14. Conclusion

In this section, we looked at various types of relations between words. We saw that words can engage a number of relations simultaneously. As Yule (2020:134) says, we characterise the meaning of words in terms of their relationship to other words. Knowing the company a word keeps helps us to understand that word. It provides us with a much wider perspective, not only of a particular word, but also of the concept and conceptual field it lexicalises. What is clear from this chapter is the fact that semantic description depends on an understanding of lexical relations. Consequently, this chapter offers statutory interpreters a simple set of semantic tools that could aide in deciphering the meaning behind words.

4. Understanding Non-Verbal Communication

It is true that the law requires linguistic interpretation from time to time, and that various interpretation theories address the approach in which courts should handle language inquiries. And, as we know by now, interpretation comes down to the question 'What does X mean?' This creates the idea that meaning is always restricted to texts like statutes and case law, or utterances and statements made by everyday people. When we talk about the linguistic tools involved in deciphering meaning, few people think of the semantics present in body language, tone of voice or text stylistics. In fact, we communicate a lot of valuable information by the way we carry our bodies and in the manner that we say things. The famous dictum *It's not what you say, but how you say it that matters* rings true when it comes to meaning making. It also means that we need to view the term *text* more inclusively, beyond mere written documents. Schmidt and Rademeyer (2021:Ch 11) point out that there is no uniformity when it comes to defining what a document is, but for the most part it refers to any device that records information, either tangible or perceptible. It would be tricky to define non-verbal communication as a type of document, for this reason *text* could be a better fit. However, when we work with text recorded as written documents, we may glean a lot more about what an author communicates through his or her style.

Allowing non-verbal communication as evidence is probably not that simple. A court must consider many things: does it qualify as witness evidence? Could it be an admissible document or credible hearsay? Is non-verbal communication something that needs corroboration? Non-verbal communication is not something that South African courts really pay attention to, which is a pity; because it could add value to the linguistic investigation that a court conducts. The reason for this is simple: speaking involves a whole lot more than words. In fact, speakers integrate verbal and non-verbal communication when they speak. This chapter will present an overview of at least three important examples of non-verbal communication, which statutory interpreters may find quite useful.

4.1. Non-verbal communication

Conversational interaction between people is quite complex. When we speak, we do not use words alone. No, we use our bodies as well – every part of them. Also, sometimes we use our bodies instead of words to convey a certain message. Additionally, we make non-verbal noises either when we listen or when we speak. In short, a lot goes on when we speak. Teachers at school often tell learners not to speak with their hands – they must rely solely on their words. Even teachers are taught never to cross their arms or frown when they stand in front of learners – it gives the impression that the teacher is dissatisfied or closed off. Before radio and television interviews, a technician tells you not to 'uhm' and 'ah' when you speak – it annoys listeners and sounds like the speaker does not know what he or she is talking about. People try to minimise non-verbal communication, because they see it as poor communication and feel it often communicates something negative. Of course, this is not true. Body language is very important to human communication. This is especially visible in efforts to improve body movements in social robots like humanoids.[1] In order for social robots to come across as lifelike, they must move like humans and use gestures and facial expressions to supplement, complement and emphasise what they express in speech (Wachsmuth and Salem 2014:1945, 1947). There is also the possibility that deceivers like liars train their bodies to express as little as possible about their deception, yet researchers believe there might be 'leakage' in the sense that small signs in their body language could expose them (Sporer 2014; Zuckerman et al 1982).

4.1.1 Body language

What is body language exactly? **Body language** concerns the human body as message transmitter. It includes aspects like contact, proximity, orientation, appearance, posture, gaze, facial expression, and movement in space (Kidwell 2013; Fiske 2011:64–65). When we speak, we position our bodies to align with our conversation partner and this framing of the body communicates a person's engagement in the conversation and his or her attitudes towards what is being said. We look at our partner and expect our partner to look at us (unless we avoid one another's gaze, which is also telling). We read facial cues to see whether our partner is listening, understanding and interpreting what we say in the way we intend.[2]

1 This is also visible in artificial intelligence; scientists and computational linguists work hard to ensure AIs mimic human communication characteristics in order to improve interaction between humans and AIs (like chat bots and computerised personal assistants).

2 At the start of the Covid-19 pandemic, I often heard people complain that they had difficulty reading facial ques behind masks. During the pandemic, most of us had to learn how to express ourselves through our eyes and eyebrows, and similarly, to read those messages sufficiently. Cultures that are used to face covers like surgical masks or burqas are better attuned to limited facial cues.

Furthermore, we use facial expressions to communicate various emotions, from surprise to anger, annoyance to confusion, and so on. Consider the following example (adapted from Moll, 2012: 83):

> 4.1 John: I wonder who will take Mike's caseload.
> Frank: (frowns)
> John: You haven't heard! Mike left the company.
> Frank: (eyebrows raised)

We can tell from 4.1 that Frank was at first confused and then surprised. His facial expression communicated the necessary information for John to continue the conversation undisturbed. Frank's use of facial expressions also functioned as his contribution to the conversation, representing his own turn-taking without uttering a single word (Moll 2012:83; Hirschberg 2017:545-546).

Body movement is of equal importance. We nod our heads to signify that we agree or follow a conversation, likewise we might pull away when someone touches us (or tries to). We may lean into people, or we might simply want to move towards other bodies (for instance, in public spaces where many bodies congregate (Kidwell 2013:105)). Additionally, we might want to convey something about ourselves in the way we dress or style ourselves (or use our appearance as a means of rebellion or association (Fiske 2011:65)).

It is equally important to note that non-verbal communication like facial expression is often culture-specific, which could (and often does) lead to miscommunication. Experiments involving Japanese and American subjects found that Japanese individuals are less likely to show negative emotions in public, masking their negative emotions by smiling (De Gelder and Huis In 'T Veld 2015:4). Conversely, the American subjects did not mask their emotions in public. These experiments also showed that the Japanese tend to focus on the eyes whereas the Americans used the mouth as a prominent cue (De Gelder and Huis In 'T Veld 2015:5). A common South African example includes eye contact – African oriented South Africans avoid eye contact out of respect, whereas Westernised South Africans see eye-avoidance as disrespectful (Nyoni 2021:5). Experiments among different culture groups found that subjects had difficulty recognising emotions like fear, anger, and happiness in the faces of other races belonging to diverse cultures (De Gelder and Huis in 'T Veld 2015:9-10). Clearly, body language plays an important role in cross-cultural communication as well.

4.1.2 Gesturing

Non-verbal communication like body language comes very naturally to all speakers and communicates a variety of information, both positive and negative.[3] **Gesturing** is one of the most common forms of non-verbal communication and is part of everyday language.[4] The verbal and non-verbal modalities of communication form part of the same system and we tend to use them together when producing speech (Goldin-Meadow 2021:1-2; Özyürek 2018:1). Gestures can substitute for speech when speech is not possible (Goldin-Meadow 2021:2). Brookes (2005:2046-2047) has identified approximately 143 gestures in townships outside of Johannesburg that function independently of speech;[5] some gestures are used to communicate over distances, while others are used in secret.

We usually make gestures with our hands, but we can employ other body parts too, like our head or feet.[6] Yule (2020:235-236) helps us to distinguish between different kinds of gesturing, like emblems, iconics, deictics, and beats. Emblems are conventionalised gestures that communicate fixed expressions: for instance, when we give someone the *thumbs up* or we show people to be quiet by *shushing* them. Iconics reflect the meaning of what is being said by depicting concrete objects. For instance, when we ask a waiter for the bill, we might *write in the air* (we mimic signing a cheque or the credit card slip). Or, entering a bar and walking straight to a table, we might catch a waiter's eye and mimic *bringing a glass to our mouths*, indicating he or she can bring a drink straight away. The term *deictic* comes from *deixis*, which means *pointing*. When we use our fingers to point at something (or someone) while talking, we use deictic gestures. We might point toward food and say 'Would you like some?' without naming the food. Or, we could point for emphasis. We may typically use our fingers to point, but we can also use our head, eyes or other limbs for deictic gestures. Lastly, beats are very quick hand

3 Even visually impaired individuals who have never seen others' gesture, use gesturing when speaking to both seeing and visually impaired people (Goldin-Meadow 2021:2).

4 Gesturing should not be confused with sign language. Gesturing is something that accompanies both speech and signing and is not used instead of speech (like signing).

5 The word *township* in South Africa refers to a neighbourhood or village outside of towns and cities that has a predominantly black population. It is often associated with poor infrastructure, socio-economic issues and informal settlement. South African townships are comparable to Brazilian *favelas*.

6 Facial gestures specifically share many similarities with hand gestures and are synchronised with speech as well, especially in face-to-face communication. See Bavelas, Gerwing & Healing (2014).

or finger movements that accompany speech, stressing parts of what is being said.

The effect of gesturing is not limited to speakers. Gesturing affects listeners too. Gestures help listeners to understand what the speaker is trying to convey, but they can also make communication more difficult to grasp (Goldin-Meadown 2021:4). So far, we know that listeners use gestures to pick up semantic information; in fact, addressees are able to relay information more accurately when gestures are involved (Özyürek 2018:9). More importantly, it seems that the brain processes gestures in the same way as it does semantic information (Özyürek 2018:9-12). In addition, gesturing can help set the context of an utterance. Imagine a husband entering the living room, saying to his wife 'they made another fort, didn't they?' He waves his hand about the room when he says that. The gesture helps us understand that the children did not build a fort outside, but instead built something in the living room. His gesture also implies that the materials of the fort are still strewn about. A typical example in South Africa across cultures is the *money* gesture. We rub the thumb and the tips of two upturned fingers together to indicate that something is expensive, someone has a lot of money or that we have no money. This can function independently of speech as a request or a statement, and we can combine it with other gestures like palms turned upwards to indicate a lack of money (Brookes 2004:194).

Gesturing is an integral part of the communication system and can express the same semantic and pragmatic meaning as the accompanying words, but can also encode additional information not expressed by speech (Özyürek 2018:2). As such, we should not underestimate the role and function of gesturing (and non-verbal communication in general) in semantic analysis.

Because body language is seldom recorded in case law, cases like *S v Visagie*, *Jonker v Davis*, *Herselman v Geleba* and *Ryan v Petrus* offer us little to go by. All four cases deal with verbal exchanges, of which some are clearly intense arguments. It would be impossible to imagine that these exchanges took place without any body language present. In each of these, one or more witnesses were present to see and hear what happened. For instance, the verbal fight in *S v Visagie* resulted in physical contact and a broken hand, which provides more than enough evidence of aggression.[7] No doubt, there would have been hands waving about and angry facial expressions. When the appellant called the complainant a *cunt* and a

7 *S v Visagie* 2009 (2) SACR 70 (W), paras 6–7.

poes,[8] accompanying facial cues and body stance would have added to their meaning.

However, the case *Rustenburg Platinum Mine v SAEWA obo Bester* does record some body language.[9] The mine in question was Mr Bester's employer and dismissed him for insubordination and for using racial remarks.[10] He tried to resolve a parking issue with the chief safety officer, Mr Sedumedi. When his attempts failed, he interrupted a meeting held by Mr Sedumedi. Present at the meeting were six other employees.[11] According to the witnesses present, Mr Bester pointed his finger at Mr Sedumedi and spoke in a loud and aggressive manner, instructing the safety officer to remove *the black man's car*.[12]

We can argue that Mr Bester used his pointing gesture as identifier, imperative and accusation. When he points to Mr Sedumedi, he identifies the person responsible for his trouble and holds him responsible for fixing it. He uses his gesture simultaneously with speaking and the gesture is accompanied by the loudness of his voice, which contributes to his hostile posture. Apparently, Mr Bester also *stormed* into the meeting,[13] which further adds to the impression of aggression. Undoubtedly, Mr Bester's behaviour (specifically, his body language) would have had a jarring effect on the people present at the meeting, and it would have coloured their perception of him and his use of *black man*. Knowing something about his accompanying intonation, could tell us more about the way he said (and meant) *black man*.

4.2. Prosody

Simply put, **prosody** concerns auditory aspects of language like the linguistic functions of intonation, stress, and rhythm. It is not surprising that the spoken form of language contributes towards meaning making, seeing as speakers acquire language mostly through auditory input and habitually engage in spoken language (Speer and Blodgett 2006:505). This means that speakers are sensitive to nuances in spoken language. Prosody can reflect a speaker's emotional state, the presence of irony or sarcasm, emphasis, contrast and it indicates the kind of utterance produced by

8 *S v Visagie*, para 6.
9 *Rustenburg Platinum Mine v SAEWA obo Bester* [2018] ZACC 13.
10 *Rustenburg Platinum Mine v SAEWA obo Bester*, para 3.
11 *Rustenburg Platinum Mine v SAEWA obo Bester*, paras 4–5.
12 *Rustenburg Platinum Mine v SAEWA obo Bester*, para 5. See also *Rustenburg Platinum Mine v SAEWA obo Bester* [2016] ZALCJHB 75, para 19. The Labour Appeal Court referred to Mr Bester's manner as *aggressive* and *belligerent*. See *Rustenburg Platinum Mine v SAEWA obo Bester*, para 19.
13 *Rustenburg Platinum Mine v SAEWA obo Bester*, para 5.

the speaker as well (like a statement, question or directive). Tonhauser (2019:494) uses the sentence *It's raining* to illustrate how an assertion can change to a request for confirmation when uttered with a rise at the end. Prosodic devices can also indicate the most salient information in an utterance. For instance, in the sentence *John killed Mzwandile*, the object (*Mzwandile*) could be stressed, revealing that John was responsible for one death only (implying that others killed more than one person). We also use prosody to distinguish between syntactic ambiguity. The sentence *flying planes can be dangerous* can mean two things (Speer and Blodgett 2006:507):

1. to operate a plane can be dangerous; or
2. planes that fly can be dangerous.

By stressing either *flying* or *planes*, we can make the distinction clear. In addition, we rely on prosody and gesturing when we negate statements (in the form of denial and rejection), often combining body movements (shake head or index finger, frowning) and sound effects (higher pitch or louder voice) (Prieto and Espinal 2020). It should be clear that prosody is second nature to speakers.

There are a number of auditory and acoustic elements which contribute towards the effect a speaker produces, and which a listener experiences. For instance, the pitch and loudness of a speaker's voice, the length and duration of sounds as well as the sound frequency (measured in hertz). We refer to these prosodic features as suprasegmentals, because they are speech features that we add to consonants and vowels (and to larger units of speech like syllables) to convey more information.

When we accent a syllable or an entire word, we refer to it as **stress**. As speakers, we may use stress to distinguish between different meanings (especially in the case of homonyms and sometimes polysemes), but we also use stress to emphasise what we say. For instance, there is a clear difference between *I'm CRAVING a slice of pie* and *I'm craving a slice of PIE*. Two different aspects are emphasised: the verb *craving* (as opposed to *hunger* or *want*) and the noun *pie* (as opposed to *cake*, *apple* or *bread*). Consider also a sentence like *He said he was VISUALLY impaired*. The stress of *visually* removes any doubt as to the impairment. Compare it to *He said HE was visually impaired*. The focus readjusts towards the subject of the sentence, eliminating confusion as to who suffers impairment.

When our vocal cords have a high frequency vibration, they create high sounds and when the chords vibrate slowly, they create low ones. We refer to this as **pitch** (as in low or high pitch). Higher pitch is often a sign of doubt, surprise or query, whereas lower pitch might be more reassuring or assertive (see Hirschberg (2017:536) for a description of pitch in terms of new or salient information). In an utterance like *You're going to Cape Town?* we would typically hear a higher pitch at the end (*Cape Town*), indicating that the information surprised the speaker. The higher pitch suggests that the speaker expected a different city, or is surprised about the addressee's travel plans altogether.

Sound length indicates how long or short a sound is. Differences in length (and duration) can result in a difference of lexical meaning, depending on the language. An English example includes the words *wood* and *wooed*, in which the latter has a much longer vowel (/wu:d/) than the former (/wud/). Speakers may lengthen sounds to over-exaggerate what they say, or to express the opposite. For instance, if someone said *The test was suuuuper easy*, they might mean it ironically, implying that the test was actually quite difficult.

Acoustically speaking, **loudness** concerns our perception of sound pressure. For our purposes, we understand loudness to signify the audibility of a speaker's voice, whether soft, audible or loud. There are various reasons why people alter the loudness of their voice. We might whisper so as not to disturb other people or we might talk softly because we want to gossip without anyone else hearing. A soft voice can also indicate underhandedness. Loudness may have the opposite effect – people may speak loudly because they have nothing to hide. But we also speak loudly when we want to be heard or when we want to emphasise something. A loud voice could indicate anger, annoyance, or aggression.

The **tone** of someone's **voice** can be telling of his or her emotional state or attitude as well. We can hear when someone is emotional, upset, angry or uncertain (Laplante and Ambady 2003). Additionally, tone of voice can convey politeness, sincerity, doubt, or fear (Nygaard and Lunders 2002). A speaker's tone can be calming or disturbing, and we can infer different things from a tremor or quiver in someone's voice. A study by Zuckerman et al. (1982) found that subjects were better able to identify deception based on tone of voice than reliance on facial expressions, which in turn was a better means to appraise truth statements than words alone.

Notably, Fiske (2011:64) reminds us that aspects like tone of voice only indicate present attitudes and do not transmit messages about our feelings last week. It is also worth pointing out that prosody (and body language) is mostly subjective perception. This does not mean that we should ignore or distrust information transferred in this way. Instead, we should realise that this type of information is very pragmatic, which means it is user-based and not easily looked up in sources like dictionaries.

When we use stress, pitch, loudness, and sound length to add extra information to what we say, we refer to this as **intonation**. Intonation contributes toward semantic and pragmatic meaning. It also tells us a lot about the speaker's emotions and attitude towards what he or she is saying. Let us look at a few examples:

4.2 John. /dʒɔn/
4.3 John? /↗dʒɔn/
4.4 JOHN! /{$_f$dʒɔn}/
4.5 Joooohn? /dʒɔːn/

In our first example, we find the standard pronunciation of *John*. It is neither stressed nor pitched high or low. It conveys nothing more than the lexical meaning; that is, a proper noun to label the person called *John*. Our second example reflects a question. This is indicated by a rise in pitch. Due to the rise in pitch, we can tell that the speaker is surprised to see John. From our third example, we see that the speaker raised his or her voice and might possibly be shouting. This can communicate either urgency or anger. The last example illustrates vowel length, which in this case could indicate that the speaker is crying out for John. Let us consider a few more examples, representing the same lexical load:

4.6 He wanted THAT man to vacate the building. (indexing – pointing toward someone specific)
4.7 He wanted that man to vacate the BUILDING. (indexing – indication of location)
4.8 HE wanted that man to vacate the building. (indexing – pointing toward someone specific)
4.9 He wanted that man to VACATE the building. (action description)

The pitch on the stressed words is level to low, asserting the most important information. If we heighten the pitch on any of the stressed words, declaratives become questions – seeking new information or confirmation. Take the example in 4.6. If *THAT* rises in pitch, the statement becomes a request for confirmation or an indication of uncertainty: he wanted THAT (/↗ðæt/) man to vacate the building?

Let us return to Mr Bester's utterance from the *Rustenburg* case.[14] Knowledge of his intonation could have provided some context on his use of the words *black man*. If he stressed *black man*, he clearly meant

14 *Rustenburg Platinum Mine v SAEWA obo Bester* [2018] ZACC 13.

to emphasise these words as identifiers. However, if he stressed other words instead, *black man* could easily fade to the background, making it less obvious and less of an intentional racial slur. Consider the following scenarios:

4.10 Remove that BLACK MAN's vehicle.
4.11 Remove that black man's VEHICLE.
4.12 REMOVE that black man's vehicle.
4.13 Remove THAT black man's vehicle.

From our first instance in 4.10, it is clear that *black man* is emphasised, increasing the chances that the words have a derogatory ring to them. However, in the remaining three examples, the intonation accentuates different parts of speech, refocusing the semantic meaning each time. If we consider Mr Bester's body language – his stormed entrance, his loud voice, his pointing gesture – together with his intonation, his pronunciation of *black man* would have been quite aggressive, adding context to the meaning of *black man* in this specific situation. Alternatively, if he stressed the word *vehicle* with the same body language, the utterance's semantic meaning changes. The semantic focus and weight are no longer on *black man*, which limits its racial connotation to a large extent.

What complicated matters for Mr Bester is his use of the modifier *black*. Word choice (lexical variation) is an important aspect of a speaker's language style and makes a world of difference to semantic interpretation.

4.3. Text stylistics and textual tone

You might wonder how non-verbal communication and prosody apply to written text. Surely, how we use our bodies and our voice system to transmit a message is quite different to how we would communicate through written form. Yes, this is true. Yet, writing can reveal similar information.

Speakers do not acquire writing as easily as speech. Instead, it comes at a much greater cognitive cost, partly because writing has additional rules and standards that apply. When we write, we give our text much more thought. We plan what we want to say, manipulating the structure and word order of sentences. When we write, we decide which words are more appropriate to get a message across. We write with different goals in mind: we might want to persuade, inform, entertain or instruct. Depending on the purpose of the text, we make the necessary adjustments to communicate successfully.

However, here is the secret: every person has an **idiolect** that functions as a **linguistic fingerprint**.[15] This is evident in the way we speak. No two people speak the same, regardless of whether they repeat the same phrase or not. Our voices are not the same, and we do not have the same rhythm when we speak. Even if we have very similar lexicons, we do not employ them in the same way. Each individual's language use is unique. Our education, location and upbringing is also audible in the way we speak. We can tell people apart by listening to them; we know where they come from and what social class they belong to. This linguistic fingerprint is present in writing as well: more so when people write without carefully considering their message. By studying written texts, we can confirm who the author of that text is, based in part on the writing style the author used. Consider the following utterance:

4.14 Girl, when I reached the office I noticed my carriage was haemorrhaging! I had to take her to the doctor. Urgh! Headache.[16]

This utterance, taken from an actual conversation, reflects the speaker's unique word choice and sense for drama. We can tell that the speaker uses an informal style to express humour and to elicit a certain response from listeners. It would be safe to argue that most of this speaker's messages reflect similar creative word choice. The example in 4.14 illustrates another important aspect: **linguistic variation**. Linguistic variation refers to the possibility of saying or writing something in more than one way. Wardhaugh and Fuller (2015:6) supply this definition:

> There is variation across speakers, that is, reflections of different ways that people speak in different regions or social groups, but also variation within the speech of a single speaker. No one speaks the same way all the time, and people constantly exploit variation within the languages they speak for a wide variety of purposes.

15 McMenamin (2002:59) cautions against the oversimplification of the fingerprint analogy. Where fingerprint analysis uses few idiosyncratic identifying points to yield reliable results, stylistics depend on language samples that vary considerably and offer either few or many identifying points. According to McMenamin, DNA offers a better analogy for stylistics, because both use a combinatorial system when analysing various data.

16 For clarity: carriage = car; haemorrhaging = leaking oil; doctor = mechanic.

Variation is a part of our linguistic fingerprint, present in written text too. Other authors might not be so easily recognisable as in 4.14. That said, all of us make mistakes when we write. We often do not know that they are mistakes, which means that we repeat them throughout.[17] Likewise, as speakers, we have certain habits when we communicate and we expose those habits when we write. We might start or end our messages the same way. Some of us might be quite pedantic and use punctuation marks religiously whereas others do not care much for commas and full stops. We might have preferences for certain words. In sum, we can read a text and get a sense of the voice of the person who wrote it.

Stylistics comes down to the study of an individual's linguistic traits that may be so rare and unique that someone else could not (easily) duplicate them either purposefully or by chance; these traits were acquired during a speaker's language development and are therefore part and parcel of that individual (McMenamin 2002:51). Writing style results from recurring choices that writers make habitually, reflecting either acceptable grammar and so-called correct forms of language, or unacceptable and ungrammatical language forms, including the mistakes we make (deviant choices) (McMenamin 2002:110).

Not only does our writing style expose our linguistic fingerprint, it also conveys meaning in different ways. The choices a writer makes show linguistic variation, which in turn can contribute towards the semantic and pragmatic meaning conveyed by the text. Style markers vary between the layout of a document or text, the punctuation, spelling, word formation, syntax, semantic variation and lexical variation (McMenamin 2002:122). Having reviewed lexical relations like synonymy, hyponymy and meronymy, we now know that lexical variation can express nuances. There is a difference in calling someone a *bitch*, *slut* or *whore*. Likewise, referring to romantic partners as *sugar*, *babe* and *mamma* express subtle differences too. When our choices and subsequent language variation express our *voice* (our attitude), we refer to it as **textual tone** or **tone of writing**.[18] Tone of writing is a representation of a speaker's (author's) personality and his or her point of view on the topic or of the recipient. A written message can therefore come across as friendly, helpful, hostile,

17 It was a unique language mistake in the Unabomber manifesto, which the FBI also found in private correspondence, that lead to Ted Kaczynski's identification.

18 This is often popularly referred to as *tone of voice*, which can easily lead to confusion. For clarity, we use *tone of voice* here only as a reference to the actual tone of a speaker's voice when speaking (see 4.2 *Prosody*). Of course, the idea is the same – that we can communicate emotion and attitude in writing as we do through voice.

rude, threatening, sarcastic or even cruel. The tone of a text can be clinical or sterile; in other words, textual tone can be devoid of emotion and rather express a corporate (business) voice (Hübner Barcelos, Dantas and Sénécal 2017). Equally important, the nature of a textual tone will dictate a person's reaction to it, either positive or negative.

S v Bresler represents in many ways a result of poor style.[19] Traffic officers stopped and apprehended Ms Bresler one evening because she exceeded the speed limit. She decided to challenge her ticket in traffic court. According to her statement, she was speeding because she thought another car was following her.[20] Ms Bresler claimed that someone attacked her when she was younger and left her for dead. This, and her father's advice to ignore traffic laws when she drove alone at night, informed her behaviour.[21] The presiding officer of that traffic court, Mr Koeries, referred to Ms Bresler's statement as *paranoid*.[22] His choice of words is a strong indication of his attitude: he does not believe her and he thinks her reasoning is ridiculous. Considering that someone just admitted to suffering from past trauma, Mr Koeries' attitude was rather insensitive, to say the least.[23] The presiding officer's response and the outcome of the case led to an appeal, driven by the accused's father, Mr Bresler (which led to contempt of court, *crimen injuria* and criminal defamation against the Breslers).[24]

Mr Bresler submitted an application and a petition for leave to appeal, and he submitted heads of argument and a summary of his argument in which he attacked the judiciary as a means to convey Mr Koeries' incompetence.[25] See the following selected excerpts from Mr Bresler's submission:[26]

19 *S v Bresler* 2002 (2) SACR 18 (C).
20 *S v Bresler*, at 22–23. The second car was also stopped and the driver ticketed.
21 *S v Bresler*, at 22–23.
22 *S v Bresler*, at 23.
23 Mr Koeries probably questioned the truthfulness of Ms Bresler's statement. Still, he could have chosen a different word in expressing his doubt as to the reason for Ms Bresler's disregard of traffic laws.
24 *S v Bresler*, at 20–22.
25 *S v Bresler*, at 21–22, marked as exhibits C, E–G.
26 Mr Bresler's submission is in Afrikaans. Satchwell J provides an English translation for every Afrikaans text; however, the translations are not always precise. I have therefore translated each example anew, where applicable. Where text is quoted in English only, we have to accept that the English is a true and trustworthy reflection of Mr Bresler's submission. Examples are reproduced verbatim.

4.15 This behaviour looks very African and seems like bundu justice.[27]

4.16 Is this man crazy?[28]

4.17 The appellant demands that this case be referred to a genuine court and that the consequences of the Mickey Mouse court be investigated.[29]

4.18 It is a simple matter to ask this Court to discard what can only be seen as an insane verdict to the lower court.[30]

4.19 The accused must assume that this magistrate is second rate and therefore incapable of making the right judgment.[31]

4.20 Unfortunately, the accused standing before a magistrate has no idea whether the magistrate or the Judge if he conforms to the racist criteria of affirmative action by being of colour, has been appointed on merit based on skill and competency or simply on the basis of his skin colour.[32]

Because we do not have the original submission in front of us, we cannot analyse Mr Bresler's style based on document format, but we can pay attention to style markers like lexical and semantic variation, and where applicable, the syntax and morphology of his constructions. In our first example (4.15), we find the words *looks very African* and *seems like bundu justice*. In both phrases, he references Africa, connoting its supposed uncivilised character. This negative connotation links directly to the noun phrase *this behaviour*, which refers back to Mr Koeries' attempt at applying the law. The implication is clearly that Mr Koeries is uncivilised, unable to apply the law and links his inaptitude to his race. This becomes even more apparent in the rest of the examples.

The expression in 4.16 is a direct reference to Mr Koeries and acts as a rhetorical question; as such, it functions as a challenge and a negative assertion: Mr Koeries is crazy (in its *ludicrous* sense, rather than *insane*). The presiding officer's unfitness is further emphasised in 4.17 by the words *genuine court* and *Mickey Mouse court*, which are juxtaposed. With these specific lexical choices, Mr Bresler says that a proper court would

27 'Hierdie optrede lyk darem baie Afrika-agtig en kom voor as bundu gereg.' At 21, exhibit C.

28 'Is die man gek?' At 21, referring to Koeries, exhibit C.

29 'Die appellant eis dat hierdie saak na 'n regte hof verwys word en dat daar ondersoek ingestel word na die konsekwensie in die Mickey Mouse hof.' At 21, exhibit E.

30 *S v Bresler*, at 21, exhibit F.

31 *S v Bresler*, at 21, exhibit F.

32 *S v Bresler*, at 21, exhibit F.

not have made the decision that Mr Koeries made. This suggests that Mr Koeries' decision is trivial and insignificant. If a court is ridiculous, then so is its presiding officer. The words *demands*, *be referred* and *be investigated* are also interesting, because they give a strong impression that Mr Bresler speaks with authority. At least, he thinks he has the authority to instruct a court and to order one court to carry out an inquiry on another. The fact that he calls for an investigation further stresses his impression of Mr Koeries, that of someone of inferior skill and status.

The statement made in 4.18 reflects a sentiment that the court of appeal will see the matter in the same light as Mr Bresler – there is no other outcome but to declare the court *a quo*'s decision unreasonable. The statement comes across as very nonchalant and assured. He refers to the issue as a *simple matter*, an obvious one that *can only be seen* as an *insane* verdict. By his word choice, he highlights the fact that it is easy to see how outrageous the previous decision was. Mr Bresler speaks plainly in 4.19, when he says Mr Koeries is *second rate* and *incapable* of making the correct decision. Both lexical items strongly express Mr Bresler's perspective of Mr Koeries. Read in the light of the other example sentences, it is clear that Mr Bresler thinks little of Mr Koeries based on his race. This notion is made abundantly clear in our last example, 4.20. By starting his statement with the discourse marker *unfortunately*, he creates the impression that what follows is indeed regrettable. His formulation positions the accused as a victim of political agendas (*affirmative action*), the uncertainty of knowing which presiding officer is simply a token appointment, and which is reliable. His words suggest that a black or brown magistrate or judge will most likely be a political appointment, which means they will not be skilled.

Mr Bresler's attitude and opinion shows quite strongly through his style. It is clear that he chose his words deliberately to express his disdain for the traffic court, presided over by Mr Koeries. Rather obvious, Mr Bresler thinks very little of Mr Koeries and his abilities as a legal practitioner. His language in his application also reflects a superior attitude, one that enables him to instruct the court of appeal on what to do. He sees himself in a position that allows him to share his superior (racist) opinion on the inferiority of the court *a quo*.

S v Bresler illustrates how the *voice* of an author can stand out in a written text. The way a speaker (author) formulates his or her text can reflect a lot about him or her. It is equally apparent how the tone of the text can communicate semantic meaning through specific lexical and semantic variation and aspects like syntax.

4.4. Conclusion

In this chapter, we briefly reviewed the basic elements known as non-verbal communication, such as body language, gesturing and prosody. Each of these contribute to semantic and pragmatic meaning when we communicate. In cases where courts have to scrutinise verbal exchanges, it could be helpful to take note of the non-verbal aspects that accompany the contested utterances. Semantic richness is also visible in written texts where the textual tone is evident. As mentioned before, it is not always WHAT you say, but HOW you say it that matters. And how you say (or write) something ultimately contributes to what you say (or write).

So far, we have reviewed the notion of meaning and the way in which word relations and body language help to create and extend it. In the next chapter, we focus more intently on the way speakers use language to create meaning through interaction, situation and context. We move from a mostly semantic approach to a more pragmatic perspective. This is followed by discussions of two resources used to verify and test meaning – dictionaries and corpora – in the subsequent chapters.

5. Understanding Language Use

The aim of this chapter is to understand language use in a multilingual society and knowing why it may potentially influence semantic or pragmatic inferences. Knowing *why* we use language the way we do, helps us to understand *how* we use it in certain contexts. It will certainly help us understand the language challenges that the justice system faces and it will help us grasp the meaning behind a speaker's words as well.

For instance, the South African Constitution states every arrested or detained person has the right to a trial in a language he or she understands.[1] If language proves to be a barrier, the state must provide a qualified interpreter to ensure the accused does not suffer unfair treatment before the law. In *S v Sikhafungana*, the court dealt with an attempted rape incident.[2] The victim is deaf and uses home signing to communicate with her sister, who is her only interpreter.[3] The sister acted as the interpreter when the police arrived at their home, but she was not allowed to be the interpreter during the hearing, because the sister was a witness as well. This left the deaf sister without proper interpreting assistance. A similar situation appeared in *S v Kruse*, in which a deaf accused person did not speak South African sign language.[4] The court ignored his request for a very specific sign language interpreter, which resulted in a situation where the court's appointed interpreter would communicate with the accused in Afrikaans in writing whereupon the accused would respond in writing in English.[5] The interpreter for *S v Ngubane* was not able to interpret successfully between isiZulu and Afrikaans, because he did not have a sufficient knowledge of isiZulu, and in *S v Tshabalala* an isiXhosa interpreter was responsible for interpreting between English and isiZulu.[6]

1 Constitution of the Republic of South Africa Act 108 of 1996, section 35(3)(*k*).

2 This is an unreported case of 2012 heard in a regional court in the Eastern Cape. The facts of the case are summarised in Docrat, Kaschula & Ralarala (2017) and Docrat, Kaschula & Ralarala (2021).

3 Not all deaf and hearing-impaired individuals can speak the dominant sign language due to a lack of necessary education. This results in these individuals developing a sign language unique to them and their family or friends. This is known as *home signing*. Because home signing is unique to the individual, an official sign language interpreter is of little use. See Baker et al (2016).

4 *S v Kruse* 2018 (2) SACR 644 (WCC).

5 *S v Kruse*, paras 10–14.

6 *S v Ngubane* 1995 (1) SACR 384 (T) at 385; *S v Tshabalala* 1999 (1) SACR 412 (C) at 425–426.

In each of these examples, the state failed because it did not understand the language challenge or its cause.

The need for interpreters stems from South Africa's language dispensation: a multilingual country that predominantly uses English in the justice system. Where there are various peoples there are language varieties and contact between them is inevitable. Language contact leads to new creations and new meanings assigned conventionally to existing words. As a means of regulating language (and the way in which the justice system should treat people), the state creates and uses language policies. To what extent these policies are helpful, sufficient or truly at the service of ordinary people is doubtful (Docrat, Kaschula and Ralarala (2021)).[7] Multilingualism presents many different challenges of which language proficiency is one of the more serious concerns (Carney 2021). It is common in multilingual societies for one language to stand out as the *lingua franca*, the language used by most to communicate across cultures and language clusters. Often, people use the *lingua franca* as a basic communication tool and not necessarily for higher functions like law. When the *lingua franca* is also the language of the state and specifically the legislature and the justice system, language proficiency becomes very important. When people do not understand, they depend on others to support their best interests. This in itself may put individuals at a disadvantage.

Another important aspect to keep in mind is the fact that grammar rules often fall away when we speak. When we speak, different conversational rules apply and the ways in which we either follow or flout those rules determine the success of the communication endeavour. Social and cultural norms play an important role in the construction of speaker meaning. It is also here that the true diversity of language is displayed.

In this chapter, we start by exploring the different ways in which language use is affected by people themselves and by official policies. From there, the focus adjusts to what is sometimes termed *speaker meaning*, also known as pragmatics. The aim of this chapter is twofold: firstly to understand how language queries that appear before a court have a history and may be more complex than simply assigning a dictionary definition to the situation at hand, and secondly to understand how meaning is created through a speaker's interaction with other speakers and with

7 Mohlahlo and Ditsele (2022) found that some national departments did develop language policies in accordance with the Use of Official Languages Act 12 of 2012, but they were not implemented. English (and sometimes Afrikaans too) is usually the default language for national service delivery.

the immediate context. It is important to realise that many factors may influence the communication effort and consequently alter the inferred meaning. This is especially true for the ordinary meaning principle.

5.1. Language variety

Because people cluster together in different parts of a geographical area, they tend to conform in many ways. One of these is the tendency to speak similarly. This entails using mostly the same vocabulary (lexicon), formulating sentences more or less the same way and speaking with an overarching accent. In other words, people might speak English natively across the entire country, but each enclave will probably display differences in the way it speaks. This is true for all speakers across the world. A speaker's (or community's) communication needs help to shape the character of each community's language. We use language for commerce, education, worship, healing and the like. We also use language to communicate for purposes that are more official, communicating with people we consider more important than us, and to communicate with people like ourselves for everyday transactions. For each of these diverse purposes, we have a different approach. What this also means is that we constantly switch between the various forms of language in order to communicate successfully. Broadly speaking, we refer to this phenomenon as **language varieties**.

Language variety is a general term that describes a way of speaking. Varieties include the standardised form of a language, as well as dialects, sociolects, style, register and genre. The **standardised** form is often a result of studious language planning. The idea is to create a variety that everyone understands, making communication across communities possible. To achieve this, official authorities use the standardised language variety for government, business, academia and medicine and they teach it to everyone at school to ensure all speakers come to know it. An important aspect of standardisation is to ensure that the grammar and spelling are uniform and that acceptable language behaviour is codified. The codification influences both spoken and written forms of language and identifies what a language commission considers deviant language behaviour. Dictionaries are notable codifications of standard and acceptable language. Unfortunately, this approach has led to a difference in status between the standardised variety and the so-called non-prestigious varieties. An example includes the difference between Standard Afrikaans and Kaaps, Griekwa and Namakwalands. Even though all four varieties share equal value, Standard Afrikaans has a much higher social status. We use the term **dialect** to indicate non-standard varieties of a language.[8]

We refer to the language a speaker grows up with and speaks daily in commonplace and social situations as a **vernacular**. This can be either the standardised variety, a dialect or sociolect. If a speaker only knows the one variety (which is often the case), he or she may have difficulty expressing him or herself when they move beyond the parameters of their language variety. For example, someone who grew up in the greater City of Tshwane area knows either Standard Afrikaans or Sepitori, a Setswana-Sepedi dialect commonly spoken in and around Pretoria. Standard Afrikaans will allow a speaker to communicate with other speakers of Afrikaans, regardless of the variety. Because Sepitori is so unique, its speakers would be able to communicate with other Setswana and Sepedi speakers too, but with greater effort.[9] A large number of vernacular speakers of sociolects like Scamto and Tsotsitaal might only be able to communicate successfully with people in their speech community.

If a speaker is familiar with both the standard variety and non-standard varieties of a language, they are able to switch between the various forms for different communication needs. Additionally, we distinguish between two domains; that is, a high and low domain. What this means is that we use a highly codified variety of language to fulfil certain functions, like academic discourse, worship and the practice of law. This higher standard of language is also visible in a respected body of literature. In contrast, we use lower language varieties for lower language functions like buying bread from the corner shop and talking to someone on the bus. This too is visible in (popular) literature. For instance, the language present in an Act of Parliament and the language present in a popular magazine are very different despite representing different varieties of the same language. The former is an example of higher domain language and the latter of lower domain language. We refer to this language situation as **diglossia**. Diglossia can cause a serious discrepancy in power relations between those capable of switching between the two domains and those who cannot. Ferguson's (2003:348-

8 The term *dialect* remains problematic and in many respects ambiguous. From a sociolinguistic perspective, all varieties of a language are considered dialect, including the standardised form. See Wardhaugh & Fuller (2015:28–29).

9 Álvarez-Mosquera, Bornman & Ditsele (2018:448–449) showed that many people who moved to Pretoria had to actively acquire Sepitori; their knowledge of Sepedi did not necessarily equip them to communicate without effort. Some individuals choose to learn (or ignore) Sepitori to become part of the in-group.

349) research has shown that speakers do not acquire higher domain varieties naturally, but have to learn it through formal education, which immediately implies prestige. This is evident in research done by Mabasso (2019) in Mozambique, where presiding officers insist accused persons and witnesses respond in Portuguese, privileging those who master the language well. Brown-Blake (2019) reported similar phenomena, exposing Jamaican judges' refusal to acknowledge the difference between Caribbean English (in this event, Jamaican) and English, even though they are speakers of both varieties themselves. Even if speakers are moderately literate, they may not be able to cope with diglossic situations. For instance, few South Africans are able to follow political and policy related speeches in English, implying that many South Africans cannot switch to higher domain English when necessary (Van der Walt and Evans 2018:188).

In multilingual countries like South Africa, most people speak at least two languages (not including dialects or sociolects, unless they are vernaculars). Because speakers of different languages are in constant contact, they will use a common language to communicate. As mentioned before, we call this a **lingua franca**. With a few exceptions, English is a *lingua franca* of Southern Africa, whereas Kiswahili is a *lingua franca* of Eastern Africa and French of most of Western and Northern Africa. Speakers use a *lingua franca* in different ways, either as a native or as an additional language (Wardhaugh and Fuller 2015:115). It might also be spoken purely at conversational level or as a higher domain variety.[10] Depending on where a speaker might be living, he or she could have more than one *lingua franca*. A Namibian citizen might use Afrikaans as the *lingua franca* for everyday purposes, but will need English when communicating with various government departments; maybe switching between the two as required.[11] The term **code-switching** signifies a speaker's movement between languages (or their varieties) as the need arises.[12] This can also take the form of code-mixing, which happens when a speaker uses two or more varieties simultaneously. See the examples below.

10 Varieties like Sepitori also function as *lingua francas*, used as a means to communicate between different cultures in the greater Pretoria regions (Álvarez-Mosquera, Bornman & Ditsele, 2018:441–442).

11 This is another example of diglossia. In this case, the Namibian government uses English exclusively as its only medium of communication, isolating English for higher domain functions in a country where English has alarmingly few native speakers (Sukumane 2000).

12 Some sociolinguists prefer the term *multilingual discourse* instead of *code-switching* (Wardhaugh & Fuller 2015:85–86).

5.1 Skud with brasse who are not afraid to wys you that you are catching on kak.[13]

5.2 It depends gore o na le bomang.[14]

Code-mixing is usually limited to sociolects. **Sociolects** are social dialects associated with social groups or classes. Where regional dialects can be geographically based (like Sepitori), sociolects originate within groups related to various factors like age, race, religion, hobbies and so on (Wardhaugh and Fuller 2015:42-43).[15] As we have seen before, words like *pure filth* belong to a specific surfing community; therefore, we can attribute it as lexis belonging to a specific sociolect, Surfspeak. The lexis associated with a surfing community in Cape Town might be different to the sociolect surfers in Durban use (Mesthrie 2014).

So far, we have noticed that different groups employ different variations of language (often as part of their identity or as a matter of association) and this sometimes requires speakers to adapt their language use and to make choices when they communicate. The way someone speaks to their boss is usually different to the way he or she speaks to friends at a fly-fishing club. We use the term **register** to denote instances of language use informed by the context and situation a speaker finds him or herself in. The use of technical vocabulary, or **jargon**, is characteristic of register and makes it easier for a speaker to communicate with others in a particular group. Jargon immediately gives an addressee an idea of the type of discourse to follow. Starting a letter with 'Dear X' instead of 'Howzit B' indicates the formality and context of the interchange. We associate register with certain occupations as well; law and its use of *legalese* is one of the best examples. Though legal practitioners practice law in a language such as English, they use a certain legal register to communicate, both in

13 vannie.kaap Instagram post, 19 February 2022. English and Kaaps. Translation: Hang out with friends (bros) who are not afraid to tell you when you are making a mess of things.

14 Slabbert & Finlayson (2002:238). English and Setswana. Translation: It depends on whom you are with.

15 We can make another distinction: ethnolects. Ethno dialects are varieties spoken by specific ethnic groups. Locally, we can consider the specific type of English spoken by South African Indians, the Afrikaans spoken by brown and Cape Malay communities in the Western Cape and sociolects like Scamto and Tsotsitaal as examples of ethnolects. However, anyone who is exposed to these dialects can master them. Also, not everyone who identifies as a member of an ethnic group necessarily speaks the associated ethnolect. Not all South African Indians speak South African Indian English and not all Cape Malays speak either Afrikaans or Kaaps. Conversely, dialects like Namakwa-Afrikaans and pidgins like Fanagalo are spoken by different ethnic groups and are therefore not ethnolects.

speech and in writing. Typically, legal language is stuffy, dense and quite complex. On the one hand, legal language ironically pursues precision and on the other, it helps to uphold the mythology of law, which works to create a distance between those who practise law and the wider public (Tiersma 2000; Winn 1996; Goodrich 1988). Acquiring a knowledge of law includes acquiring a good command of its register.

How does all of this relate to statutory interpretation? As a starting point, it should make the judiciary more sensitive to the fact that a person's vernacular often sets their limits. Moreover, most people do not comprehend legal register, whether they are proficient in a language such as English or not. It is unreasonable and unproductive to expect someone to understand the English of the legislature and of the judiciary when he or she is limited to conversational English. Capability in the one variety does not equate linguistic skill in the other. Courts must be aware of literacy levels and know that people who appear before the law seldom understand enough to help themselves (Carney 2021). Research by De Vries and Docrat (2019:97-99) and Legal Aid South Africa (2016) indicated that litigants' English language proficiency in criminal cases was reasonably low – less than 23% of litigants had a good command of English in terms of comprehension and speaking as well as reading and writing. About 43% of litigants in civil suits had good English proficiency.

Also, if someone speaks a dialect or a sociolect as their vernacular, then a court must be sensitive to that fact and find a solution that best fits the problem. If a Scamto speaker appears in front of a magistrate or judge, there is no use in calling on isiZulu or Setswana interpreters to assist.[16] Instead, a court must use an interpreter who can translate directly between the language of the court and the dialect / sociolect, without clarifying reformulation (Moeketsi 2000:236).

Furthermore, presiding officers from multilingual societies will sometimes have to interpret words from any of the varieties spoken in the country. Word conundrums may range from the unique slang of *pure filth* seen in *Wells v Atoll Media*,[17] to exploring the gender of the Tshivenda word *muloi* as in *S v Mafunisa*.[18] In the latter case, the presiding officer dealt with

16 See once more *S v Kruse* 2018 (2) SACR 644 (WCC). Álvarez-Mosquera, Bornman & Ditsele (2018:442) indicated that Sepitori is the first language of many generations and is closely associated with the founding of Pretoria. For many, Sepitori is their vernacular with English and Afrikaans as their additional languages.

17 *Wells v Atoll Media (Pty) Ltd* [2010] 4 All SA 548 (WCC) (9 November 2009).

18 *S v Mafunisa* 1986 (3) SA 495 (V).

an accusation of witchcraft in terms of the Witchcraft Suppression Act.[19] The question was whether the genderless *muloi* should include the male gender and whether a translation of *wizard* would then have the same meaning as *witch*. Cognisance of the fact that *muloi* means both *witch* and *wizard* in Tshivenda not only shows understanding of how languages differ, but also how they sometimes need different approaches to reach the same legal conclusion. The magistrate, Mr Netshilindi, used his knowledge of Tshivenda and English to solve a language riddle. Unlike the Jamaican and Mozambican examples cited, local presiding officers should be willing to step away from the current monolingual language policy and employ the languages they know when necessary.

Lastly, it should be clear by now that the judiciary is in need of properly trained and readily available interpreters. They are indispensable, yet many are poorly trained, over-worked, under-paid and scarce (Moektesi 2000; Hale 2010; Lebese 2014).[20] Worse yet, presiding officers and legal practitioners do not always understand the role and responsibilities of interpreters, often expecting them to go beyond what is expected of them (Moeketsi 2000:234-235; Lebese 2011:348-349, 351). The complexity of language variety calls for a different approach to employing interpreters.

5.2. Language contact

We have already established that people are in constant contact. As a people, we live in close proximity, we travel and work together, and we interact at supermarkets and social settings like restaurants and bars. We use social media, where diverse people meet. We might attend a meeting in English, but revert to different languages during the tea and smoke break. As a result, the continuous interaction exposes us to different languages and language varieties. **Language contact** has many interesting consequences. For one, language varieties often originate because of language contact. We are already familiar with the concept of a *lingua franca*, a common language variety necessitated by the fact that many people from different language backgrounds need to understand one another. Three more concepts include language maintenance, language shift and language death.

19 Witchcraft Suppression Act 3 of 1957.

20 The situation presents a greater challenge to foreign language interpreters, whose proficiency in South African vernaculars are lacking. Usadolo and Kotzé (2014) found that many foreign African language interpreters had no formal training in the languages they interpret in court and they lacked cross-cultural knowledge to assist them.

Language maintenance is the continuous use of a certain language despite competition from more powerful languages, often due to various reasons like money, status and institutional support (Mesthrie and Leap 2011:245-251). This is visible in South Africa where Afrikaans is still widely spoken even though other languages like Sepedi or isiZulu might have a greater number of speakers in a particular area. Factors like economy, culture and institution (church and school) help to sustain Afrikaans in rural areas. It also applies to English in South Africa, despite the fact that there are by far more native speakers of isiZulu and isiXhosa in South Africa than English.[21] The government is a strong driving force behind the use and maintenance of English, as well as South Africans' perspective on the status of English (Webb 2010; Deumert 2011:401). Increasingly, South Africans are raising their children in English – this is visible in the increase in numbers of English native speakers and the decrease in numbers of native African language speakers (Ditsele 2014:215-216). Immigration and migration are important factors in language maintenance as well and directly link to economic influence (Mesthrie and Leap, 2011:249-250). Those who either move to South Africa from abroad or who move from one province to another, bring with them a need to adapt linguistically. However, they not only try to acquire the prominent language, they also bring with them their own language.

Similar factors are at play when language shift takes place. **Language shift** refers to the replacement of one language by another as the primary means of communication and socialising (Mesthrie and Leap 2011:245). Once again, immigrants might shift from their home language to that in their new surroundings. Also, the immigrant community might be large and isolated enough to maintain its language. For instance, a Spanish-speaking immigrant might shift to English in South Africa, but a Mandarin or Cantonese-speaking immigrant might not. Instead, a Chinese worker who lives and works predominantly in a Chinese enclave in Johannesburg might have less use for English (or any South African vernacular).

Language death can occur due to various reasons. The most obvious reason is the systematic extinction of its speakers. Yet, other forces are also at work to encourage speakers to shift from their native language to a prominent language variety. Once again, because of factors like economy, status perception and institution, speakers might choose another language making it difficult for a threatened language to maintain its status among its speakers. Mesthrie and Leap (2011:247) remind us that we

21 According to Stats SA's 2011 census, 9.6 percent of South Africans were native speakers of English, compared to 16 percent isiXhosa and 22.7 percent isiZulu speakers.

consider some languages dead (like Latin), but they have actually evolved into other varieties over generations (like Italian, Spanish, Portuguese and French) and are therefore not necessarily dead.

A very prominent aspect of language contact is lexical borrowing. **Lexical borrowing** signifies the incorporation of words (and phrases) from one language into another. We can borrow a word from another language and use it in its original form or we can adapt that word to the sound pattern and spelling convention of our own language variety.[22] Notably, using borrowed words does not imply that the speaker has any usable knowledge of the source language (Mesthrie and Leap 2011:243). The term *borrowing* is a bit of a misnomer too, because once the recipient language incorporates a borrowed item, it remains and forms part of the lexis of the recipient language. The words *kaia*, *donga*, *imbizo*, *foendi* and *aikona* are all listed in the *Handwoordeboek van die Afrikaanse Taal* (Odendal and Gouws 2010) as Afrikaans words – note the spelling has changed in some items (as well as their pronunciation). The dictionary does indicate them as borrowings from Nguni, Sotho or Indian languages, but they now form part of the Afrikaans lexicon in the same way that isiXhosa derived *ihempe* and *inkantolo* from Afrikaans (Brandford and Claughton 2002:203). Languages borrow words from one another because one speech community might already express a particular ideation that another speech community is looking for. An example is *tsunami*, which was a known concept in Japan long before the rest of the world came to know it in 2004. Sometimes, we borrow words related to technology or inventions created by speakers of other languages, for example *megabytes*, *bluetooth* and *airfryer*. Borrowing often depends on the dominant language it has the most contact with. Due to the international position and status of English, many words come from there. Proximity is another important factor. Brandford and Claughton (2002:203-204) showed how isiXhosa speakers incorporated words based on their proximity to either English or Afrikaans. Some speakers would use *iplasi* (Afrikaans: plaas), while others would use *ifama* (English: farm), depending on the region.

22 A few years ago, a listener sent a WhatsApp voice note to a Johannesburg based radio station, correcting the newsreader on her pronunciation of the proper noun *Gauteng* (a province in South Africa). She stressed the first syllable, GAUteng and he insisted that the second syllable should be stressed, *GauTENG*. The newsreader stated that she was a Setswana speaker and that *Gauteng* was a Setswana word, which means that her pronunciation was correct. Although the newsreader was right, the listener was also correct, because in his language (Afrikaans) the stress often falls on the second syllable. This is another example of loan words adapting to the sound systems of the recipient language as it forms part of the lexicon.

Of significance to statutory interpretation is the realisation that borrowed items do not always keep their original lexical meaning. Brazilian Portuguese borrowed the English word *nerd* and turned it into the verb *nerdear*, which means to surf the internet (Yule 2020:60). Scamto borrowed the English word *clever* and turned it into *kleva*, which is either a noun or adjective signifying someone who is street smart (Mzansi Taal 2022; Brookes 2005:2062). This means presiding officers must be aware of the semantic shift that takes place and should be careful to assign a word's original meaning when a contested word has clearly undergone a semantic change due to borrowing and language contact.

5.3. Language planning and language policy

Few people probably realise that their language behaviour is a result of language planning and language policy as well as the politics that surround it. We speak the languages that we do in the way that we do because someone either interfered or left us to our own devices. Deumert (2011:371) points out that interference in language use is a common phenomenon. Examples of interference include:

> complaints about slippery grammar in letters to newspaper editors, spelling reforms, questions of 'political correctness', advocacy of 'plain language' use in insurance policies, the role of minority languages in education, [...] the selection of official languages – the list seems endless (Deumert, 2011:371).

Language planning is an intentional attempt to change the language behaviour of speakers in a given country or speech community. Cooper (1989:45) defines it slightly differently: 'Language planning refers to deliberate efforts to influence the behaviour of others with respect to the acquisition, structure, or functional allocation of their language codes.' To him, language planning does not always amount to change but rather influences language behaviour and is therefore a much more realistic goal. He also sees language planning as either a result of social change or an instrument to facilitate social change (Cooper 1989:164).

Though the results are not always advantageous to everyone, language planning is often a necessary step. A multilingual society must decide what language a government must use to speak with its citizens. Because language is central to service delivery, we must know which languages to prioritise. This is known as *status planning*, in which one or more languages are identified and promoted to serve various functions within government and a country in general.[23] Of course, prioritising one or more languages also means that other languages (and their speakers) are left behind. The implementation of language plans usually takes the form of **policies**, some supported by legislation. Status planning commonly involves other types of planning as well, like *corpus planning* and *acquisition planning* (see Cooper, 1989:31-35). Corpus planning may include standardising a language variety, changing the status of a language altogether, or introducing politically correct lexis to replace contentious vocabulary. Acquisition planning involves the actual teaching and spreading of the identified language(s). A government will achieve little through its status (or corpus) planning if a country's population remains incapable of speaking or understanding the selected language. The apartheid government prioritised English and Afrikaans as the two official languages. As a result, both languages were compulsory subjects in every school. This was an important part of its acquisition planning strategy, ensuring that citizens were able to use both languages to a certain degree (which had its own negative consequences). After 1994, the democratic government of South Africa declared eleven official languages; however, the government has done very little in terms of acquisition planning. English and Afrikaans remain the default school languages in many schools throughout the country and English literacy levels remain poor.

Language planning can play a vital role in restoring balance after a turbulent past or in modernising a society and its economy (Deumert 2011:377, 388). It could also serve to both nationalise a country and promote a monolingual society, as well as to protect language minorities with a multilingual language policy (Wardhaugh and Fuller 2015:373-381). Ultimately, language planning is about literacy (acquisition planning) – training people to use one or more languages for daily use (Hornberger 2003). Hornberger (2003:452) points out that language planning is not political in itself; instead, it is the goal of a literacy planning endeavour that gives it a political agenda. Because language planning and subsequent policies deal with literacy, it affects education and economy directly, and

23 An obvious result of status planning is the use of language in public spaces, which include print, broadcast and social media. Signs, posters, advertisements, slogans, notices, pamphlets, radio campaigns, television news reports, social media posts all form part of a linguistic landscape that government and the private sector uses. Preferring one language to another in these public spaces supports the status and use of selected languages (Shohamy 2005:111-114). The linguistic landscape of South Africa is overwhelmingly English. Government departments use English inside their buildings and English on their social media platforms.

when it is not successfully executed, it easily creates a visible discrepancy between literate and illiterate people.

South Africa's post-apartheid government set a specific language planning agenda in motion with the founding provisions and the Bill of Rights entrenched in the Constitution.[24] Section 6 of the Constitution not only declares the official status of selected languages, but it also mandates government to use a minimum of two languages at all times and to regulate and monitor their language use.[25] The Constitution manifested the Pan South African Language Board to manage and monitor official languages and to develop neglected South African languages like Khoikhoin, Nama and sign language.[26] Unfortunately, the South African government has done very little to realise section 6, which resulted in *Lourens v President van die Republiek van Suid-Afrika.*[27] Justice Du Plessis found that the South African government failed to give effect to section 6(4) of the Constitution; consequently, he instructed government to finalise and implement language legislation.[28] This led to the Use of Official Languages Act,[29] which forces all government departments, entities and enterprises to create and uphold a language policy that gives effect to section 6 of the South African Constitution.[30] Despite the Constitution and the Act's directives, national departments like the South

24 Constitution of the Republic of South Africa Act 108 of 1996. Keep in mind that informal language policies were already present in pre-colonial times, enabling trade between people. The Dutch East India Company gave way to more official policies, which the British vigorously expanded (Thompson 1995:68, 144). The Christian church (and associated schools) played an equally important role in standardizing spoken local languages and in maintaining colonial languages through missionary efforts (Ross 2000:26, 36–37, 45). Arabic and Arabic-Afrikaans were maintained by Muslim schools in the same way (Conradie & Groenewald 2014:52). Today, the bilingual language policy of the apartheid state is well known.

25 Section 6(3) and 6(4) of Constitution of the Republic of South Africa Act 108 of 1996. In many respects, government depends on English and Afrikaans as the minimum two languages. Many official documents like civil service application forms and government issued certificates are still only available in those two languages (or English only).

26 Section 6(5) of Constitution of the Republic of South Africa Act 108 of 1996. Perry (2004) dubbed the Pan South African Language Board the 'toothless watchdog', because it has no real authority to act on language rights abuses.

27 *Lourens v President van die Republiek van Suid-Afrika* (49807/09) [2010] ZAGPPHC 19.

28 *Lourens v President van die Republiek van Suid-Afrika*, at 14.

29 Use of Official Languages Act 12 of 2012.

30 Constitution of the Republic of South Africa Act 108 of 1996.

African Police Service and the judiciary primarily use English (Mohlahlo and Ditsele 2022; Carney 2021: 8; Docrat and Kaschula 2019:73-74).

From a practical point of view, the use of English as the only language of the judiciary and the justice system can be advantageous, because, ideally, government can better spend its limited resources on record keeping and service delivery in a single language. Yet in doing so, it marginalises a great many people. This is visible in examples like *Cape Killarney Property Investments (Pty) Ltd v Mahamba* and *South Durban Community Environmental Alliance v Minister of Forestry, Fisheries and the Environment.*[31] In both cases, the court dealt with situations where stakeholders were either not properly notified of certain events, or the notices were communicated in English only. The effected parties in the respective cases are predominantly isiXhosa and isiZulu speaking. Government has a responsibility towards citizens who cannot easily switch between two or more languages or between the low and high domains of English to support themselves when they enter the justice system. This is where the real problem currently lies – a monolingual policy is restrictive, even more so when a legal register is the chief medium of communication. Once more, the existing language policy necessitates services from legal-linguistic aides.

As long as South Africans' English proficiency remains limited, the government (and judiciary) has a responsibility to support its citizens linguistically in the form of well-trained interpreters and translators.[32] Poor interpretation services seriously hamper the judicial process and harm those depending on these services. A proper standard for legal interpretation is still lacking, both in courts and at police stations (Lebese 2014; Carney 2021). Moeketsi (2000:234) cites the following example of poor interpretation in Sesotho with interference from the interpreter:

5.3 Prosecutor: State your name.
Interpreter: (in Sesotho) What is your name?

31 *Cape Killarney Property Investments (Pty) Ltd v Mahamba* 2000 (2) SA 67 (C), paras 15-18; *South Durban Community Environmental Alliance v Minister of Forestry, Fisheries and the Environment* (17554/2021) [2022] ZAGPPHC 741 (6 October 2022), paras 86-88, 90, 92-94.

32 This is not limited to English. Even if the justice system truly uses a multilingual approach, the difference between low and high domain language functions remains a problem. If a person is not able to switch between the two varieties, the probability of miscommunication persists. One way to solve this problem is by eliminating diglossia. This means that a plain language register must completely replace the existing legal register.

> Witness: Thabiso.
>
> Interpreter: (in Sesotho) There are many Thabisos, man. What's your surname?
>
> Witness: Thabiso Tseka.
>
> Prosecutor: Where do you live?
>
> Interpreter: (in Sesotho) Where do you live, then, Mr Thabiso Tseka?
>
> Witness: (in Sesotho) I live in Pretoria.
>
> Interpreter: (in Sesotho) When Pretoria is so big, man, how do you expect this court to know where you actually live? Provide an address.

There are many examples that correspond. Steytler (in Deumert 2011:404) cites interpretation between a prosecutor and an isiZulu speaker: The prosecutor asks the accused how he pleads. Instead of providing an impartial translation in the first person, the interpreter poses a leading question: 'Do you find yourself guilty?' The accused replies: 'I do have a case against me.' Interpreter: 'I plead guilty.'[33]

It is not only the standard of interpreting services that may cause problems, but access to information in general may also prove challenging. Documentation used within the justice system often appears in a legal register that could be too difficult for ordinary, low domain language speakers to understand. Yet, different role players within the justice system expect everyone to read and sign these documents. Presiding officers and legal council should question whether litigants actually understood any of the documents used against them. For instance, the SAPS form 14A provides arrested and detained persons with their rights, and stipulates what they were arrested or detained for. SAPS 14A is an important document in legal proceedings, yet its authors pitched its language register at a level comprehensible to university graduates (Carney 2021). How must someone with little comprehension of formal language (of any vernacular) sign a document he or she does not fully understand? How is it acceptable that a court holds such a person accountable because he or she signed a document that court officials simply accept the litigant understood?[34]

33 See Lebese (2011; 2014) for more examples.

34 Police officers explain the contents of SAPS 14A to arrested and detained individuals before they are expected to sign the form. However, as Carney (2021) indicated, various factors contribute to individuals not grasping what is being said to them at that moment.

The current language policy extends to the ritualistic nature of court language. Linked to the legal register employed in courts, language plays an important role in upholding the mystery and authority of law. A study by Eades (2012b:481) revealed that 'lawyers and judges appear to be overly preoccupied with courtroom procedure, which is bound by rigid discourse patterns'. Goodrich (1988:153) illustrates this by a magistrate's insistence that a defendant uses 'the language of the court':

5.4 Clerk: Do you plead guilty or not guilty?

Defendant: Yes, I did it. I said I did it.

Clerk: Do you plead guilty or not guilty?

Defendant: Yes, I did it. I just want to get out of here...

Magistrate: Do you plead guilty or not guilty?

Defendant: Yes, I did it.

Magistrate: No. I'm asking whether you plead guilty or not guilty. You must use either the words 'not guilty' or 'guilty'.

Defendant: (looking towards probation officer) She said, 'Say guilty'.

Magistrate: No. You must say what you want to say.

Defendant: Yes, I'll say what you like. I did it.

Magistrate: You must use the language of the court.

Mabasso (2019:45) cites a similar example in Mozambique:

5.5 Judge: (in formal Portuguese) Can you tell us what the matter is?

Defendant: (in Portuguese) I will speak in Shangaan.

(in Shangaan) I don't speak any Portuguese.

(in Portuguese) I did not go to school.

Judge: (in formal Portuguese) Tell us your story in Portuguese, we can understand you!

Defendant: (in Shangaan) I don't speak any Portuguese!

The traditional and ritualistic use of court language favours no one, least of all litigants. A language policy must serve everyone who enters the justice system. Because language is one of law's most important instruments, everyone should benefit from it.

This makes the signed copy of SAPS 14A a valuable record of a person's guaranteed rights.

5.4. Intercultural communication

By now, it should be evident that people from different backgrounds interact constantly. In fact, interaction is almost inevitable, even more so in multicultural countries. When people from different cultures interconnect, it encompasses more than language. **Intercultural communication** relates to both verbal and non-verbal communication between people from different cultures, but includes factors like beliefs, norms and identity.[35] As a result, successful intercultural communication involves transaction and negotiation. Conscious negotiation is very important; without it, miscommunication is bound to happen. Speakers must be aware that the person they are talking to might hold beliefs concerning status (age, gender and social standing), behaviour (who is allowed to do what), cultural communication practices, and their relationship with the speaker. Who is to speak first and how must they adapt their language accordingly?

Doubtless, intercultural communication can be quite complex. For instance, certain contexts might only allow the discussion of specific topics whereas the status of the speaker could dictate the allowable response (and the appropriate language style). Is it allowable for a speaker to call a conversational partner by his or her first name? Should a speaker use particular honorifics? What topic or lexis is inappropriate in one context but expected in another? What about non-verbal communication like touching, smiling and eye contact? What is expected of interlocutors when silence between turn-taking lasts too long and becomes awkward? Different cultures have different response rates and pauses between turns (Hua 2013:106-107). How do interlocutors negotiate physical space? May speakers express emotion in public, and how should those around them react? If a speaker negotiates the communication effort without much awareness, not only can it lead to misunderstanding, which will cause a setback in message transmission, but it can also lead to a breakdown because one of the interlocutors either cannot make sense of what is happening, or they may have lost face (Hua 2013:113). As we will see later, speech acts and Grice's co-operative principles play an important role in maintaining politeness. Politeness strategies are important for successful intercultural communication (Hua 2013:100-103) and could be of great value to police and court officials.

Misunderstanding can also occur when an interlocutor speaks to a conversational partner in an additional language that he or she is not very proficient in, resulting in mishearing, mispronunciation or lexical

35 Not be confused with *cross-cultural communication*, which is a comparison of communication practices between different cultures.

comprehension problems (Hua 2013:115-116). This applies equally to a situation in which both parties use a *lingua franca* that neither speaks fluently, as well as incidents where people speak different languages to one another. For example, a situation quickly got out of hand when a white woman asked for a shopping basket in a Pretoria department store (Francke 2018; Sibiya 2018). The woman used the Afrikaans word *mandjie*, which her black interlocutor misunderstood as the English word *monkey*. The potential misunderstanding led to an enraged altercation.

Gumperz (2003:140) adds another dimension to intercultural communication: contextual cues. Contextual cues comprise the verbal and non-verbal signs that interlocutors need to help them make sense of the messages each speaker transmits. This includes accessible and available linguistic and encyclopaedic information. It varies between factors like prosody, code-switching and word choice (Gumperz 1992). Gumperz (1992) illustrates a prosodic mismatch between Indian and Pakistani cafeteria staff and their British supervisors: The Indian and Pakistani staff had to ask customers if they wanted gravy with their food. Instead of using a rising pitch towards the end to indicate a question (/↗greivi/) (like the British), they used a falling intonation instead (which is how the Indian and Pakistani immigrants ask questions). This created the impression that the cafeteria staff were rude and uncooperative. Likewise, Chick (2002:265) found that South African Indian students were very direct in their responses of disagreement, whereas white students found disagreement face-threatening and preferred to hedge their responses as a means to resolve potential conflict. He argues that the white students could interpret the Indian students' responses as rude and problematic.

Additionally, pragmatic mismatch can cause misunderstanding among speakers as well, especially when someone misunderstands a particular speech act for another. Gumperz (2003:142) uses the following example of an American husband and his British wife:

5.6 Husband: Do you know where today's paper is?
Wife: *I'll* get it for you.
Husband: That's O.K. Just tell me where it is. *I'll* get it.
Wife: No, I'LL get it.

The husband only wanted information (the whereabouts of his newspaper), but his wife misunderstood it as a request to fetch the paper for him. The fact that the wife stresses *I'll*, implies that she will get it if he does not. He accents the same words in reply, stressing the fact that he only wanted information and nothing more. His wife reads his response with annoyance.

Intercultural communication has serious implications for law as well. Eades (2012a:409) indicates that the most obvious intercultural communication challenges take place in situations involving people who do not speak the dominant legal language, either during police interviews or when providing evidence in court. Either speakers have to communicate by means of their limited language proficiency or they must depend on interpreters. Even when highly skilled interpreters are involved, pragmatic and linguistic challenges persist (Eades 2012a:410-411). For instance, speakers of Spanish, Portuguese, Italian and Korean habitually omit personal pronouns, which means that contextual information becomes very important. Likewise, many Bantu languages have no personal pronouns, depending on context to indicate the first, second and third person. This, and pragmatic issues like the interpreting of tag questions pose additional challenges to interpreters, especially when the necessary context is unknown to the interpreter or linguistic devices like tag questions do not exist in the target or source language. For instance, English has a far more extensive range of tag questions than many other languages (Eades 2012a:410). Another common issue includes the fact that interpreters face semantic challenges in the sense that an appropriate equivalent word does not necessarily exist in either the source or target language (Eades 2012a:410).

Eades (2012a:412-413) further argues that the justice system should treat those who speak dialects or sociolects as vernaculars in the same way as they do any other additional language speaker.[36] Of course, this extends to hearing impaired individuals who depend on some form of sign language. And, as Moeketsi (2000) has pointed out, such evidence must be interpreted (and recorded) without adjustment into the standard variety.

Challenges of intercultural communication run deeper than pure linguistics, however. Rather, they include various factors like cultural practices bound by language and speakers' worldviews. From her research,

36 Interestingly, Eades (2012a:415–416) refers to *second dialect speakers*. They are speakers who cannot speak the dominant variety, but instead speak a stigmatised dialect. She argues that they are at a greater risk of being misunderstood, because people tend to think they understand / speak the dominant language. As pointed out previously, speakers of Scamto might be misunderstood as speakers of isiZulu, expecting them to understand and respond accordingly, when in fact they may not be able to speak isiZulu at all (or very poorly). The same applies to mixed languages like Sepitori, which is the vernacular of many speakers and can be misrecognised as either Setswana or Northern Sotho varieties.

Eades (2012b:481) has proven that a lack of understanding often resulted from cultural differences as opposed to linguistic differences, made worse by limiting linguistic practices (like courtroom discourse). This is known as *cultural presupposition*, preconceived ideas about a speaker and his or her cultural background.[37] Speakers from different cultures may view and employ silence differently, or they may view legal authority in a certain way (Eades 2012a:417, 423-424; Eades 2012b:478). For example, language speakers of English and Afrikaans tend to interpret silence as an indication of communication trouble or as a sign of untruthfulness; speakers who keep quiet have something to hide (Eades 2012b:478). However, Australian Aboriginal speakers of English use lengthy pauses as communication practices, indicating that they are thinking of what is said, or enjoying the other person's company (Eades 2012b:478). According to Eades (2012b), police and lawyers could mistake silence as ignorance, evasion and confusion. Kaschula and Maseko (2012:330) make a similar observation about amaXhosa: South African English is succinct and to the point whereas isiXhosa proceeds at a steady pace. Police and lawyers may misinterpret drawn-out responses as a sign that the litigant or witness is babbling because he or she does not know what to say, or is trying to buy some time.

In the same vein, Kaschula and Maseko (2012) indicate how a difference in worldview can cause semantic challenges. They cite a case surrounding the adoption of a child according to amaXhosa customary law. Because the word *adoption* has no equivalent in isiXhosa, some might argue that adoption does not exist in amaXhosa culture (even though it does) (Kashula and Maseko 2012:329, 331). As the amaXhosa understand adoption (and its legal responsibility) differently, it is difficult to express their view and cultural practice fully in English to a Roman Dutch and common law court. Doing so ends either in confusion or disadvantage.[38]

37 Cultural presupposition extends to what speakers expect 'everyone' to know as common knowledge, even if it is not so common. It creates unreasonable expectations. An example of this includes behaviour in court. In 2015, I attended an interpreting demonstration during a criminal trial in Guangzhou, China. The case involved a Nigerian drug smuggler who faced the death penalty. During the proceedings, the accused broke down and cried several times. After one of the accused's emotional episodes, the presiding officer reprimanded the accused, saying that a courtroom was no place for emotion and that the accused should pull himself together. The reprimand established the court as rigid, cold and imposing, a place that lacks compassion. The accused was expected to know this.

38 A more appropriate solution here would be for a court to adopt the isiXhosa words instead, rather than translating an untranslatable concept.

The importance of an awareness of, and sensitivity for, cultural differences and cultural practices in general, and their influence on language and communication is evident in Thetela's (2002) study on police interviews with women who were sexually assaulted or raped. Her study focused on a dialectical Sesotho speaking community in Lesotho and parts of South Africa, and this speech community's approach to sex discourses, highlighting the difference in cultural linguistic practices between men and women. Because speakers of this Sesotho dialect consider sex talk in public taboo, particularly for women, a vast range of euphemistic expressions exist to vaguely refer to human genitalia and sexual activities (Thetela 2002:180). When the police interview women who have been assaulted, they expect them to provide an accurate record of events, including what the accused said. But this is not culturally possible for Southern Sotho women raised to avoid sex talk in public, especially with men, resulting in a vague retelling of events (Thetela 2002:183). This poses many problems. Not only does the justice system undermine these women's cultural gender identity, but it also creates an impression that the rape or sexual assault did not take place or that the victim was to blame (Thetela 2002:185). A refusal to use explicit lexical items that directly describe sex organs and sexual activities may come across as childishness, non-compliance and stubbornness on the victim's part (Thetela 2002:184-185). Instead, police and legal practitioners should consider what this cultural insensitivity does to these women. Experiences of rape and sexual assault are deeply traumatising; forcing them to use language that clearly embarrasses them, could in fact make matters worse and could prevent other victims from coming forward. Undoubtedly, even worse scenarios could result if interviewers are from different linguistic and cultural backgrounds than the victim. The scope for miscommunication is significant.

Of course, even if an interviewer is aware of, and sensitive to, a cultural practice preventing women from speaking candidly, a vague police record might pose its own legal challenges when used to prosecute an accused offender. Evidently, intercultural communication presents obstacles for statements, police and court records, interviews and interpreting. Finding solutions to intercultural exchanges in legal contexts will only start taking shape once the justice system acknowledges that these differences exist. In the meantime, role players in the justice system must be cognisant of and sensitive to intercultural communication practices.

5.5. Context

So far, we have referred to *context* on more than one occasion. It is a term and concept widely used in both law and linguistics, but as Huang (2013: 13) reminds us, it is a notion that remains difficult to describe with precision. *Context* signifies the relevant features that form part of a setting in which we use language, either spoken or written. According to Yule (2020:151), context includes the pre-existing assumptions speakers have about a message.

Generally, we distinguish two types of context: physical and linguistic. **Physical context** consist of a spatio-temporal location; the use of language in the world we live in. It ranges from conversations and other verbal interactions between speakers in real-world settings like street corners and coffee counters to text written on buildings, banners outside shops and signs next to the road. It involves background knowledge about a situation and utterance or text. The background knowledge includes common ground or assumptions that speakers share with one another. **Linguistic context** concerns the surrounding words of an utterance or written text. Here, we look at what someone said before and after the contested utterance. And, in written texts, we look at the words, sentences, paragraphs, headings and layout that surround the contested word or phrase. It concerns conventions that speakers agree to about writing and genre.

Physical context would typically concern verbal interactions (which often include linguistic context), whereas linguistic context would typically focus on legislation, case law, schedules, treaties and other written documents that serve as evidence. In the case *Kiepersol Poultry Farm v Phasiya*,[39] the court considered the meaning of the words *reside* and *occupier*. The case concerns Mr Phasiya senior who worked for a poultry farm for 28 years and who resided on the premises as part of his employment contract.[40] After a vehicle accident, Mr Phasiya could no longer work and retired as a result. Shortly thereafter, he moved in with one of his sons, who owned his own house in Honeydew.[41] Because he left, his employer saw this as a sign that Mr Phasiya terminated his right to continue residing on the farm. Consequently, his employer sent him an eviction notice to vacate the premises in terms of the Extension of Security of Tenure Act.[42] Initially, the retired employee agreed to vacate the house

39 *Kiepersol Poultry Farm (Pty) Ltd v Phasiya* 2010 (3) SA 152 (SCA).
40 *Kiepersol Poultry Farm (Pty) Ltd v Phasiya*, para 2.
41 *Kiepersol Poultry Farm (Pty) Ltd v Phasiya*, para 3.
42 *Kiepersol Poultry Farm (Pty) Ltd v Phasiya*, paras 4, 6–7; Extension of Security of Tenure Act 62 of 1997.

and even asked for a short extension. However, soon he claimed that he was still an occupant and that his former employer unlawfully forced him to leave.[43]

The physical context[44] revolves around Mr Phasiya's actions: it includes the conversations between Mr Phasiya and his employer as well as his health and his relocation. It also involves conversations between his family and the other farm workers who continue to reside on the premises. The employer's limited means and its obligation to house new employees in Mr Phasiya's stead is of equal importance. The court must (and did) interpret the meaning of *occupier* against this backdrop. The linguistic context[45] revolves specifically around the definition of *occupier* in sections 8(4) of the Act, read together with sections 8(1), 9(2) and 9(3). For more clarity, the presiding officer considered case law's comprehension of the word *reside* as well. In this instance, Mpati P extended the linguistic context to include another word and read the applicable legislation with its broader context in mind.

It is probably redundant to stress the importance of context to statutory interpreters, because its necessity for semantic inference is obvious. We should always seek meaning within context. The trouble is rather to decide where the borders of context lie. In law, legal scholars and practitioners tend to limit the context to the very immediate surroundings. This approach might (sometimes) work for semantic inquiries, but an examination into pragmatic meaning depends more strongly on a broader linguistic and physical context (Huang 2013:215). This will become apparent in the next subsections.

5.6. Spoken language

Spoken language engages more than talking. We have already seen how non-verbal communication (facial cues, gesturing, prosody) adds to spoken language. However, when we scrutinise spoken language, we realise that it too has many nuances. Before we explore aspects like speech acts, maxims for successful communication or the impact of politeness, we must carefully consider what spoken language is. We will briefly look at features such as utterances, turn-taking, adjacency pairs, deixis, transcriptions and annotations to better comprehend spoken language's relevance to law.

43 *Kiepersol Poultry Farm (Pty) Ltd v Phasiya*, paras 4 and 5.
44 *Kiepersol Poultry Farm (Pty) Ltd v Phasiya*, paras 10–18, 29.
45 *Kiepersol Poultry Farm (Pty) Ltd v Phasiya*, paras 7–9, 25–29.

5.6.1 Utterances

Simply put, an **utterance** is the smallest unit of continuous speech. It starts and ends with a clearly audible pause, which means it is bounded by silence.[46] In other words, an utterance is always spoken output as opposed to written text. We can represent an utterance in written form using a language's orthography or a transcription alphabet and we can capture utterances through voice recording. Utterances contain plenty of information in intonation, pauses, voice quality, accent and word choice that aid in the meaning making process. When courts study utterances, they do so either as voice recordings or as reported speech documented in police dockets. Both the police and litigators use cross-examination to verify and test the truthfulness of what someone said. Sometimes they use cross-examination to manipulate what someone said. Verification of utterances often leads to a he-said-she-said situation in which person A claims that person B uttered a certain phrase, which person B denies and tries to disprove. Paying close attention to non-verbal cues (as part of the facts of a case) could assist in detecting which version of an utterance may be the most truthful. Examples of familiar utterances include *Herselman v Geleba* and *Ryan v Petrus*.[47]

5.6.2 Turn-taking and adjacency pairs

When we observe two people talking, it might look as if there is little effort in conversing with one another. One person speaks, followed by his or her interlocutor. In fact, it is much more complex. For any conversation to succeed, participants must be fully aware of one another and employ conversational norms such as turn-taking. **Turn-taking** is an organisational feature of conversation which allows each interlocutor to have a turn at speaking. This means that each listener must pay close attention to the words used by a speaker, signalling when the listener may take his or her next turn at speaking.

There are different cues that signal alternating turns like timing, eye contact, body posture, prosody and word choice. These cues may be cultural and could cause intercultural confusion, especially when certain cues are unfamiliar or avoided by particular groups. These cues include eye contact or acceptable forms of address. Successful turn-taking also depends on norms that prevent interruption or overlap. Or, when one

46 This is true for vocal languages. Signed languages employ many different techniques to indicate the boundaries of utterances, like facial expressions, eye gaze, torso movements, etc.

47 *Herselman v Geleba* (231/2009) [2011] ZAECGHC 108 (1 September 2011), para 2; *Ryan v Petrus* 2010 (1) SACR 274 (ECG), at 277.

speaker feels compelled to interject, he or she must use acceptable means to do so without causing the conversation to break down.

Certain utterance types tend to co-occur: greetings, questions, requests and offers, complaints and apologies (Wardhaugh and Fuller 2015:282). These types of utterances consist of a single person speaking and another person responding. We refer to these as **adjacency pairs**. For example, a question leads to an answer, a speaker makes an offer and the interlocutor accepts or rejects it. Adjacency pairs are not only conventional, but are culture-bound as well. The utterance *thank you* prompts *you're welcome* in American English and *my pleasure* in British English, whereas speakers in Greece and Egypt respond by *not at all*. In South Africa, the greeting ritual almost always takes the form of a three-part interchange:

5.7 'Hallo, how are you?'
'I'm fine.'
'I'm also fine.'

Turn-taking plays a vital role when investigators try to piece facts together based on what two or more parties said. It plays an equally important role during interviews, cross-examination, interrogation and courtroom narratives, where power relations are present and suspects and witnesses' accounts are vulnerable to manipulation and coercion.[48] Consider the following example in which the litigator uses the word *suggest* strategically to introduce an alternative version of events to the court, taking control of both the facts and cross-examination (May et al 2020:21):

5.8 Q: I am going to suggest to you that you did keep controlled drugs. What is your answer to that?
A: No.

The example in 5.8 illustrates that a speaker can control both the turns (when and how often they alternate) and the type of answers he or she

48 For valuable research on power relations during cross-examination, and multimodal approaches, see the work done by Gregory M Matoesian and his associates. A good place to start is his 2013 chapter, which illustrates the powerful contribution that non-verbal communication can add. See his seminal work of 1993, in which he describes cross-examination as a 'weapon of domination'. This is also illustrated by Thetela's (2002) account of police interviews with women who were raped. Furthermore, read the work done by Heydon, 2005 and 2019 as well as May *et al* (2020). Please see the bibliography for details.

wants to elicit. One speaker can use turn-taking to steer a conversation deliberately in different directions. This makes turn-taking a powerful tool, for both honest inquiry and manipulation.

During the Oscar Pistorius trial,[49] senior counsel Mr Gerrie Nel cross-examined Mr Pistorius on the details of the incident. At some point, Nel asked Pistorius why he mentioned in his plea explanation talking to Reeva Steenkamp after hearing noises coming from the passage, but failed to include this detail in his bail application:[50]

5.9 Nel: So why did you not say that in your bail application?

Pistorius: I'm not sure, my lady, I can't explain.

Nel: In your, when you prepared for court, you wanted the Court to understand that you knew she was on the bed. That's why you invented a discussion with her.

Pistorius: I didn't invent a discussion with her, my lady.

Nel: During your bail application, you did not think that there would be a need to invent a discussion. Isn't that so?

Pistorius: I didn't invent any discussion that was in my bail nor that was now, my lady. I haven't invented anything.

Similar to our example in 5.8, Nel uses the word *invented* to control Pistorius' responses, to create a strong impression that the accused's version is flawed and to apply pressure on him.

5.6.3 Deixis

Deixis involves *pointing* and is present in both spoken and written language. This means that a speaker points to something when talking (or writing). The act of pointing relates to the uttering speaker as well as the place and time of the utterance (Huang 2013:136). As a result, we distinguish three kinds of deixis, that is person, time and place.

Speakers identify conversational partners through personal pronouns, kinship terms, vocatives and honorifics. For instance, speakers identify interlocutors by their names, titles or even terms of endearment. Speakers also use pronouns to indicate interlocutors as a first, second or third person, in either singular or plural form, sometimes signifying their gender. The use of personal pronouns can indicate whether an interlocutor

49 *S v Pistorius* (CC113/2013) [2014] ZAGPPHC 793 (12 September 2014).
50 The transcript was taken from Patrick Malone Associates' analysis of the cross-examination.

considers him or herself part of the in-group (the inclusive *we*) or as someone identifying others.

Time deixis helps to position an utterance or conversation in terms of temporal measurements. Time is always relative to the time at which a speaker produces the applicable utterance (Huang 2013:144). It varies between words that indicate calendrical time such as *Monday*, *September* or *five o' clock* and includes adverbs of time like *next*, *then*, *tomorrow*, *this* and *almost*. Speakers can express time deixis grammatically through tense as well, indicating whether something is happening, already happened or still needs to take place.

Space deixis concerns the specifications of location relative to the applicable utterance. Space concerns distance, position, proximity and visibility. Proper nouns, nouns of locality and prepositions help to indicate space deixis. We can tell where someone or something is based on the words we use. Consider the following example:

5.10 John went to Cape Town.

5.11 John is somewhere near Cape Town.

In 5.10, the proper noun *Cape Town* signifies John's spatial whereabouts. However, it is the preposition *near* in 5.11 that communicates his proximal location. Similarly, the case *S v Molefe* revolved around the meaning of the word *disposed*.[51] A mother tried to dispose of her baby's body after it was born dead.[52] When police searched her home, they found its body concealed inside a bucket, ready for the mother to dispose of it somewhere else. The presiding officer argued that the body was still clearly visible and therefore its mother did not dispose of it. Following precedent cases, the presiding officer used the preposition *on* to indicate visibility: if a body were on a bed or on a table, it would be clearly visible to anyone who entered the room.[53] Yet, when we consider the actual location of the body (the bucket), the preposition changes to *in*, which alters our understanding of location. We can no longer argue that the body is easily visible, because items *inside* of containers are more difficult to see (Carney 2018). The difference between *on* and *in* invoke two different verbs as well: *seeing* and *looking* (or even *searching*). If an item is *on* a table, we can easily *see* it; if an item is *in* a container like a bucket, we probably have to *look* for it, because its location is not that obvious (Carney, 2018).

51 *S v Molefe* 2012 (2) SACR 574 (GNP).
52 *S v Molefe*, paras 2, 6.
53 *S v Molefe*, para 7; *R v Dema* 1947 (1) SA 599 (E), para 4.

5.6.4 Fillers, hedges and discourse markers

Spoken language is further characterised by what we call fillers, hedges and discourse markers. A **filler** is a sound, word or phrase that means nothing in itself, but generally indicates that the speaker is pausing to think. During turn-taking, fillers indicate that interlocutors must still wait their turn and not mistake the pause as an opportunity to start talking. Common examples include *um*, *uh*, *actually*, *and stuff*. It is important to pay attention to fillers, because they can reveal something about the speaker's uncertainty, or even the truthfulness of what comes after the pause. As indicated before, pauses may be culturally significant in the sense that pauses and fillers can indicate respect for interlocutors and serve as a sign that a speaker is honestly thinking about what is said, considering his or her words carefully.

Hedges are words or phrases that speakers use when they want to be cautious, vague or ambiguous. Speakers may hedge what they say when they are not entirely certain of the facts or when they need to protect conversational partners from the harshness of a truth or when facts must remain private (like financial or medical records). There is a clear difference between *John stole the yellow bike* and *John might have stolen the yellow bike*, or *John contracted Chlamydia* and *I think that John contracted something like Chlamydia*. Hedging can imply that a speaker does not want to commit fully to what he or she says or to what they know to be true. Thetela's (2002) study on the language of Sesotho women who avoid speaking about sex openly in public, illustrates how these women use hedges and euphemism to talk about sensitive topics to police officials who are more empowered than they are.

Discourse markers are words and phrases that help manage the flow and structure of spoken and written discourse. They include lexical items like *oh*, *well*, *you know* as well as connecting words such as *because*, *then*, *but*. Discourse markers signal where a conversation is going and what interlocutors can expect from the speaker. They also signal when turns may be alternated. For instance, using a word like *then* indicates a sequence of events just as the phrase *first of all* implies that this is the first of a number of points raised by the speaker. Speakers often use the word *so* to introduce a topic or fact, *I mean* indicates a rephrasing and *because* provides a reason (causality) for what preceded.

Let us briefly consider the following example (adapted from May et al 2020:20):

5.12 Police interviewer: So, is it fair to say then, that before you had sex with her, she was certainly saying to you she didn't want to have sex with you?

Interviewee: She says she don't know, I think.

The example of turn-taking in 5.12 presents us with a number of utterance related aspects. Firstly, it is clear from the use of personal pronouns (person deixis) that the incident involved the interviewee and a woman, and from the syntax we gather that the woman is the object of the discussion and the object of the violation. The police interviewer takes control of the interview and steers the conversation in a very specific direction by using the phrases *is it fair to say* (also a hedge) and *she was certainly saying*, strongly suggesting that the interviewee raped the victim, leaving little room for other possible outcomes. The police interviewer uses the word *before* (time deixis) to highlight a sequence of events, clearly positioning consent prior to sex. He or she also uses the phrase *is it fair to say* as a discourse marker to stress the fact that the woman said she did not want to have sex with the accused.[54] Because the accused has very few options, he hedges the reply to make it as vague as possible. The accused uses two hedges: he is not certain what the victim consented to (*I think*), and the victim was herself not certain (*she don't know*). Through hedging, the accused implies that he was not deliberately at fault – she did not say 'no', after all.

As we can see, different features of an utterance can provide us with a lot of valuable information. However, if voice recordings are not very clear and transcriptions are sloppy, spoken evidence can quickly lose its value.

5.6.5 Transcriptions and annotations

Usually, various officials within the justice and civil systems record spoken language as a crime report at a police station (statements) or during a criminal investigation (interviews, interrogations). It may also form part of conversations with legal representation in support of criminal or civil cases. More spoken language evidence might be recorded during a trial (cross-examination). Even though voice and video recordings of conversations, interviews, interrogations and cross-examinations are typical, courts mostly deal with a transcription of the spoken language.

54 Fraser (2009) would label this phrase an *inferential marker*, because it provides a basis for inferring information. The phrase is posed as a question but meant as a statement. The police interviewer is telling the accused that the woman said 'no'.

It is important to realise that the transcription is only a representation of the spoken output and when it is incomplete and inaccurate, so is the evidence. In South Africa, a police or court **transcription** simply reflects the words of a verbal interchange based on what the transcriber hears and comprehends. It does not indicate paralinguistic features like intonation and prosody and it seldom (if ever) contains notes when something is inaudible or if the transcriber is unfamiliar with words or phrases.

Transcriptions could lack accuracy and linguistic value for different reasons. The spoken text might not be audible (a person speaks too softly or might have a strong accent), the transcriber might be an additional language speaker, interpreters could interfere or confuse the transcriber and a transcriber's education and training could be lacking. Courts and legal firms use stenographers, who are supposed to be trained in shorthand but require no official linguistic (phonetic and phonological) training. At police stations, it is often police officers who act as both interpreters and transcribers. Ralarala's (2014) research has revealed that police officers are often responsible for interpreting, translating and transcribing when a victim reports a crime or during investigations. The majority of these police officers have no post-school academic training, least of all training as interpreters, translators and transcribers. Language proficiency of both police officials and the public pose further challenges to the accuracy (and trustworthiness) of statements and transcriptions of verbal interchanges (Harding and Ralarala 2017).[55] The version that serves as evidence might not be a true version of what was said. Take as an example the phrase *she wasn't breathing*, which Oscar Pistorius reportedly said during his first trial for the death of Reeva Steenkamp. Different news outlets reported that Pistorius described Steenkamp as not breathing when he found her body. However, as the forensic phonetician, Dr Helen Fraser (2014) pointed out, he was actually saying *she was everything*. Does a transcription mistake like this make a huge difference to the case as a whole? Not in this occasion. But, if mistakes like this creep in, so can many others.

55 A colleague once told me of an instance when he reported a crime at a police station. The police officer insisted they record the statement in Afrikaans, even though he was an additional speaker himself. The intruders came through the door, but because the police officer did not know the Afrikaans word for *door*, he chose *window* instead (because he knew that word). Though the police officer tried his best to accommodate my colleague, his limited language proficiency changed the facts of the case.

Transcriptions serve primarily as a record of facts, but they are texts rich in linguistic data as well. A transcription is not simply a record of what was said; instead, it offers a lot of linguistic evidence that can contribute immensely to the facts of a case. In order for transcriptions to be of greater value, the justice system must find better ways to ensure their accuracy. A great way to do this is through training interventions. This is not to say that stenographers and transcribers (like police officers) must receive training in linguistics. However, a protocol or accredited guide for transcription could serve the justice system well. Such a protocol or guide should emphasise what kind of paralinguistic information should be captured through annotation, and how to transcribe spoken language in such a way that it could reflect valuable phonological information.[56]

If counsel and presiding officers are satisfied with a transcription, they should consider which prosodic information is relevant to their case, along with the characteristics of utterances present in the transcription. The following transcription by Harding and Ralarala (2017:165) serves as an example of a non-phonetic transcription that includes paralinguistic information. Duration of pauses are indicated between single brackets (measured in seconds) while double brackets contain notes on voice quality and non-verbal sounds. The interchange is between a woman assaulted by her boyfriend and a police officer taking her statement.

5.13 Police officer: Yoh! (0.8) What you done to your boyfriend, ma'am?

Complainant: (0.5) Nothing (.) maybe it's because I talk too much ((in a very soft voice))

Police officer: (.) You talk too much anden?

Complainant: (0.2) Maybe he doesn't like that (.) that I talk too much [...]

Police officer: What he like you must keep quiet?

Complainant: Mmh

Police officer: (.) So w-w-why you talking too muts?

Complainant: (0.3) Coz it's my right to talk (.) I can't keep quiet ((crying))

Police officer: Mmh?

Complainant: I can't keep quiet when something is wrong ((crying))

56 Some tertiary institutions do offer training in transcription as part of their language practice qualifications. However, they seldom include proper training in phonetic or sociolinguistic transcription.

The transcript tries to capture as much of the phonetic data as possible, without using a phonetic alphabet. From the transcript, we can see that the police officer is not very sympathetic nor sensitive to the complainant. He starts by blaming her of being the abuser, followed by a reprimand of sorts for talking too much (and therefore affirming the cause for the abuse).

5.7. Speech acts

The language philosophers of the early twentieth century insisted that sentences and utterances be described in terms of logic and their truth-value. According to them, if a sentence had no truth-value it did not qualify as a sentence. In other words, sentences had to describe some state of affair or contain facts that could be evaluated for their truth or falsity. John L. Austin was the first to argue that instead of trying to work out whether a sentence was true or not, we should pay more attention to the way speakers use language. Ludwig Wittgenstein preceded the concept of language-as-use through his language-games examples, but it was Austin's work on the performativity of language that paved the way for speech act theory. Austin's student, John R. Searle, improved on his ideas and most of what we now understand about speech act theory is due to Searle's thorough work.

The basis of **speech act theory** is simply that speakers perform certain tasks by talking, or as Huang (2013: 93) defines it: saying is (part of) doing, and words are (part of) deeds. Austin (1962:5) uses the following examples to illustrate his point:

5.14 I name this ship the Queen Elizabeth (as uttered when smashing the bottle against the stem).

5.15 I bet you sixpence it will rain tomorrow.

Austin (1962:6) argued that utterances like those in 5.14 and 5.15 do not describe any event nor do they convey any facts. They also do not describe what the speaker is doing. Instead, it shows the speaker is actually performing an act while he or she is talking; the speaker is busy naming an object or busy betting on chance. It is a performance like any other physical act such as eating, driving or walking. This means that certain utterances (and sentences that are made to be uttered) have the function of performance. In fact, speakers perform a number of tasks by talking, many relevant to law. A very good example is a judgment. A judgment is an order by which a presiding officer tells the parties what to do: *I order you to pay damages of R60 000*; *I dismiss the appeal*. In this section, we will look at the different components of speech acts, as set out by Austin and Searle.

5.7.1 Performatives

We understand that uttering certain words engages us in the act of doing, like naming and betting. However, not all utterances qualify as performances. If a speaker says *Hello!*, he or she is not performing an act. So, how do we tell the difference? We can tell if an utterance is a performative by paying attention to the **performative verb**, that is, the verb that names the action while performing it. The following examples all include performative verbs:

5.16 I pronounce you man and wife.
5.17 I sentence you to 18 months in prison.
5.18 I promise to phone you when I get there.
5.19 I apologise for leaving without saying goodbye.
5.20 I order you to leave the room immediately.

From the examples above, we can see that when a speaker says the verb, he or she is also performing the act. To sentence someone to prison partly takes place through the verb itself. The same applies to apologies – an apology only comes into existence once it is said. These sentences are clearly different from the following, which do not contain performative verbs:

5.21 John and Mary are married.
5.22 John was sorry that he left without saying goodbye.
5.23 He received an 18-month sentence for what he has done.

Examples 5.21 to 5.23 all describe facts or a state of events; their verbs do not describe a performance as it is taking place. To help us, Austin (1962:57, 61) suggested we use the adverb *hereby* to reinforce the performative, though it is somewhat formal (see also Huang 2013:96; Chapman 2011:60; Cruse 2015:366). This means that we can insert *hereby* to test if an utterance is a performative: *I hereby order you to pay the remaining fee*; **I hereby find your joke funny*. When someone says *I hereby order you*, he or she is still engaging in the performance of ordering. The same is not true when someone says *I hereby find / experience [...]*. A speaker does not engage in the act of finding (experiencing) just by saying so. In fact, the speaker most probably experienced pleasure in hearing a joke and then described his or her pleasure by saying they thought it was funny.

To complicate matters slightly, speakers can perform acts implicitly without using a performative verb. Compare the following examples:

5.24 I promise to attend your lecture tomorrow.

5.25 I will attend your lecture tomorrow.

5.26 I am sorry I cannot attend your lecture tomorrow.

In 5.24, the performative verb *promise* describes and engages the act of promising. However, in 5.25 the speaker still performs a promise grammatically through the future tense, specifically through the auxiliary verb *will*. Sometimes the performative verb is absent but implied. If a speaker shouts *Go away!* he or she is actually saying *I order you to go away*. The same applies to a speaker who asks *Interested in the new Steven Spielberg movie?* The speaker is actually saying *I request you to accompany me to the latest Steven Spielberg movie*. This is apparent in 5.26; the speaker apologises without using the performative verb *apologise*.

So far, we can tell that performatives have certain characteristics. They can be both explicit (containing a performative verb) or implicit. A performative can be aided by the adverb *hereby*. They are also grammatically restricted (Cruse 2015:366). This means that we must use them in the simple present tense, either in active or passive constructions. In the active voice, a performative must be in the first person. Consider the following examples:

5.27 I (hereby) declare the meeting closed.
*I have (hereby) declared the meeting closed.

5.28 The meeting is declared closed.
*The meeting was declared closed.

5.29 *He declares the meeting closed.

Once we use the performative verb in any other way, it becomes a descriptive verb instead. In other words, it describes a state of affairs and does not perform simultaneously. As we will see in the next subsection, speech acts must adhere to certain conditions before they can truly perform.

5.7.2 Felicity conditions

During his 50th birthday celebration in 2018, King Mswati III announced that the world would henceforth know Swaziland as Eswatini. He performed an implicit speech act by declaring 'our country will now be called Kingdom of Eswatini'. Because he is the absolute monarch of the country, the name change was immediate.[57] As the king, he had the authority to change the name without consultation or due diligence. No one else has this kind of authority or clout. So, when a random speaker shouts from a crowd *I hereby rename South Africa 'Mzansi'*, it means nothing. No speech act occurred. No name change was affected. For a speech act to realise, it must meet certain criteria. Austin (1962:25-38) referred to these as **felicity conditions**.

Felicity conditions are a set of criteria that must be present in order for a speech act to be successful. If a speaker ignores any of the conditions, a misfire is said to take place. Felicity conditions range from the authority of the speaker and the conventions involved, to the appropriate circumstances and a speaker's intentions. For instance, to enact a statute, the agent must have the necessary authority and there must be evidence that people followed the conventional procedures before either parliament or the president can enact legislation. A random person cannot stand on a street corner and call out a new law by his or her own authority. The same applies to a registered minister who officiates a wedding or a clergyman who baptises a baby. If the wedding breaks the law (either statutory or religious), then it does not matter much that the minister pronounced the couple married. If a priest baptises the wrong baby, then the speech act also misfired, because in each instance the speech act is infelicitous and therefore invalid. If a speaker performs a promise with every intention of breaking it, or a speaker congratulates someone knowing that person achieved something through cheating, then the speech act is still performed but abused (Huang 2013:100).

Searle (1965:259-263) refined the criteria and distinguished between preparatory, sincerity and essential felicity conditions (see also Cruse 2015:376; Huang 2013:104-106). Preparatory conditions hold that a speaker has the appropriate authority and operates within the accepted circumstances. The king of Eswatini has the authority to rename the country because he is an absolute monarch. But the king of the United Kingdom does not have the same authority, which means that he cannot rename Britain just by saying so.

In order for sincerity conditions to hold, a speaker must have the appropriate beliefs and feelings. This means that a speaker must be grateful when he or she thanks someone; a speaker must be committed to

57 The immediacy of the name change is reflected in the Government Gazette of May 2018, stating that the renaming was effective as of the day the king announced it (Motau 2018).

keeping a promise or a speaker intends to adhere to the conditions of a bet. The last condition (essential condition) defines the act being carried out. It means that a speaker undertakes the obligation to carry out the act. If a speaker makes a promise, he or she undertakes to fulfil the promise. If a speaker requests something, then he or she intends to see to it that the addressee fulfils the request. If a speaker inquires, then he or she intends on receiving an answer.

Another condition that needs to be present for some speech acts to realise is the uptake. An uptake is not always necessary. For instance, if person A apologises to person B, the latter may or may not accept the apology. A refusal of the apology does not render person A's act of apologising invalid. Yet, if you are making a bet, the addressee must agree to the venture and its conditions. If there is no uptake, there is no bet.

5.7.3 Locution, illocution, perlocution

In order to distinguish between the form and function of speech acts, Austin distinguished three types of acts: locutionary, illocutionary and perlocutionary speech acts. As Chapman (2011:62) reminds us, the three forms are constituent parts of what a speaker says. When we study speech acts, we deal with all three of them simultaneously, although we might focus on one at a time. The distinction comes down to the actual words spoken, the intention of the speaker and the effect of a speaker's words on the audience.

A **locutionary** act is the basic act of speaking and involves the *actual words* a speaker produces. In other words, locutionary act represents a speaker's physical speech output. As such, it conforms to grammar and convention and contains extra-linguistic references too.

An **illocutionary** act expresses the *intent* or purpose of an utterance; it refers to the function or action that a speaker intends to accomplish or fulfil by producing an utterance. What we have come to know as speech acts or performatives are in fact illocutionary acts and they include permitting, nagging, warning, blaming, refusing, swearing, accusing, and so on. The intention or function of an illocutionary act is also known as the **illocutionary force**. In fact, there is no communication without illocutionary force. An utterance might be a request, a wish or a command. For example, if a speaker says *I will see you soon*, the utterance can be either a promise or a threat. Even though the speaker made a statement, he or she did not mean simply to convey information about a specific state of affairs. Instead, the speaker intended to bind him or herself to a future event. We would then refer to the utterance as having the illocutionary force of a promise or commitment.

A **perlocutionary** act is the *consequence* of the speaker's words on the listener. It represents the effect or by-product of a speaker's words. If a speaker intends on persuading the listener, then the act is only successful once the listener performs the act because of the persuasion. When a speaker requests information, the perlocutionary act succeeds once the speaker receives what he or she requested. This is also known as the **perlocutionary effect**. Imagine a bank robbery during which a robber points a gun at the teller and says *Hand over the money or I will shoot*. His locution has two illocutionary forces: instruction and threat. Once the bank teller pushes the bag filled with money towards the robber, the teller affects the robber's illocutionary act. The robber walks away with the money; which means the perlocutionary act was successful.

Apart from the form-function distinction, we also discriminate between different classes of speech acts.

5.7.4 Classification of speech acts

A number of scholars have suggested a typology for speech acts, but Searle's classification remains the most authoritative. He identified five groups: assertives, directives, commissives, expressives and declaratives.

Assertives commit a speaker to the truth of the expressed proposition and express facts. This means they express a speaker's beliefs and hold a truth-value. It includes asserting, claiming, reporting, complaining, boasting, warning, suggesting, stating, and so on. For example:

5.30 (I hereby claim that) John stole the money.

Directives represent the attempts of a speaker to get the listener to do something. They express a speaker's desire or wish and include advising, commanding, ordering, begging, questioning, requesting, asking, recommending, and so on. For example:

5.31 (I hereby recommend that you) Don't use too much garlic!

Commissives commit a speaker to some future course of action. They reflect a speaker's intention to do something later on. They include offering, promising, vowing, pledging, refusing, threatening, contracting, undertaking, and so on. For example:

5.32 (I hereby promise that) I will be back by tomorrow.

Expressives represent speech acts that express a psychological attitude or state of emotion such as joy, sorrow, and the like. They include thanking, apologising, congratulating, blaming, praising, condoling, forgiving, and so on. For example:

5.33 Congratulations on your promotion!

Declaratives are speech acts that bring about change in reality. This means the world is no longer exactly the same once the words have been spoken. They include resigning, dismissing, declaring (war, for instance), firing, excommunicating, naming, opening (an exhibition or financial venture), sentencing, consecrating, and so on. For example:

5.34 (I hereby declare that) This shop is now officially open for business.

Knowing the different classes of speech acts is helpful when we need to distinguish between direct and indirect speech acts.

5.7.5 Indirect speech acts

Searle (1975) indicated how speakers tend to say one thing but mean something entirely different. He used the classic example of guests sitting around a table and someone asking *Can you reach the salt?* The speaker is clearly directing a question at another table guest, but he or she is not enquiring about the addressee's physical ability. The question is not whether the person has the physiological means to pick up a saltshaker. Instead, the speaker wants the addressee to pass the salt to him or her. Thus, the speaker uses a question indirectly as a request. Speakers can decode indirect messages because they share common background information and adhere to principles of cooperation (see the next section).

Most languages distinguish between three or four basic sentence types: declaratives, interrogatives, imperatives and exclamatives.[58] The declarative sentence is a statement that conveys factual information. The interrogative sentence poses a question with the sole purpose to elicit information. The imperative sentence imparts a command and tells people what to do. Lastly, the exclamative sentence expresses an emotional state. When the sentence type corresponds with the basic illocutionary force, namely stating, asking, commanding and expressing, we have a direct speech act. However, when there is no direct link between the sentence

58 Basic sentence types must not be confused with the classification of speech acts. These represent types of sentences and are therefore grammatical classifications. The typology of speech acts represents pragmatic classification.

type and the illocutionary force, we have an indirect speech act. See table 5.1 below.

Table 5.1: Indirect speech acts			
Utterance	**Sentence type**	**Direct speech act**	**Indirect speech act**
Do you have a light? (flirting)	Interrogative (question)	Directive (asking) Can you light my cigarette?	Directive (ordering) Speak to me.
It's stuffy in here.	Declarative (statement)	Assertive (stating) It is hot and humid inside.	Directive (requesting) Open a window or start the air conditioner.
Money. Bag. Now!	Imperative (command)	Directive (commanding) Hand over the money immediately!	Commissive (threatening / promising) Give me the money, or else.

As we can see from the examples in the table above, speakers essentially convey a lot of information at the same time and say more than one thing simultaneously. If a speaker says *Please clear out your office*, it is formulated as a request, but it has two distinct (related) illocutionary forces: an order and being fired from a job. Non-verbal communication like intonation and body language assist speakers to minimise miscommunication and help speakers to decode what is actually being said. A shared background also aids speakers. We know conventionally that if someone tells you to clear out your office, the speaker is ordering you to leave, unless the context indicates otherwise (like clearing your office for maintenance purposes). Indirect speech acts are very common; they make up a major part of daily communication. As such, they form an important part of legal language output as well as crimes of language.

5.7.6 Speech acts and the law

Legal documents like statutes, judgments, wills and deeds all function as speech acts and may contain more than one type of act. A statute usually starts with the performative verb *enact* and may perform other acts as well, like permitting, ordering and prohibiting (Kurzon 1986:15–16). Let us take the Children's Act as an example.[59]

Government published the Act in the Government Gazette with a short explanation as to the purpose of the legislation. It also contains a preamble elaborating on its goal, followed by the passive construction 'be it therefore enacted by the Parliament of the Republic of South Africa'. The Act starts with Chapter 1 that defines a number of words, which is an illocutionary act (legislative directive). The Act commands users to use the words in the way that Parliament has defined them here. The Act furthermore orders the organs of the state to implement this law in national, provincial and local government.[60] The illocutionary force of ordering is present in the use of the word *must*. The word appears 236 times throughout the document, which confirms that this (and any other) law is a directive, specifically an order and command. The Act also permits and prohibits certain behaviours. For instance, it allows only the High Court to confirm, amend or terminate a person's parental responsibilities as they relate to a specific child.[61] But, when it comes to marriage, a child may not be married off to someone when the child is below the minimum age set for marriage.[62] The illocutionary forces of permitting and prohibiting are expressed through the performative verb *may (not)*. Laws often contain directives in the form of warnings as well. For instance, section 12(9)(a) states 'Circumcision of male children older than 16 may only be performed if the child has given consent to the circumcision in the prescribed manner'.[63] The conjunction *if* is conditional and serves as a warning here. The implication is that should anyone force a male older than 16 to undergo circumcision against his will, there will be consequences. This is a perfect example of an indirect speech act, because it is formulated as a statement (declarative sentence), but it carries the illocutionary force of a warning (directive speech act).

Contracts and wills function in a similar fashion. A lease asserts certain speech acts, like stating who the tenant is and what the owed rent is, and it permits and disallows the tenant to do certain things in the property. Similarly, a will orders an executor to distribute items, to sell assets or to set up a trust. Although the agencies in all three legal documents are vastly different, they employ similar speech acts – mostly assertives, directives and commissives.

59 Children's Act 38 of 2005.
60 See section 4 of the Children's Act.
61 See section 22(7) of the Children's Act.
62 See section 12(2)*(a)* of the Children's Act.
63 Children's Act 38 of 2005.

Speech acts are also present in legal text types like one's right to remain silent, legal orders such as restraining orders and subpoenas as well as interdicts. Legal orders command people to either stop or start specific behaviour and they often permit the holder of the order to behave in a certain way. For instance, if an employer receives an interdict against unlawfully striking employees, the legal order usually allows the employer to act against the striking employees should their behaviour persist. For example, an employer might be permitted to withhold pay or start disciplinary proceedings against striking staff members.

In South Africa, when the police arrest or detain someone, that person receives a Notice of Rights in Terms of the Constitution.[64] A police officer explains the rights contained in the Notice and then hands a copy of the Notice to the arrested or detained person. In its current form (written in the passive voice), the Notice contains a number of speech acts. It starts by asserting that the police are detaining the individual. It proceeds to inform the individual of his or her rights as a detained person ('you have the right to consult with a lawyer...'). The formulations take the assertive form of both informing and stating. The Notice tells the individual what he or she is rightfully allowed to do. Equally important, the Notice contains warnings: 'you have the right to remain silent and anything you say may be recorded and may be used as evidence against you'. The South African Notice has two certificates at the bottom of the document as well. Here, arrested or detained individuals must certify that they understand their constitutional rights. Because warnings are interwoven with the individual's rights, certification implies that the signee also understands the cautions (in other words, the rights of the state). Isolated, the speech acts in the Notice look like this:

5.35 I hereby *state* that we detain you for the possession of an unlicensed firearm.

I hereby *inform* you that you have the right to challenge the lawfulness of your detention.

I hereby *warn* you that we will only release you once you have satisfied reasonable conditions.

64 The Notice of Rights is also known as SAPS 14A (see section 5.3, this chapter) and is equivalent to the American Miranda warning as well as the Caution used in many Commonwealth countries. The South African caution is not recited to an individual upon arrest or detention, but only shared with the individual once they are taken to a police cell. For linguistic analyses of these, see Carney (2021), Kaplan (2020), Rock (2012) and Solan & Tiersma (2005).

> I hereby *certify* that Mr X has informed me in Setswana of my Constitutional rights.

All four assertive speech acts found in the Notice carry the various illocutionary forces of stating, informing, warning and certifying. In addition, we find these type of speech acts in language crimes like threats, perjury, bribery, conspiracy, and incitement. Examples of speech acts in a conspiracy and bribery case are evident in *S v Shaik*.[65] The case centred around Mr Schabir Shaik, a business owner who, along with many others, were involved in corrupt dealings between 1995 and 2002.[66] In some of the dealings, Mr Shaik conspired with others to pay large amounts to or on behalf of Mr Jacob Zuma, who held different positions in government throughout this time, to the benefit of everyone involved.[67] One of those to benefit from the bribery was Mr Alain Thétard, who wanted protection from a special investigation in South Africa.[68] As the go-between, Mr Shaik wrote many letters to Mr Thétard including the following:

> Kindly expedite our arrangement as soon as possible, as matters are becoming extremely urgent with my client.[69]

In this excerpt, Mr Shaik uses two illocutionary acts of which the first is indirect. The first comes across as a polite request ('*Kindly expedite our arrangement…*'), but due to the urgency (seen in the second sentence), it is actually an order (*I hereby order you to do this as soon as possible*). The second sentence asserts a factual situation; it makes known the urgency of the situation. In another letter to Thétard, Shaik writes:

> I assume the first service arrangement payment to occur before the 15th December 2000 so that I could give effect to its intended purpose before we close.[70]

Here too we can see an instruction: *pay the money for me to protect you*. The letter contains an indirect warning or threat: the payment must happen before the set date, or Mr Shaik will not be able (or willing) to do his work (namely, protect Thétard in the investigation).

65 *S v Shaik* 2007 (1) SA 240 (SCA) (6 November 2006).
66 *S v Shaik*, para 2.
67 *S v Shaik*, paras 3–5.
68 *S v Shaik*, para 6.
69 *S v Shaik*, para 193.
70 *S v Shaik*, para 195.

There are many examples of language crimes, some committed by infamous individuals like the Unabomber, Ted Kaczynski, and well-known individuals like Donald Trump and Elon Musk. Kaczynski wrote a letter to *The New York Times* in 1995 insisting that they (or another national publication) publish his manifesto. His letter mainly contains a threat (*publish my article or else*), but as Van den Berg and Surmon (2019:169) argue, threatening language is multi-layered because it communicates meaning both directly and indirectly. Kaczynski's letter is a good example of this. His letter contains a number of illocutionary forces. Although mainly a threat, the letter states that he has a document he wants published. He instructs the reader how and where to publish his document. He promises to stop the bombing once someone has printed and distributed his message. In asserting the reasons why he will desist from bombing, he indirectly persuades the reader to give him what he wants (a national audience) and in doing so, he proceeds to manipulate the reader (Van den Berg and Surmon 2019:272). His assertions, persuasions and promises are all linked to his conditional threat of bombing, should his request (instruction) be ignored. All of the speech acts have the potential to realise, because the speaker (Kaczynski) meets the necessary felicity conditions. As the Unabomber, he has the authority to act on both his threat and promise. Based on his past behaviour, he also has the sincerity to follow through on both illocutionary acts (the threat and the promise). Furthermore, he satisfies the essential condition, because he has proven himself as someone who carries out his threats and therefore also his promises.

Threatening language includes incitements of fear of terrorist acts. Sometimes, individuals post jokes not realising the effect of their words. In 2014, a Dutch teenager jokingly tweeted a terror threat to American Airlines, which very quickly escalated and resulted in turning herself in at a police station in Rotterdam. Her tweet contained a vague threatening speech act (Abdelaziz 2014):

> hello my name's Ibrahim and I'm from Afghanistan. I'm part of Al Qaida and on June 1st I'm gonna do something really big bye.

Similarly, Paul Chambers was initially convicted for publishing a menacing message contravening British communication legislation (*The Guardian*, 2012). When his flight was delayed due to bad weather, Chambers posted his joke, which authorities took very seriously (*The Guardian*, 2012):

> Crap! Robin Hood airport is closed. You've got a week and a bit to get your shit together otherwise I'm blowing the airport sky high!!

As ordinary people, both Chambers and the Dutch teenager have the agency and the authority to commit terrorist acts. Yet, the sincerity and essential felicity conditions are not present. There is no evidence that either person has the genuine intent to carry out a terrorist attack on either the airline or the airport with sincere conviction or motivation. Although the illocutionary speech act of a threat is present in both tweets, an abuse is clearly visible.

Incitement to violence is often present to some degree in political speech. After losing the elections, Donald Trump delivered a speech at a rally in 2021, which might have incited the storming of the United States' Capitol building. In his speech, Trump stated that the Republicans could not allow Joe Biden to govern the country as its illegitimate president, that they should 'stop the steal' (Savage 2021). It was the following words that looked suspiciously like incitement and that many of his followers understood as a call to arms (Savage 2021):

> [...] we're going to walk down, and I'll be there with you ... We are going to the Capitol [...] we are going to try and give them the kind of pride and boldness that they need to take back our country.

If we study his words in isolation, we can see that he asserts facts – he is telling his supporters what they will be doing. Yet, the assertion has the indirect illocutionary force of an instruction: *march to the Capitol and take back the country*. Of course, we must be careful not to read his words out of context. He repeatedly said that they (the Republicans, his supporters) must fight ('if you don't fight like hell, you're not going to have a country anymore'), which strengthens his continuous war metaphor. That said, he was specifically referring to the weaker Republicans working in Congress when he said that they should 'go down there'. He was implying that they should encourage and reinvigorate the weak Republican Congressmen, who he partly held responsible for losing the election. He was not actually explicitly saying that anyone should storm the Capitol and prevent Biden from taking office. Yet, his speech contained many indirect messages, which followers could understand as an encouragement.

As can be seen, it is easy for someone's word to incite violence, or be misunderstood as incitement of violence. Following the incarceration of South Africa's former president, Mr Jacob Zuma, riots broke out in KwaZulu-Natal and Gauteng. The riots claimed 72 lives and caused large-scale damages to businesses, forcing closures. The South African Police allegedly investigated at least twelve individuals who might have incited the riots through social media, among them Mr Zuma's daughter, Duduzile Zuma-Sambundla, who tweeted that the riots would not have happened if Mr Zuma was not arrested (Cele 2021). In her tweets, she called on people to 'let it burn' and directed a warning to current president, Mr Cyril Ramaphosa: 'you shall reap what you have sown' (Du Plessis 2021). Her tweets represent illocutionary forces like threats, orders and assertions.

A more precise example of incitement to cause harm is present in *South African Human Rights Commission v Khumalo.*[71] Justice Sutherland found Mr Velaphi Khumalo guilty in terms of section 10(1) of the Equality Act[72] for publishing the following words in 2016:

> I want to cleanse this country of all white people. [W]e must act as Hitler did to the Jews. I don't believe any more that the is a large number of not so racist white people [...] white people in south Africa deserve to be hacked and killed like Jews. U have the same venom moss. look at Palestine. noo u must be bushed alive and skinned and your off springs used as garden fertiliser.[73]

Mr Khumalo's text is an example of direct assertive and commissive speech acts. He expresses his desire for a future South Africa; through his words, he suggests future action to be taken. Indirectly, his words carry the illocutionary force of recommendation or advice (which is a directive – *we must act, we must bush and skin people alive, we must use offspring as fertiliser*). We can see his message as an indirect declarative speech act as well. It holds the illocutionary force of purging (ridding South Africa of white people – and the world of Jews), thus bringing about change in reality.

Language is also at the heart of personality infringements like insult, defamation and related hate speech. We have already seen the power of words in cases like *Wells v Atoll Media*, *Herselman v Geleba* and *Rustenburg Platinum Mine v SAEWA obo Bester.*[74] Another example of personality infringement is Elon Musk's tweet in which he referred to the British cave explorer, Vernon Unsworth, as *pedo guy*. Musk claimed that *pedo guy* was a common South African English insult when he was young

71 *South African Human Rights Commission v Khumalo* 2019 (1) SA 289 (GJ).

72 The Promotion of Equality and Prevention of Unfair Discrimination Act 4 of 2000.

73 *South African Human Rights Commission v Khumalo*, para 1.

74 Of course, there are more prominent cases of personality infringement and hate speech, like *Heroldt v Wills* 2014 JOL 31479 (GSJ); *Isparta v Richter* 2013 (6) SA 529 (GNP); *Le Roux v Dey* 2011 3 SA 274 (CC); *Afriforum v Malema* (18172/2010) [2010] ZAGPPHC 39; *ANC v Sparrow* (01/16) [2016] ZAEQC 1 (10 June 2016); *South African Human Rights Commission v Qwulane* (EQ44/2009) [2017] ZAGPJHC 2018.

and did not denote that someone was an actual paedophile (Chokshi and Taub 2019). Of course, Unsworth did not see it that way. In another tweet, Musk stated 'Bet you a signed dollar that it's true', which he countered during the lawsuit, saying 'I also did not literally mean that he was a pedophile. I meant he was a creep' (Chokshi and Taub 2019). Van den Berg (2019:311) mentions that illocutionary force sometimes misaligns with the perlocutionary effect of language output. This means that the intent behind a speaker's words does not always match the outcome that he or she tries to affect with their words. Musk intends on expressing his uneasiness with someone like Unsworth (calling him a creep) but produces a completely different effect (suggesting he is a paedophile). Labelling someone a paedophile is much more destructive than labelling them a creep. Van den Berg (2019:310) further reminds us of how difficult it is to pinpoint intention in something like hate speech. Even though defamation does not rely on a transgressor's intention, we do see Musk's intention shine through in his tweet stating he is pretty certain that Unsworth really is a paedophile. Regardless, there is little doubt his intention was to hurt or harm Unsworth in some way.

In this section, we have looked at what speech acts are and how speakers employ them. To understand the principles underlying the successful decoding of speech acts (especially indirect speech acts), we turn our attention to Grice's principles for communication.

5.8. Implicature

Looking at speech acts, we have seen that there often is a big difference between *what is said* and *what is meant*. It begs the question of how listeners are able to know what a speaker actually means by saying one thing and implying something completely different. The philosopher H. Paul Grice considered how speakers and their listeners encoded and decoded implied messages and how these messages adhered to an agreement of sorts between participants. He proposed the Cooperative Principle, a theory of cooperation to ensure successful communication. Grice's principle also identified potential reasons why communication failed and why listeners decoded messages incorrectly. His theory is not perfect and has been challenged and elaborated on by many scholars over the years, but it remains a cornerstone in pragmatics.[75] In this section, we

75 Do not confuse this with Grice's (1991a) theory of meaning, which is different from his theory of conversational implicature (Grice 1991b). In the former, Grice distinguishes between sentence and speaker meaning. Sentence meaning is often equated to what is written as opposed to what is intended (the speaker's inference). According to Davis J, *Endumeni*

take a closer look at Grice's ideas as well as one of the major pragmatic theories that Dan Sperber and Deirdre Wilson derived from Grice's work, Relevance Theory.

5.8.1 Conversational implicature

Grice (1991b:306-307) distinguishes between a speaker's utterance – what someone says – and what their words implicate. He refers to the implicated (the implied) meaning as an **implicature**. Consider the following examples:

5.36 A: Has John bought the newspaper?
B: I saw him return a while ago.
Implicature: Yes, he bought a newspaper.

5.37 A: I need a coffee real bad.
B: The kitchen is to your left.
Implicature: There is coffee (or coffee-making things) in the kitchen.

In 5.36, speaker A uses an imperative (a question) to gain information and instead of providing a direct answer, speaker B makes a statement to imply that, according to B's best knowledge, John went out with the sole purpose to buy a newspaper. The fact that John has returned means that he was probably successful. The implication is that John bought a newspaper.

In 3.37, speaker A expresses his desire for coffee. B's reply addresses that desire by implying that A can either find coffee in the kitchen, or at the very worst, A will find what he or she needs to make some. In both examples, speaker A's utterance holds the characteristics of agreement

expects interpreters to determine Grice's speaker meaning when interpreting statutes, although according to him this is not entirely possible. See *Starways Trading 21 CC v Pearl Island Trading 714 (Pty) Ltd* [2017] 4 All SA 568 (WCC), paras 41–50, and *Commissioner for the South African Revenue Services v Daikin Air Conditioning South Africa (Pty) Ltd* (185/2017) [2018] ZASCA 66 (25 May 2018), paras 32–35, footnotes 1–2. Davis J's arguments why contextual information like the headings of provisions or additional sources like explanatory notes do not aid in the construction of speaker meaning, is not wholly clear. The essence of Grice's theory of meaning is about expressing and recognizing intention (Huang 2013: 24). The speaker makes his/her intentions known and trusts that the intention is recognizable to the audience. Seen in this light, the legislative speaker (Parliament) makes their intention clear when they use obvious and precise headings for provisions or when they include schedules and descriptions. See also Wallis's (2019) reply to Davis.

and contradiction. This means that speaker B can either agree or disagree with the utterance or B can contradict it. For example:

5.38 A: Has John bought the newspaper?
B: Yes. / No. (John does not read newspapers.)

5.39 A: I need a coffee real bad.
B: Yes, you do. / No, you do not. (You do not drink coffee.)

In contrast, implicatures do not share the same characteristics. A speaker cannot agree / disagree with or contradict an implicature:

5.40 A: I need a coffee real bad.
B: *The kitchen is not to your left. / *We do not have a kitchen.

Conversational implicatures come down to at least four criteria: context dependency, cancellability, non-detachability, and calculability. Because an utterance's meaning is implicated, it can simultaneously have many different implicatures. This means that the utterance stays the same, but the implied meaning differs in each context. Context is therefore a key factor in pinning down what a speaker implicated. Consider the following:

5.41 A1: I need a coffee real bad.
B1: The kitchen is to your left.
Implicature: There is coffee in the kitchen.
A2: Does this office have a fridge by any chance?
B2: The kitchen is to your left.
Implicature: Yes, we have a fridge.

It is also possible to cancel or nullify an implicature by providing additional information. Cruse (2015:416) argues that the cancellability criterion forms part of the wider context. For example:

5.42 A: Has John bought the newspaper?
B: I saw him return a while ago. But he was empty-handed.

In addition, implicatures are non-detachable. This means that if we use the same utterance in the same context it will always produce the same implicature. This is because implicatures are tied to meaning and not form. Lastly, implicatures are calculable, which means that listeners are generally able to work out (infer) what a speaker implicates. In other words, a listener understands that when a speaker says X they actually mean Y.

Implicating is a common practice among speakers; it is something that we do constantly. At this point, the question remains how listeners are able to infer what speakers implicate with their utterances. Grice suggested that speakers use a system of cooperation. Let us have a closer look.

5.8.2 Cooperative principle

Grice (1991b:307–308) saw conversation as a cooperative effort between speaker and listener during which both parties agree to general principles of communication. This shared effort aids speakers to implicate a specific meaning and helps listeners to infer that implicature by means of the **Cooperative Principle** and its underlying maxims.

In a nutshell, the Cooperative Principle simply expects both speaker and listener to cooperate when conversing. This means that they should try to observe the maxims. There are four main maxims, mostly containing submaxims: quality, quantity, relevance and manner. The **maxim of quality** expects speakers to be truthful. This means speakers must always speak the truth and only provide facts that they have evidence for. The **maxim of quantity** expects speakers to provide sufficient information, in other words no more and no less than what is necessary. The **maxim of relevance** is straightforward and always expects a speaker to provide relevant information. Lastly, the **maxim of manner** expects speakers to speak clearly. This implies that an utterance will be brief, unobscured, unambiguous and follow a chronological order of events. For instance:

5.43 A: When does your flight depart?
B: 22h30.

The implicature in 5.43 is that the airplane departs at 22h30. In this case, the utterance complies with the maxim of quality, because it expresses a fact that anyone can verify. Also, B expresses what he or she believes to be true at that point in time. In terms of the maxim of quantity, B provides a sufficient amount of information, namely the departure time. Of course, the question of *when* the flight departs could apply to the date as well. In that case, B's reply does not comply with the maxim of quantity, because it lacks enough information to be satisfactory. As a result, it could lead to a follow-up question (*Yes, but on which day?*), which means that the first communicative exchange was unsuccessful.

If B said the airplane departs on Wednesday evening at 22h30, he or she upholds the maxim of relevance, because B provides an answer that contains relevant information to A's question. However, in 5.44 below, we see that B's reply does not comply with the maxim of relevance, because it provides irrelevant information.

> 5.44 A: When does your flight depart?
>
> B: You need to go through security, followed by passport control. Only then can you walk to your gate.

Providing irrelevant information will inevitably lead to confusion and consequent follow-up questions. Alternatively, if the implicature is too much effort to decipher, it could also lead to a breakdown in communication. The implicature in 5.43 adheres to the maxim of manner as well, because B's reply is brief, clear and orderly. However, the following example illustrates how a speaker may infringe the maxim of manner.

> 5.45 A: I am out of petrol.
>
> B1: There is a garage 1 km down the road.
>
> B2: I know a place where they fix cars.
>
> B3: That's a pity! This happens to me all the time. But I always manage to reach a petrol station just in time. I'm lucky that way. Now, if you turn left at the next traffic light and continue for about 4 kilometres, you will reach a butchery. You can't miss it! It's a peculiar red and blue shopfront. They will know where the nearest garage is. Definitely ask them.

The reply from speaker B1 in 5.45 expresses the implicature that A will find petrol at a garage close by. His or her implicature complies with the maxims of quality, quantity and relevance, because B1's reply is factually correct (at least, to B1's knowledge) and contains the necessary amount of information relevant to A's statement. It complies with the maxim of manner to some extent: it is brief, clear and unambiguous. Yet, it might be too brief and lack some clarity. For instance, speaker B1 does not mention whether the garage will be open for business. The implicature therefore extends to include this assumption.

The same is not true for replies B2 and B3. Both infringe the maxim of manner, which prevents the listener from calculating the implicature. In B2, the reply is absurd, making any logical link between A and B2 difficult to understand. The reply in B3 infringes both the maxims of quantity and manner by being very elaborate. The implicature is that speaker B3 does not know how to assist. It is therefore not clear from either B2 or B3 how A can fix the petrol problem.

It is very important to note that Grice's maxims are not rules or laws that govern communication. As Saeed (2009:214) explains, we should rather view the maxims as *a baseline for talking*. In other words, a listener assumes that the speaker produces an utterance with the listener in mind. This means that the speaker packages the utterance in such a way that the listener can infer the implied message by ensuring that the implicature is brief, clear, relevant and true. Speakers are not only aware of the maxims; they usually try to follow them.

However, because maxims are not rules, a speaker might deliberately fail to fulfil a maxim (Grice, 1991b:310). For example, if a speaker lies (on moral grounds), he or she **violates** the maxim of quality in order to mislead. A speaker can also choose to opt out of the Cooperative Principle by making it plain that he or she is unwilling to fulfil a certain maxim. Examples of this include hedging or the use of metaphor. When a speaker hedges an utterance, he or she is clearly signalling that they are being intentionally vague. In other words, the speaker ignores the maxims of quality or manner on purpose. Sometimes speakers infringe a maxim for linguistic effect. This means a speaker deliberately produces a sarcastic, ironic or a metonymic utterance. When this happens, a speaker is said to **flout** or exploit the maxims. In order for flouting to succeed, the listener must be fully aware of the fact that the speaker is intentionally infringing maxims without opting out of the Cooperative Principle. The listener is familiar with figurative language like sarcasm or metonymy and is therefore able to infer the utterance in this way. Of course, if a listener is unfamiliar with a device like metonymy or irony, the implicature might not succeed because the listener is unacquainted with the form of the specific linguistic device.

For example, if a speaker said *The mushroom omelette wants his coffee with*, the implicature is that the person who ordered an omelette in a restaurant wants coffee as well (Cruse 2015:422). The speaker expresses the implicature through metonymy, which means that he or she flouted the maxim of quality (the utterance is itself untrue, because an omelette is not a living entity that consumes coffee). The following example illustrates how a speaker flouts the maxims of quality and relevance through metaphor without opting out of the Cooperative Principle:

5.46 A: John really likes his new partner.
B: John showers him with gifts.
Implicature: Yes, John likes his new partner.

As with the omelette example, the implicature in 5.46 is quite plain. Because the implicature is calculable (inferable), we can accept that the speaker cooperates while flouting the maxims. The listener is likely familiar with the metaphor (*to shower with gifts*) and therefore realises that the speaker still operates within the Cooperative Principle. In the same sense, B can cancel the implicature by adding *to get him off John's back*. If B's utterance contained the hedge *as far as I know*, this would be a signal that B is opting out of the Cooperative Principle.

What should be clear by now is that both speaker and listener are aware of the maxims for successful communication and are therefore able to send and receive implied messages. They are able to do this based on the speaker's attempts to communicate successfully the first time, and the listener's assumption that a speaker aims to communicate successfully. Miscommunication takes place when there is an obvious misalignment between speaker and listener. We can trace the misalignment back to many different sources of which the most important is probably a difference in background knowledge. For instance, if an international business partner is unaware of load shedding, he or she might not understand when the South African partner indicates an absence from the next meeting. Not knowing the importance of certain tones in spoken language could also lead to a misunderstanding in the semantic load of certain words and consequently give rise to a completely different inference.

How does all of this apply to law? First of all, we may use the Cooperative Principle to determine whether spoken or written conversation contains any implicatures. This will help to determine whether a conversation is straightforward or whether it has any implied messages as well that need further scrutiny. Let us take *S v Shaik* as our example once more.[76] In another letter to Thétard, Shabir Shaik writes:[77]

> 5.47 I refer to our understanding Re: Deputy President Jacob Zuma and issues raised. I will appreciate it if you can communicate to me your availability to meet.

Seen objectively, the message looks plain. However, let us consider the maxims of conversation to be sure. Quality (be truthful): The message qualifies as truthful, because it refers to an existing issue and requires Thétard to provide verifiable information in order to meet up. Quantity (be sufficient): Although the message suffers from wordiness, it does not lead to confusion. Shaik refers to existing information without repeating said information. Relevance (be relevant): The message is relevant by referring to existing information and by requesting a meeting because of the existing information. Manner (be clear and orderly): The intention of

76 *S v Shaik* 2007 (1) SA 240 (SCA) (6 November 2006).
77 *S v Shaik*, para 185.

the message is clear – they must meet. Also, there is a chronological order present – the meeting is a consequence of the 'issues raised'.

Based on this evaluation, there is no implicature in 5.47. The message is rather simple. Shaik is not trying to say one thing and mean something else. It is clear that something happened which Shaik, Zuma and Thétard had to discuss. When one of the participants in the corrupt dealings seemed to be dismissive of Shaik, he said the following:[78]

5.48 They can play hardball, but we can play political ball.

The utterance in 5.48 contains an implicature. This is a good example of a speaker flouting maxims by deliberately using a metaphor. He does this without opting out of the Cooperative Principle. Let us consider the maxims once again. Quality (be truthful): The expression itself infringes this maxim, because neither party is playing baseball. However, Shaik believes the other parties are being intentionally difficult and he has enough evidence to support this (the fact that they are obviously dismissive of him). Quantity (be sufficient): Shaik uses figurative speech to convey both the other parties' attitude as well as his own influence and intentions. Because the expression is well known, it provides a sufficient amount of information to convey the message. Relevance (be relevant): The expression relates directly to the difficulty he is experiencing with one of the other participants, and the consequences that could follow. Manner (be clear and orderly): The assumption here is that Shaik's audience was familiar with the figurative expression. If not, the audience would be very confused as to what his words implicate. Implicature: We can make things difficult for them too.

The utterance consists of two independent clauses. The first contains the conventional figurative expression and the second contains Shaik's own metaphor. The successful inference of his metaphor depends on his audience's understanding of the conventional expression. This is where the implicature lies. By means of the two figurative expressions, Shaik not only cautions others not to cross him, but he also asserts his own political influence and further implicates the type of relationship he has with Jacob Zuma. The utterance in 5.48 furthermore illustrates how Grice's Conversational Implicatures work together with Austin and Searle's Speech Act Theory. Shaik's implicature contains obvious indirect speech acts with the illocutionary force of boasting, warning as well as threatening.

78 *S v Shaik*, para 130.

In *Rustenburg Platinum Mine v SAEWO obo Bester*, we saw that Mr Bester allegedly uttered the words *remove that black man's car* to the safety officer, Mr Sedumedi.[79] His utterance is a speech act that instructs the listener to do something specific. It does not contain an implicature. Apart from using the word *black*, there is nothing weird about Bester's expression. However, Sedumedi's alleged conversation with Bester does contain an implicature:[80]

5.49 You don't want to park next to a black man's car, that is your problem.

Sedumedi's utterance takes the form of a statement and expresses the illocutionary force of blaming and accusing. The implicature is that Bester is a racist. The utterance itself infringes the maxim of quality, because the speaker does not offer any verifiable facts that Bester does in fact not want to park next to a black man. These are allegations only.

In *Jonker v Davis*,[81] Mr Davis's utterance contained a clear implicature, that he is of superior status and that Mr Jonker is of a lower caste and therefore inferior to him:[82]

5.50 You must remember that I am the son of a rich man and that I have been well educated. I will not stand for a boy like you, who grew up in a 'krot' [...].

Davis' utterance further implicates that the difference in their status disallows Jonker from addressing or even reprimanding him.

As can be seen from the examples above, Grice's Cooperative Principle can help us better understand the meaning that a speaker expresses as well as the audience's inference thereof. Can we apply the same to statutes? That might be a bit trickier, even though courts do it all the time. To start, we have to accept that the legislature is a speaker and that every enactment is in fact a written form of a conversation between the state and its people. As addressees, the citizenry assumes and accepts that the legislature intends on communicating truthfully, sufficiently, relevantly and clearly. However, knowing what we do about the legal language employed in statutes we also know that laws are often wordy and ambiguous. Sometimes, acts may contain obscure wording and unnecessarily complex lexical items and syntax. This means that

79 *Rustenburg Platinum Mine v SAEWA obo Bester* [2018] ZACC 13, para 5.
80 *Rustenburg Platinum Mine v SAEWA obo Bester*, paras 6–7.
81 *Jonker v Davis* 1953 (2) SA 726 (GW).
82 *Jonker v Davis*, at 726.

legislation regularly infringes the maxims of quantity and manner. Due to the nature and purpose of legislation (its need for clarity), acts should not include implicatures. Legislative drafting must aim to eliminate implied meaning as much as possible. Consider the following example taken from the Genetically Modified Organisms Act,[83] which deals with offences and penalties for contravening the Act. Section 21(3) states:[84]

> 5.51 Notwithstanding anything to the contrary in any law contained, a magistrate's court shall be competent to impose any penalty or make any order prescribed by this Act.

The implicature of this statement is that a higher court could also impose penalties or make orders if another law allows it. The implicature is further that the lower court should be the first port of call if no other law applies and binds this Act to a higher court. These implicatures might be obvious to legal scholars and practitioners, but it might not be that plain to the public. Once again, this begs an old question of who the true audience is: the educated few or the masses?

A Gricean approach to statutory interpretation could help a court understand why two parties assign diverse meanings to a word or phrase and it may help a court decide which assigned meaning applies to the context at hand. For instance, in *Starways Trading 21 CC v Pearl Island Trading (Pty) Ltd*,[85] the court had to decide whether Starways Trading repudiated its contract with Pearl Island Trading and whether the word *ex-warehouse* excluded the operations set out in section 59 of the Customs and Excise Act.[86] The parties entered into a sugar contract. As the importer and initial seller, Starways Trading carried the responsibility of paying import duties, which they recovered from the purchase price they levied. When the excise was lowered between August and September of 2016, it affected Pearl Island Trading's purchase price as well.[87] When they insisted on paying the reduced price, Starways Trading claimed that the word *ex-warehouse* meant that the agreement was contrary to section 59 of the Act, which allows deductions in the event of lowered excise duties.[88]

From the facts of the case, it is clear that Starways Trading and Pearl Island Trading understood *ex-warehouse* differently: Starways Trading

83 Genetically Modified Organisms Act 15 of 1997.
84 Genetically Modified Organisms Act.
85 *Starways Trading 21 CC v Pearl Island Trading (Pty) Ltd*, 2019 (2) SA 650 (SCA) (3 December 2018).
86 Customs and Excise Act 91 of 1964; *Starways Trading 21 CC v Pearl Island Trading (Pty) Ltd*, para 8.
87 *Starways Trading 21 CC v Pearl Island Trading (Pty) Ltd*, paras 5 and 7.
88 *Starways Trading 21 CC v Pearl Island Trading (Pty) Ltd*, paras 6–7.

understood the word to denote that a price is free of any fluctuations in excise and that the risk is carried over to the purchaser once the goods arrive at the buyer's warehouse.[89] Pear Island Trading understood the word to indicate from where the seller will deliver the goods.[90] In order for *ex-warehouse* to indicate more than its ordinary meaning (denotation: out or in front of the warehouse), it had to have an extended definition clearly indicating that a contract excludes any excise fluctuations. Measured against the maxims of conversation, Starways Trading would also have to prove that the potential technical meaning is more widely accepted than the ordinary meaning (which must be easily verifiable). Alternatively, they should be able to prove that the ordinary meaning of *ex-warehouse* is either too short or too long to be fully comprehensible and that it is irrelevant. More importantly, the onus is on them to indicate to what extent the existing ordinary meaning is obscure or ambiguous, which it is not.

Their sugar contract did not define *ex-warehouse* nor was there any clear indication that it should be read contrary to section 59 of the Act. Clauses 7 and 8 of the sugar contract contain no implicature; none was vested in the word *ex-warehouse*.[91]

Let us now move to Relevance Theory and its potential application in statutory interpretation.

5.9. Relevance theory

Sperber and Wilson derived their theory from Grice's ideas on implicatures. As a result, their theory does contain some similarities but for the most part, it departs from Grice's. In Relevance Theory, the Cooperative Principle is replaced with the Principle of Relevance. In consequence, all the conversational maxims fall away, save the maxim of relevance. According to this theory, an utterance conveys the information that is relevant enough for an audience to decode. This means that if a speaker says something, the receiver of the utterance can assume the speaker communicated something that is worth the receiver's time and energy to listen to and interpret. Put differently, the addressee accepts that the speaker tried to communicate in the simplest way possible. This falls within the human ability to sort through the mass of information that reaches us every day in order to focus on what is more important at

89 *Starways Trading 21 CC v Pearl Island Trading (Pty) Ltd*, para 10.

90 *Starways Trading 21 CC v Pearl Island Trading (Pty) Ltd*, para 16. See also *Starways Trading 21 CC v Pearl Island Trading 714 (Pty) Ltd* [2017] 4 All SA 568 (WCC), paras 12, 15–17.

91 *Starways Trading 21 CC v Pearl Island Trading (Pty) Ltd*, para 3.

that particular point in time. In other words, humans constantly isolate relevant information from irrelevant information. This cognitive ability is quite important and useful for identifying underlying intentions and attitudes as well (Yus 2015:642).

Relevance Theory is rather complex and is not always well-defined or described. What follows is a summary of its essence, which is sufficient and useful for our purpose.

5.9.1 Principle of Relevance

At the heart of it, Relevance Theory sees the comprehension of utterances as an inferential process that combines what a speaker says with contextual information to yield an interpretation of what the speaker meant (Wilson 2017:81). Two principles ground the theory: the Cognitive Principle of Relevance and the Communicative Principle of Relevance.

The **Cognitive Principle of Relevance** states that human cognition is aimed at maximising relevance. This involves both new stimuli and existing information. Input leads to a variety of cognitive effects. For instance, new information can combine with existing information to reach new conclusions or strengthen existing ideas. New input can also contradict or delete what a speaker already knows (Carston and Powell 2008:342). In order to reach certain cognitive effects (new conclusions or confirmation of existing ideas), humans expend cognitive effort by processing the input. The processing of input depends heavily on context. According to Sperber and Wilson, context comprises mentally represented information that includes beliefs, doubts, hopes, plans, wishes, intensions, questions, sounds, smells, memories, conclusions and so on (Wilson 2017:82). A receiver selects the most relevant context during the comprehension process that applies best at that particular point in time. More importantly, a person expends less cognitive effort when the information is at its most relevant.

Because people are overwhelmed by constant input and because individuals select the most relevant information for comprehension processing, a speaker must work that much harder to capture an audience's attention. A prerequisite of successful communication is that the addressee must accept an utterance is relevant enough to attend to (Wilson 2017:85). The **Communicative Principle of Relevance** states that when a speaker produces an utterance, he or she is also communicating its optimal relevance to the listener. In other words, when speaking, a speaker is simultaneously proposing that what he or she is saying is worth an audience's time and effort. The principle works through two conditions and two practical heuristics (Wilson 2017:85-86):

The conditions:

1. An utterance is relevant enough to be worth the addressee's processing effort.
2. It is the most relevant utterance within the speaker's ability and preferences.

The first condition states that an audience will presume every utterance is relevant enough to be worthy of processing, otherwise an addressee will not attend to the utterance. We can liken this to an employee scanning through an e-mail inbox. The person will open an e-mail because he or she thinks that e-mail contains relevant information. The second condition states that an audience will presume a speaker has gone to the trouble to ensure that what he or she says is always relevant to the addressee. The speaker does this by deliberately reducing the audience's processing effort and increasing the cognitive effect. In terms of our e-mail example, an employee will presume that the sender will not waste his or her time by forwarding a fruitless message or one that is unnecessarily long and complex.

The heuristics:

1. The addressee follows the path of least effort when interpreting an utterance.
2. The addressee will stop once the expectations of relevance are satisfied.

The first heuristic states that an addressee will expend the least amount of effort to process an utterance. The audience expects the speaker to make the utterance as easy to interpret as possible, which means that an addressee is always prepared to expend the least amount of energy. This is especially true for vague and ambiguous or overly complex input. The receiver of an ambiguous utterance will grab at the meaning that comes to him or her first by as little cognitive exertion as possible. Lastly, the second heuristic states that an addressee will stop the comprehension process the moment their expectation of relevance has reached saturation. This means a receiver will stop attending to an utterance once he or she finds an interpretation that is the most relevant at that particular point in time (and through little processing effort). Our fictitious employee will scan through the existing emails and only read what they think is important and which requires the least effort to read through. If the first paragraph of an e-mail is sufficient to draw the necessary conclusion, the employee will probably not continue reading. Further, he or she will definitely not attend to any emails that appear less relevant.

So, what does all of this mean? Because a speaker wants to convey meaning, he or she must knowingly communicate it in such a way that their audience will willingly spend cognitive effort to interpret what the speaker said. The speaker conveys the message knowing that the audience will use a varied context to process the message and that the audience will stop once they have drawn a conclusion. A speaker exploits the fact that an audience will select the very first conclusion available. Knowing this can help a speaker communicate as successfully as possible the first time around. Yet, it also makes it possible for misunderstandings to take place or for speakers to manipulate the audience. Let us illustrate this by means of four examples.

Our first example concerns an experiment where a team randomly stopped strangers on the street and asked *Do you have the time, please?* According to Wilson (2017:87–88), the prediction was that the strangers would round off the time by at least five minutes in an effort to optimise the relevance of the utterance and its consequent reply. Indeed, the majority of strangers either rounded off or gave a general indication of the actual time. However, once the team changed their question and asked strangers *Do you have the time, please? I have an appointment at 4.00*, the strangers aimed at providing more accurate time readings. In this case, the audience interpreted the reference to an appointment as more relevant and therefore maximised the relevance of the information in return.

Our second example concerns the Clicks-Monkey incident that we discussed previously. Remember that a white woman supposedly asked a black woman for a shopping basket, using the Afrikaans word *mandjie*. The black woman heard *monkey* instead. If we examine this incident through Relevance Theory, it means that the black woman used the most relevant context available to her (a white woman connected to a history of racist slurs like *monkey*). She used this context to process the input (*mandjie / monkey*) and accepted the very first conclusion that the cognitive processing allowed (*monkey*). Once she had drawn her first and most relevant conclusion, she stopped processing. At that particular moment, she heard a white woman calling her a monkey. Because comprehension processing reached saturation the moment she realised that she was insulted with a racial slur, she no longer had a cognitive need to consider any other possible facts like the shopping basket, the woman speaking Afrikaans or the sheer randomness of it all. From a Relevance Theoretic perspective, the problem lies with the white woman's output. Choosing to speak Afrikaans in that situation, she did not consider the option that her utterance will necessitate greater processing effort, which could result in a breakdown in communication.

For our third example, we consider the consternation involving the supermarket franchise, Spar, and the well-known South African singer, PJ Powers. For a specific winter marketing campaign, Spar's liquor affiliate, TOPS, published advertisements with the wording *PJ Powers* on it. The campaign apparently referred to the power of pyjama parties (*PJs*), using slogans like *no sleep only party*. However, it failed miserably because many South Africans misunderstood *PJ Powers* as referring to the South African recording artist, PJ Powers, and not to pyjamas. The singer's personal history as a recovering alcoholic made the reception of the campaign worse. Grundlingh (2016:249-250) points out that here too readers followed the path of least cognitive processing effort based on the available context. The context consists of South African music culture and shared memories as well as the wording *PJ Powers* and images of alcohol. The logical conclusion would be that TOPS referred to the singer. In fact, the images of alcohol and the slogan *grab a drink* could strengthen reader's reference to the singer (Grundlingh 2016:250). Once readers have reached this conclusion, they will stop looking for possibilities that are more relevant. This also means that the readers would not pay much attention to the rest of the advertisement, because the processing effort reached saturation the moment they started thinking of the singer instead. Even though *PJs* is a well-known abbreviation for pyjamas, the co-occurrence of *PJ Powers* is not so common. In fact, if one uses *PJ* as a search term on Google South Africa, the immediate result is PJ Powers, the recording artist (Grundlingh 2016:253-255). To search pyjamas, one has to use the search term *PJs*. This means that the cognitive processing effort is simply too high; it is very unlikely that an ordinary audience would read the advertisement and first think of a pyjama party. The sender of the message did not produce an output that was easy for an audience to interpret and therefore did not allow them to reach an interpretation the sender intended. Due to the status of the singer, TOPS's use of the words *PJ Powers* immediately provided South African readers with input that required little processing effort and that was by far the easiest to interpret (Grundlingh 2016:266).

Our last example engages the words *faggot* and *fagott*. Carney, Grundlingh and Knobel (2023) studied an incident on Twitter in which person A referred to person B as a *fagott*. Person A's Twitter followers understood *fagott* as a homophobic slur. He then replied with another tweet, explaining that *fagott* was the German word for a bassoon, a musical instrument. He insisted that the word referred to person B's last name, Basson, which was the French for *bassoon*. He denied calling B a *faggot*, which is the homophobic slur. Once again, the sender of the tweet expected too much cognitive processing effort from his audience.

For his Twitter followers to know that *fagott* is equal to *bassoon* and that both refer to the family name *Basson*, they need to have a broad knowledge of musical instruments (and the instruments' names in different languages) as well as genealogy. The Twitter followers would not come to this conclusion first. Because *fagott* looks so similar to *faggot*, it is easy for an audience to misread the one for the other. In fact, Carney, Grundlingh and Knobel (2023) provided evidence that *faggot* is often misspelt, supporting the possibility that Twitter followers thought *fagott* referred to a homosexual male. By means of a small experiment, Carney, Grundlingh and Knobel (2023) also showed that readers misread *fagott* to mean *faggot*. Participants did this because the processing effort was less in assuming that *fagott* meant *homosexual male* as opposed to *bassoon*. Once readers concluded what *fagott* meant, their processing effort stopped. As reasonable readers, they assumed that the author of the tweet produced an output that contained the most relevant information and that expected the least processing effort. In other words, readers assumed that the author of the tweet intended for them to understand *faggot*. This begs the question whether the author of the tweet was deliberate in his use of *fagott*. If a sender produces an utterance knowing that the receiver will draw the easiest and quickest conclusion based on the input he provides, then he would expect readers to see *fagott* and think *faggot*.

Relevance theory allows us to understand why an audience understood words and phrases the way they did, and it provides us with a way to work out the intention of the speaker (author). We now shift our focus to a linguistic phenomenon related to speech acts, implicatures and intended speaker meaning: politeness.

5.10. Politeness

Generally speaking, politeness is socially correct or appropriate language and behaviour. But it is not just something our parents taught us; it is also an important linguistic device. We use it to attend to 'the feelings and expectations of those one is interacting with so that social interaction proceeds smoothly' (Brown 2017:383). As an important aspect of social interaction, politeness forms part of the cooperation between conversational partners. Speakers employ different strategies to maintain a positive self-esteem and to prevent any kind of imposition. It is primarily the work of Erwin Goffman, and later that of Robin Lakoff as well as Penelope Brown and Stephen Levinson, that gave rise to politeness theory. Understanding the language involved in politeness strategies provides necessary insight into how and why speakers offend others. To be certain, politeness is central to language crimes like hate speech, insult, personality infringement and trolling, to name only a few. Because politeness is itself an implicature – an utterance that may be inferred – linguistic politeness strategies relate to pragmatic devices like speech acts and conversational implicatures, which is familiar territory by now. In this section, we take a closer look at the basic premise of politeness theory and how the principles of politeness link to legislation like the Hate Speech Bill, the Equality Act and law of personality.

5.10.1 Face

People have impressions of themselves and others. When they partake in social encounters, they partly express what they think of themselves and what they think of their interlocutors, whether they know it or not. Mostly, participants of an encounter will assume that the individual presents his or her view of the self and others wilfully (Goffman 1967:5). To describe this view of self, Goffman (1967:5-6) used the term **face**. We understand *face* as the positive public image people claim for themselves. Face includes what an individual assumes others think of him or her. During an encounter, things may happen to make speakers feel good or bad about their self-image. We refer to this as having or losing face. Someone who has face feels good about the self, whereas someone who loses face could feel embarrassed or ashamed. Put differently, both verbal and non-verbal situations during an encounter can have either a positive or a negative effect on a person's self-image and therefore his or her self-worth. This can leave a person feeling validated or bad about who he or she is. People will therefore do what they can to avoid any situation that could potentially threaten their face. Because it is so important to speakers to maintain face constantly (theirs and their interlocutors' face), face-work becomes a vital condition of interaction (Goffman 1967:12).

Brown and Levinson (1987:61) distinguished between positive and negative face. For them, **positive face** represents an individual's desire to be accepted, respected and liked by others. **Negative face** represents a person's fear of being forced into unwanted and uncomfortable situations, which means that an individual's freedom of action is impeded. To save negative face, interlocutors must have options to either opt out or continue the line of conversation willingly. We use the term **face-threatening acts (FTAs)** to describe verbal and non-verbal incidents that could cause individuals to lose either positive or negative face (Brown and Levinson 1987:65-67). These FTAs cover a number of potential threats ranging from impositions like offers, requests, threats, warnings and suggestions to expressions of disapproval, criticism, complaints and reprimands. FTAs include expressions that make it clear that a speaker does not care about the addressee's positive face by means of violent and offensive language, incorrect or inappropriate terms of address, taboo language and topics as well as the raising of sensitive and divisive topics. Face-threatening acts depend on three variables: the social distance between the speaker and the addressee, the power relation between them and the ranking of the imposition (Brown and Levinson 1987:74). Put differently, we tend to be more polite to people we do not know; we tend to be more polite to our social superiors (but they are not necessarily equally polite in return), and our cultural norms and values determine which impositions are graver than others (Brown 2017:386). Let us consider the following two examples:

5.52 A: Professor, here's my assignment.
B: Late as usual, John. Why do you even bother?

5.53 A: I think we should go back to your place and watch the match. Your TV is bigger.
B: Uhm, okay. Sure. What time?

In 5.52, there is a clear power relation between professor and student. The professor's reply in B threatens John's positive face in terms of his desire to be accepted and liked. John might seek his professor's approval, which makes the professor's reply (an accusation and disapproval) that much worse. In 5.53, speaker A makes a suggestion that leaves B uncomfortable, which means that A is imposing on B. Speaker B feels as if he or she does not have a choice to decline A's suggestion.

To avoid or navigate potential face-threatening acts, a speaker employs **face-saving strategies**. These include avoiding people and situations altogether, increasing physical space between people and even choosing certain communication channels above others (sending text messages instead of telephoning). One of the best techniques is to use polite language. Speakers generally know what to say (and how to say it) in order to reduce threats to their own face and that of their interlocutors. We will look at some of the face-saving acts in the next sections.

5.10.2 Linguistic devices for politeness

Brown and Levinson (1987:13, 62) maintained that politeness – and specifically the notion of *face* – is universal; a phenomenon present in all languages and cultures in some shape or form. However, it is important to realise that different cultures will practice politeness differently (and for different reasons). We saw previously that some cultures use eye contact and silence as politeness devices. Individuals in some Southern African cultures will avoid eye contact as a sign of respect in the same way certain

Australian cultures will insert long pauses when they formulate a reply to an interlocutor. We also saw how Southern Sotho women use euphemisms to talk about sex and body parts. Actually, the use of euphemism is one of the most common techniques to talk about various taboo subjects in public and to strangers. According to Lakoff (1973:299, 302), employing euphemisms is one of the face-saving strategies that aims at making people feel good (or less awkward).

In some cultures, speakers will use honorifics to ensure respect and politeness. Honorifics may include both official titles and kinship terms but also extend to forms of address that include the use of polite pronouns. Here, speakers often distinguish between older and younger individuals, as well as those who might have a higher status. It is an impersonalisation strategy that helps to insert social distance between speaker and addressee, and aids in communicating respectfully with strangers or people who acquire conventional status through age or position (Brown and Levinson 1987:22-23). Where a system exists in which speakers have to use certain terms of address, either formal or informal, it could be disrespectful or impolite to address people in any other way. For instance, there is a difference between saying *Excuse me, sir* and *hey, you*. Terms of address blend with taboo words when a speaker uses particular lexical items or pejoratives to address someone or to refer to a third party. The chosen words can conjure up a variety of concepts and connotations, which will contribute both semantically and pragmatically to a situation. This applies to known slurs as well as ordinary words. The word *bomber* has no impolite connotations by itself, yet if you refer to a Muslim colleague as *the suicide bomber*, this could be very insensitive and Islamophobic. Even if the speaker did not intentionally use the phrase as a racist slur, it still affects the addressee's positive face and could cause unnecessary legal woes.

Another technique is to use hedges and vagueness willingly.[92] This means that speakers might not be certain about the facts or the truth of a matter, or they do not want to commit to the consequences. Instead of saying *John stole the petty cash* you could say *John is sort of involved in the petty cash theft*. Hedging the sentence helps to protect the speaker's negative face (because the speaker is put in an awkward position to report on John's involvement) but protects John's positive face too (because it is still not clear how John is involved and therefore his reputation is

92 This is described as avoidance-based politeness. Together, the use of honorifics, hedges, indirect speech acts and other mechanisms to impersonalise utterances serve to avoid losing face and to increase agreement. See Brown (2017:386).

not ruined just yet). The opposite could also apply – a speaker knows exactly what the truth is or what the facts are but do not want to reveal them due to the sensitivity of the information (think of economic or medical data). For example, some cultures consider talking about money as rude. It is impolite to ask someone what they earn or how much they paid for something. Instead of saying *You must've broken the bank on this TV* you could say *This TV is pure quality*, implying that the TV is expensive. Hedging this sentence provides the interlocutor with options – he or she can volunteer more information on what the TV cost, or the interlocutor can opt out by discussing the features of the TV. Similarly, people might consider questions about health as impolite. If a colleague is on sick leave for mental health reasons, a co-worker might hedge references to the colleague's exact medical status: Instead of saying *I think John has lost it* you could say *I think John is not feeling his best lately.* In this case, vagueness helps to save both the speaker's negative face and John's positive face.

Of course, the easiest way to practise politeness is simply to use formulaic expressions meant for the task, which include *please* and *thank you* as well as typical complimentary expressions (Brown and Levinson 1987:26; Brown 2017:385). The adverb *please* and modal verbs like *may* and *could* go a long way in expressing politeness. We can also construct polite expressions by changing statements to questions. Instead of saying *Purchase the transport token before 12h00* you could say *Please purchase the token before 12h00*, or *Could you (perhaps) purchase the token before 12h00.* That said, the power relation between speaker and listener can render polite words ineffective. Lakoff (1973:295) illustrates this with the example *Please shut the window.* She argues that, as a polite request, the speaker is asking the recipient to perform a favour on the speaker's behalf. This is only the case if both parties have more or less the same status. If so, the recipient can refuse (either politely or impolitely). Yet, if the speaker is superior to the recipient, then *please* is merely used conventionally and not as a true politeness marker. In other words, the speaker is saying *I'm being a nice guy, but I can force you to do what I say.* The recipient does not have much of an option to refuse, which imposes him or her and threatens the recipient's negative face. In this vein, Brown (2017:389) reminds us that polite utterances do not necessarily express feelings about an interlocutors' persona; rather, polite utterances express expected concern for face. As such, the use of honorifics, hedges or politeness formulas do not guarantee politeness. A range of contextual and non-verbal cues as well as semantic criteria can override any politeness expressed through an utterance. For instance, if a speaker says *Please shut the window* in a loud voice and stresses *PLEASE*, he or she is not being polite at all.

Brown and Levinson (1987:103–129) proposed a number of strategies to save or maintain positive and negative face. According to them, a speaker must take an interest in the addressee to give positive face. Speakers can do this by complimenting (*Wow, you had a haircut!*), exaggerating (*Your hair looks FANTASTIC*) and by using terms of endearment for those closest to them (*The haircut suits you, babe*). Using familiar terms of address when speaking to strangers or people who are less familiar helps to soften any imposition a speaker might cause. Words like *dear* and *friend* are common: *Would you mind reaching the rice on the top shelf, dear?* Speakers maintain positive face by sticking to safe topics of conversation and by agreement. The latter represents token agreement, which means that a speaker pretends to agree in order to save face and avoid disagreement. This is achieved through adapting utterances by introducing agreement before moving on to a contrary opinion: *Yes I understand, but... I completely agree, however...* The use of white lies is a similar strategy to avoid disagreement. The speaker will tell a lie not to damage the listener's positive face (*Yes, your new haircut suits you*). Other strategies to maintain positive face include giving (or requesting) reasons for certain decisions or propositions, and joking. Jokes between people who share a common background help to put a listener at ease, especially when something embarrassing just took place, when a speaker aims at relaxing a conversation, or when he or she wants to make up for an obvious blunder.

Because negative face is about preventing imposition, Brown and Levinson (1987:129–210) proposed strategies to minimise any form of coercion. This means a speaker should try his or her best not to force the audience into awkward situations in which they have little to no choice. Some of the best ways to achieve this is through indirect and impersonal constructions. Speakers either implicate through indirect speech acts (*Can you possibly pass the salt?*) or by using the passive voice and indefinite pronouns (*all rights reserved*). The use of pronouns includes the plural form of the second person, *we* (*We regret to inform you...*). These strategies help to soften the blow, so to speak, because the directness of an imposition and the main agent (the speaker) are less obvious to the listener. Other strategies that work well are hedging, questioning, and apologising. When a speaker damages the addressee's negative face in any way, the speaker can start by acknowledging the imposition and his or her reluctance to impose (*I know you are very busy, but...; I hope this won't put you out too much, however...*). The speaker should continue with an actual expression of apology and include convincing reasons for the imposition (*I'm really sorry for approaching you with this issue, but I need help and have no-one else to turn to*).

In the next section, we take a closer look at pragmatic devices that serve to express politeness.

5.10.3 Maxims of politeness

Brown and Levinson's elaborate work on politeness was preceded by those of Lakoff (1973) and Leech (1983). Because politeness is often expressed through implicatures, it makes sense that Lakoff and Leech formulated maxims to function within or alongside Grice's Cooperative Principle. Lakoff's (1973:298) Rules for Politeness consist of three maxims:

1. Don't impose.
2. Give options.
3. Make the audience feel good – be friendly.

Speakers apply these rules depending on the situation they find themselves in – on occasion only one rule applies, sometimes more than one applies. The first maxim means to stay out of people's business. If a speaker needs to intrude, they should ask permission. Here, conventional and formulaic expressions are common goods. A speaker will also typically use passive constructions, impersonal expressions and technical terms to increase the distance between speaker and audience (Lakoff 1973:299).

In the same vein as Brown and Levinson's negative face-saving strategies, the second maxim provides the audience with an opportunity to make their own decisions. Hedges and euphemisms help an audience to avoid feeling put on the spot. Using a euphemism for sexual acts will lessen the blow for someone who avoids talking about sex in general. Both medical terms and taboo words could embarrass an addressee and threaten that person's positive and negative face (their assumption of what others will think of them as well as their freedom to act). This maxim sets out to provide an audience with the option either to opt out of a conversation or to continue in some way (Lakoff 1973:300-301).

The first and second maxims work together to make an audience feel good (they help people maintain face), but the third maxim is aimed at making the audience feel wanted. One way is to close the gap between speaker and audience. This can be done by eliminating formal language between the two, using nicknames if interlocutors are familiar with one another and by employing the second person *you*. This works to establish a 'state of camaraderie' (Lakoff 1973:301-302).

Leech's (1983) approach is a lot more formal and structured. He proposed the Principle of Politeness to work alongside Grice's Principle of Cooperation. The aim of Leech's principle is for speakers to choose expressions that will belittle an audience's status as little as possible (Cruse 2015:426). Belittling acts include reducing people to subservient roles (expecting them to expend effort and so minimising their freedom), saying bad things to or about them, expressing pleasure in their misfortune, disagreeing (and so indicating your opinion of their thoughts) and praising oneself (Cruse 2015:426). To combat this type of behaviour, Leech (1983:104; 131) introduced the tact maxim and maxims of politeness. Leech (1983:107-108) described the tact maxim in terms of a cost-benefit scale. The least polite expression is uttered at a much greater cost to the addressee (*Answer the phone!*), whereas the most polite expression comes at a greater cost to the speaker in an attempt to reduce the cost for the listener (*Could you possibly answer the phone?*). At the heart of it, the tact maxims endeavour to soften any imposition by offering an audience the option to refuse. This is achieved by using questions or by using indirect expressions. Questions provide the opportunity to refuse and indirect expressions disguise the imposition to some extent, making the cost less obvious (Leech 1983:108-109; 123-127).

His maxims of politeness consist of five more maxims that tend to work in pairs: generosity maxim, praise maxim, modesty maxim, agreement maxim and the sympathy maxim (Leech 1983:133-139). The generosity maxim works with the tact maxim and aims at putting the audience first at the cost of the speaker. However, instead of being overly polite the speaker is very direct: *Let me take out the trash* (not *Would you mind if I took out the trash?*). If the benefit was for the speaker (in terms of the tact maxim), he or she would formulate their expression in such a way as to minimise the cost for the listener.

The praise maxim works with the modesty maxim and is concerned with positive and negative opinions. The aim is not to say anything nasty even when the speaker has a negative opinion. Consider the following:

5.54 A: Do you like my new haircut?
B: No, it looks terrible. (impolite)
It suits you, although I quite liked your previous style. (polite)

The modesty maxim tries to minimise self-praise. Because boasting is seen as impolite behaviour, the speaker not only reduces bragging, but tries to minimise praise by the audience as well. Compare the following:

5.55 A: You were fantastic!
B: Yes, I'm pretty great. (impolite)
Oh, I barely managed. (polite)

5.56 A1: Please take this huge present as a sign of our gratitude. (impolite)

A2: I don't think you will be able to do much with this tiny gift, but please accept it as a token of our appreciation. (polite)

The example in 5.55 is typical of an attempt at reducing self-praise by replying modestly. However, Cruse (2015:430) points out that an audience will easily notice when a speaker's modesty is insincere and could therefore be less impolite. A person could reply modestly simply by saying *thank you* and leaving it at that. In 5.56, utterance A1 exemplifies how a speaker makes the gift about his or her greatness, whereas the speaker in A2 tries to stress their appreciation. However, once again A2 can come across as insincere, especially when the gift is not small at all. By focusing attention on the size of the gift, the speaker is still relaying the focus to him or her in some way.

The remaining maxims of agreement and sympathy aim at mitigating any negative effect caused by disagreement and by offering an addressee congratulations or condolences, which Leech sees as inherently polite acts. Non-verbal communication like body language and intonation plays an important role when disagreeing in polite fashion or being congenial. Frowning or loudness of voice, as opposed to smiling and solemn facial cues, immediately contribute towards the pragmatic load of utterances. Of course, this is true for all politeness strategies as well as face-threatening acts.

A familiar strategy to mitigate FTAs is indirect language use. Let us have a quick look at this in the next section.

5.10.4Indirect language

Noticeably, one of the most common ways speakers express politeness, is by using indirect language such as indirect speech acts. According to Searle (1975:64), speakers employ indirect speech acts because it is simply too awkward to issue direct imperatives or requests (*Leave the room!* as opposed to *I wonder if you would mind leaving the room?*). Indirect speech acts (as well as other indirect expressions) are therefore seen as an ideal politeness strategy (Brown and Levinson 1987:142). Indirect language offers an audience the opportunity to opt out of an uncomfortable situation or imposition. The indirect utterance makes the condition of the utterance clear without forcing the audience into a corner. Asking a stranger *You don't happen to have any change for a loaf of bread?* makes it immediately obvious that the speaker wants money, but the utterance provides the listener with the option to politely reply with *yes* or *no.*

Furthermore, it helps to provide an explanation for a request as opposed to the direct request itself: *This room is really stuffy* versus *Will you open the window?*

When responding to indirect speech acts, Clark (1979:435, 437) points out that most can adequately be answered with brief replies. For instance, if someone asks *Can you tell me what the time is?* the listener can respond with *It's six.* Yet, many people reply with *Yes, I can – it's six.* Adding the redundant first part (*Yes, I can*) is considered more polite and serves as a sign that the listener understood the indirect speech act, which in turn means that the listener is actively cooperating with the speaker. Clark (1979:446-448) also reported experiment results that showed most speakers would initiate their request with formulaic expressions like *would you..., could you..., do you mind..., I was wondering..., I am sorry to bother you, but...* In most cases, the recipient replied with *no (I don't mind).* This serves as a sign that indirectness helps to diminish the threat from requests and orders, or softens threats provided by disagreements and interruptions (see also Saeed 2009:247).

Although many conversational participants will aim at being polite to some extent, the same cannot be said of everyone. In the next section, we review impoliteness, which is a prominent part of politeness theory.

5.10.5 Impoliteness

The politeness strategies proposed by scholars in the previous sections are meant for ideal encounters. Successful communication is primarily concerned with clarity, yet if the communicative aim is not to offend, then politeness overrides the need for clarity. Seeing as no-one is perfect, the rules of conversation are more honoured in the breach than in observation (Lakoff 1973:297). People say hateful things easily and habitually. We can view this as a form of interactional conflict, which distinguishes between being rude (forgetting or ignoring polite behaviour) and overt attacks on face (insults, threats, verbal aggression) (Brown 2017:396).[93] When someone deliberately affects another person's face negatively, this is known as **impoliteness**. Culpeper, Bousfield and Wichmann (2003:1546) define *impoliteness* as communicative strategies designed to attack face and thereby cause social conflict and disharmony. At its core,

93 The term *face-attack* is associated with Culpeper (2011:20, 118), who describes it as communication that is intentionally aggressive in which a speaker says something on purpose to impair an audience's self-image and self-worth.

impoliteness is an intentional face-attack, or at least perceived as such by the addressee.[94]

Remember that speakers communicate with a purpose in mind. Even though the interaction between conversational participants leads to a joint construction of meaning, a conversation is still directed by communicative intent in some shape or form. Culpeper (2011:49) indicates that desire and belief underlie intention: a desire for an outcome and the belief that the intended action will lead to the desired outcome. A speaker produces an utterance because he or she wants to effect something through their words and believes that they will achieve this. The outcome is sometimes an offence against face in the form of communicative aggression (Culpeper 2011:21). In other words, a speaker might attack another person's face wilfully. This is where communicative and criminal intent seem to meet.

Culpeper (2011:50-51) discriminates between a speaker's actual intentions and what an audience might perceive to be the speaker's intentions. Perception can easily lead to miscommunication, or accidental rudeness. He cites the classic example of a man asking a woman when her baby is due, only to find out that she is not pregnant. This is known as failed politeness. The man's intention was (possibly) not to offend, but the woman was offended regardless because he focussed unnecessary attention on her weight. The distinction between intentional and perceived impoliteness is seen in *S v Van der Merwe*.[95] Here the court dealt with four university students who filmed a video in which they ridiculed a decision to racially integrate a male residence on campus. The content of the video was fake but created an impression of abusing and humiliating black people. Understandably, it caused an uproar. However, the Court of Appeal agreed that the four men were not intentionally racists or evil; as a result, the court lowered their sentence. That said, even though the men were not intentionally racist and meant the video as a joke, the result was still insensitive and caused widespread offence.

Rudanko (2006:834) goes further and differentiates between overt and covert intentions. Overt intention is a speaker's recognisable intent. This means the speaker's audience can easily infer his or her intentions. At its opposite end, covert intention is a speaker's hidden intent. The speaker tries to hide his or her true intentions, which means the speaker has a

94 Once again, it is worth pointing out that non-verbal communication in the form of body language and prosody plays an important role in a listener's perception and decoding of an utterance. Loudness and pitch are vital cues to understanding whether spoken words are aggressive or not and meant abusively or not (or at least, perceived that way).

95 *S v Van der Merwe* 2011 (2) SACR 509 (FB).

hidden agenda and that the audience is being misled to achieve a certain goal. Both types of intention relate to Grice's maxim of manner – the need to avoid ambiguity and obscurity – and to the maxim of quality – the need to be truthful. Messages based on covert intentions are deceptive, because they maintain the impression that both speaker and addressee are cooperating in a conversational exchange, when in fact the speaker is manipulating his or her audience (Rudanko 2006:835-836).

It is important to note that conflictive talk takes many forms and is expressed with different communicative goals in mind; not all are meant as face-attacking strategies. Think of a professor's criticism of a student's work, teasing between friends, fights in parliament, military training and even courtroom discourse (see Culpeper, Bousfield and Wichmann 2003:1546; Brown 2017:396). All of these may be perceived as verbal aggression, but they are not necessarily aimed at affecting an audience's self-image and self-respect. Yet, some acts are strategic or instrumental assaults on another person's face, a conscious attempt to damage a person's identity resulting in being offensive (Culpeper 2011:1). Rudanko (2006:838) views levels of impoliteness on a continuum, politeness on the one end and what he calls *aggravated impoliteness* on the other end (see figure 5.1 below).

POLITENESS → RUDENESS → IMPOLITENESS → AGGRAVATED IMPOLITENESS

Figure 5.1: An example of a politeness continuum.

To him, certain politeness strategies are a more 'serious manifestation of ill will or malice' and must be seen at a much higher end of the politeness scale (Rudanko 2006:837). He considers aggravated impoliteness as a one-sided act for the speaker's own benefit, a strategy that has been given some thought and which is neither accidental nor a misunderstanding (Rudanko 2006:838). A speaker is guilty of aggravated impoliteness when he or she knowingly and by design attacks the addressee's dignity (inclusive of worth, image, respect or reputation). Reactions to impoliteness are usually emotional and can lead to a negative attitude towards the speaker. Impolite language, especially aggressive communication, can also cause social harm. Tedeschi and Felson (in Culpeper 2011:4) say that social harm involves damage to an individual's social identity and lowers their power or status. Likewise, Appellate Justice Streicher cites Lord Nicholls of Birkenhead in *S v Hoho*:[96]

> Reputation is an integral and important part of the dignity of the individual. It also forms the basis of many decisions in a democratic society which are fundamental to its well-being: whom to employ or work for, whom to promote, whom to do business with or to vote for ...

Appellate Justice Streicher continues:[97]

> There is in my view no reason why the state should oblige and prosecute in the case of a complaint in respect of an injury to a person's physical integrity but not in the case of a complaint in respect of an injury to reputation, which may have more serious and lasting effects than a physical assault.

The same sentiment was echoed by Justice Cory in the seminal Canadian case *R v Lucas* when he said that defamatory remarks could cause psychological harm, therefore people should be discouraged to 'expose another individual to hatred and contempt'.[98] He goes on to say:[99]

> Defamatory libel can cause excessive, long-lasting or permanent injuries to the victim. The victim may be forever demeaned and diminished in the eyes of her community. The conduct which injures reputation by criminal libel is just as blameworthy as other conduct readily accepted as criminal, such as a deliberate assault or causing damage to property.

It should come as no surprise then, that there is a clear link between aggression and impoliteness; the term *verbal abuse* is a reflection of this (see Culpeper 2011:4). Human dignity abuses often come down to impoliteness; they lie somewhere on Rudanko's politeness continuum. A speaker's expression might be perceived by the addressee as defamation, but the speaker's intention is overt enough to realise that he or she never intended attacking the addressee's face. Or, a speaker's intentions seem innocent, but are actually covertly aimed at manipulating an audience

96 *S v Hoho* 2009 (1) 276 (SCA) (17 September 2008), para 30.
97 *S v Hoho*, para 35. See also Culpeper (2011: 4).
98 *R v Lucas* [1998] 1 SCR 439 ((1998) 50 CRR (2nd) 69 (SCC)), paras 15 and 73.
99 *R v Lucas*, para 73.

in order to damage a third party's social identity and social respect. Understanding what (aggravated) impoliteness is and how it relates to defamation, hate speech, insult and similar delictual claims could assist a court in understanding the real transgression. The next section goes into more detail.

5.10.6 Politeness and law

What we now understand as facework (concerning both positive and negative face), is actually protected by law in the form of human dignity. The South African Constitution mentions human dignity right off the bat,[100] and it is mentioned again in the Bill of Rights.[101] Equality is another important protection, shielding every individual from unfair discrimination by the state and by every individual's fellow man.[102] The Constitution tries to ensure respect in different ways. One way is to protect every individual's right to have a name.[103] Another is through the establishment of the Pan South African Language Board with the task to ensure respect for all the languages used in South Africa.[104] The constitution also guarantees everyone a number of reasonable freedoms, just as it prohibits discrimination and lived-out hatred.[105] Dignity, equality and freedom all align with politeness: an individual's want to be respected and accepted and a desire not to be imposed upon.

Building on what the Constitution has set out, other pieces of South African legislation outlaw impolite behaviour outright. The Equality Act is probably the best example of this. The Act aims at preventing and prohibiting discrimination, harassment and hate speech and it does so in relation to section 9 of the Constitution.[106] Of special interest is section 10,[107] which prohibits any language use with the clear intention to:

1. be hurtful;
2. be harmful (or that incites harm);
3. promote or propagate hatred.[108]

100 Constitution of the Republic of South Africa Act 108 of 1996; section 1(a).
101 Sections 7(1) and 10 of the Constitution.
102 Section 9 of the Constitution.
103 Section 28(1)(a) of the Constitution.
104 Section 6(5)(b) of the Constitution.
105 Sections 9, 12–19 and 21–22 of the Constitution.
106 Read together with item 23(1) of Schedule 6 of the Constitution.
107 Promotion of Equality and Prevention of Unfair Discrimination Act 4 of 2000; section 10(1)(*a*), (*b*) and (*c*).
108 The Prevention and Combating of Hate Crimes and Hate Speech Bill 9 of 2018 has similar wording in section 4. The Bill tries to cover every possible type of communication, including electronic dissemination and visual display. The contested hate speech is also evaluated against

Any language that a court finds to be hurtful, harmful or hateful qualifies as hate speech. This ties in with a speaker's negative evaluation of an audience's positive face – a clear indication that a speaker does not care about the feelings and desires of the audience (Brown and Levinson 1987:66-67). Face threatening acts include contempt or ridicule, insult and expressions of disapproval. These FTAs may take the shape of expressions of violence, the spreading of bad news about an addressee or third party and the use of terms of address (in its widest sense). This relates to Leech's tact maxim as well – an attempt not to belittle anyone, and that of Lakoff – to be friendly. Referring to a black man as a baboon, or to gay men as animals, or to state that you want to hack and skin white people and use them as fertiliser,[109] all qualify as intentionally tactless, violent and disapproving words and would be at the end of the politeness scale (aggravated impoliteness). Words like these are harmful and hurtful because they affect the receiver's positive face and they promote hatred, which feeds discrimination. There is no way that unfriendly words like these do not affect a person's self-worth, what they think of themselves and what they assume others think of them. In fact, the victim of impolite language may view him or herself in the same way that the offender views him or her, which compromises the victims' social identity (Carney 2014:338).

The law of delict, specifically the law of personality, relates to politeness as well. Here we see the protection of a person's good name and his or her dignity. The right to a good name is linked to the right to human dignity and applies to every individual's status and reputation in society on the one hand, and humaneness on the other (Neethling 2019:199; 271). Central to defamation and injury to dignity is the question of whether a speaker's words are damaging to an addressee's reputation and standing in society, and whether a person was insulted or degraded (Neethling 2019:205; 272-273). This marks a person's self-respect. Once more, this can be linked to a speaker's positive face; the want to feel accepted and respected. People who resort to defamatory or injurious remarks do so with little to no regard for their audience; instead, they act impolitely.

a number of prohibited grounds like race, gender, sexuality and so on (see section 1(xxii) of the Act and section 4(1) of the Bill). The difference between hate speech and impoliteness, then, is the fact that hate speech is committed based on one or more of the prohibited grounds of either an individual or a group, whereas impoliteness is much less restricted (Culpeper 2021:5).

109 *Herselman v Geleba*; *SAHRC v Qwulane*; *SAHRC v Khumalo*; see also *Afriforum v Malema*.

Of course, it is important to realise that politeness / impoliteness would hardly form the main criteria to appraise infringements of personality rights or hate speech. A court will use established legal grounds to determine whether an incident is truly wrongful or not. For instance, politeness may not assist a court in determining whether a supposed defamatory publication was made in the public's interest or whether a statement qualifies as free speech. The fact that *Le Roux v Dey* has three diverse opinions is telling of the complexity concerning defamation and dignity claims. That said, politeness could assist in gauging the alleged intention of an offender and it can assist in measuring the level of insult and indignity present in particular cases.

In *Gordhan v Malema*,[110] it transpired that during a speech Mr Julius Malema referred to Mr Pravin Gordhan as 'a dog of White Monopoly Capital. We must hit the dog until the owner comes out...'. He also said that Mr Gordhan 'hates Africans' and 'he's no good this guy'.[111] According to Justice Sutherland, Mr Malema's utterances did not qualify as hate speech, because they did not infringe any of the defined prohibited grounds, and because some of the references (Pravin as a dog that needs hitting) are purely metaphorical and therefore not to be taken literally.[112] Metaphors are carriers of semantic and pragmatic meaning too and in this particular instance, it conjures up images of inferiority and physical abuse. Does this metaphor incite hatred for people like Mr Gordhan? Maybe not. But implicating that Mr Gordhan is a racist (*he 'hates Africans'*) is a clear and deliberate attack on Gordhan's positive face – his perception of what others think of him and his reputation in society. The same applies to Malema's accusation 'you must know Pravin is going to fight dirty'.[113] The implicature is that Gordhan is corrupt and unscrupulous.

A similar case with a different outcome is that of *Manuel v Economic Freedom Fighters*,[114] in which Justice Matojane found the respondents guilty of defamation. The Economic Freedom Fighters (EFF) published a statement on Twitter, expressing their dissatisfaction in the appointment of Mr Edward Kieswetter as the new Commissioner for the South African Revenue Service (SARS).[115] The tweet contains a number of implicatures and illocutionary force. It implied that Mr Manuel, the chair of the selection committee, was nepotistic and corrupt and that he partook in

110 *Gordhan v Malema* 2020 (1) SA 587 (GJ).
111 *Gordhan v Malema*, para 1.
112 *Gordhan v Malema*, paras 9 and 15–16.
113 *Gordhan v Malema*, para 1.
114 *Manuel v Economic Freedom Fighters* 2019 (5) SA 210 (GJ).
115 *Manuel v Economic Freedom Fighters*, paras 31–32.

secretive and unlawful processes.[116] The tweet furthermore referred to Mr Kieswetter as 'dodgy', unethical and corrupt and as having held unlawful appointments at SARS previously.[117] These implicatures are clearly impolite and an attack on both Manuel and Kieswetter's face (which includes their good name and dignity).[118]

In *S v Motsepe*,[119] a senior journalist published an article in which he claimed that a white magistrate imposed a much heavier sentence on a black man than on a white woman who committed the same crime.[120] The journalist based his facts on a remark made by a lawyer who assisted him during his investigation. He published the article without verifying the lawyer's version of the facts.[121] Subsequently, he published an article containing false information and insinuated that the magistrate in question was a racist who acted unfairly. Even though the published article (one in a series) unjustly exposed the magistrate to public hatred and contempt, the court found the journalist's intentions were essentially good even though his behaviour was reckless.

In *Pieterse v Clicks Group Ltd*,[122] the second respondent was working as a cashier when she thought she saw a customer put something in her handbag. When the customer readied herself to leave, the cashier called her back and said something to the effect of 'I saw you put something in your bag'.[123] Allegedly, the cashier proceeded to search the handbag. The plaintiff claimed that the cashier's words and conduct were intentionally mean and implied to everyone present that she had stolen items and that she was a dishonest person, a thief.[124] It is very unlikely that the cashier wilfully attacked the customer's face and meant to damage the customer's self-worth, but the customer's perception of intentionality was strong enough to feel embarrassed or humiliated by the incident, especially

116 *Manuel v Economic Freedom Fighters*, para 34.

117 *Manuel v Economic Freedom Fighters*, para 32.

118 In the legal battle between two of Johannesburg's mayors, Schippers JA found Mr Parks Tau innocent of defamation. He said during an address at a funeral that Mr Herman Mashaba viewed women working in local government as prostitutes or sex traders and that Mr Mashaba does not want to be black, insinuating that he is a sexist chauvinist who is ashamed of his race. Tau's utterance did not satisfy the various criteria for defamation, but it still affects Mashaba's face, more so because Mashaba's own words were taken out of context and used to present an offensive image of him. See *Tau v Mashaba* 2020 (5) SA 135 (SCA).

119 *S v Motsepe* 2015 (2) SACR 125 (GP).

120 *S v Motsepe*, para 3.

121 *S v Motsepe*, paras 10–16.

122 *Pieterse v Clicks Group Ltd* 2015 (5) SA 317 (GJ).

123 *Pieterse v Clicks Group Ltd*, para 3.

124 *Pieterse v Clicks Group Ltd*, para 4.

because it happened in front of people. As a result, it injured her social identity and the court concurred.

In the infamous *ANC v Sparrow*,[125] the Equality Court dealt with a Facebook post in which Ms Penny Sparrow commented on beachgoers during New Year's Eve. The post included the following:[126]

> These monkeys that are allowed to be released on New Year's Eve and onto public beaches, towns, etcetera, absolutely have no education whatsoever. So to allow them loose is inviting huge dirt and troubles and discomfort to others.

The text includes a number of implicatures: black people are animals, as animals they are (and must be) contained, they have little intelligence and are dirty and problematic. Black people's presence cause irritation / pain. These implicatures serve to debase a group of people and in doing so degrades their social identity – what people think of them and how they must think of themselves. Sparrow's words can also be placed at the extreme end of the politeness scale, because Sparrow wilfully (and by design) attacked the social identity of a group of people, causing social conflict and disharmony (Culpeper, Bousfield and Wichmann 2003:1546).

Similarly, the Congress of South African Trade Unions' (Cosatu) secretary of International Relations, Mr Bongani Masuku, caused a stir when he addressed students at the University of the Witwatersrand regarding the conflicts between the Israeli government and the Palestinian Hamas group in the Gaza Strip. His speech was preceded by written exchanges on a Zionist blog. The blog contained statements like 'Even when all the monkeys in Cosatu have died of AIDS (even those who were cured by raping babies), I will not return [to SA].'[127] During his address, he warned families not to send their sons and daughters to join the Israeli Defence Force, implicating that something will happen to those families if they did support Israel: '... we will do something that may necessarily be regarded as harm ...'.[128] The Equality Court found Mr Masuku guilty of hate speech, but the Supreme Court of Appeal (SCA) set the order aside.[129] The SCA agreed that Masuku's words might have been hurtful or distasteful, but argued that Masuku did not incite imminent violence

125 *ANC v Sparrow* (01/16) [2016] ZAEQC 1 (10 June 2016).

126 *ANC v Sparrow*, at 33.

127 *Masuku v South African Human Rights Commission* 2019 (2) SA 194 (SCA), para 5. Of course, the blog entry is very problematic too. Cosatu members are dehumanised, stigmatised and depicted as rapists.

128 *Masuku v South African Human Rights Commission*, para 7.

129 *Masuku v South African Human Rights Commission*, paras 11 and 31–32.

against or advocate hatred of the South African Jewish community. The judgment is an interesting one, especially because Masuku's words qualify as aggressive communication. His words carry the illocutionary force of a warning and a threat. He issued a strong ultimatum: if you support the Israeli army we will harm you. He specifically mentions Orange Grove in his speech, a suburb in Johannesburg with a historic Jewish community. This, and the fact that his speech concerns Israel's military action against Hamas, makes it obvious that violence against South African Jews were implicated.

Hate speech is framed in terms of incitement to discriminatory behaviour and expresses an intention to commit a harmful act either personally or by way of someone else (Culpeper 2021:5–6). Culpeper (2021:6) aptly observes the following:

> Hate speech can be about engineering a specific behaviour ... but it can also be about engineering a particular change in mind. In this light, it is more about persuasion, which opens up a complex area.

This engineering of the mind could be aimed at making people think less of a specific individual or group or it could be aimed at belittling and degrading someone's good name. It can also cause people to act against targeted individuals or groups. Sometimes it can be quite direct like *Ryan v Petrus* in which the respondent openly calls the plaintiff a *naaier, poes* and *hoer* in Afrikaans.[130] This qualifies as a message containing a speaker's overt intention. The respondent's main aim was to openly degrade the plaintiff, to insult her and make her feel small. The same applies to Ms Sparrow's Facebook post; it too is an overt message meant to openly insult and belittle. Our *fagott / faggot* example from earlier qualifies as a message containing covert intentions. There is a strong probability that the author of the tweet used *fagott* deliberately because he knew that his audience would read *faggot* instead. The insult is therefore layered. And, because the play on words is a brilliant form of deceit, he has an excuse to hide behind; his use of *fagott* is deceitful.

Before we end this chapter, it would be helpful to remember that as with law, a linguistic investigation may involve a number of different linguistic tools simultaneously. This chapter presents different tools separately that often work together. When a court considers a potential hate speech or defamation case, it is necessary to consider politeness together with implicature, speech acts, relevance theory, and non-verbal elements. Let us once again look at *S v Motsepe*. The journalist published

130 *Ryan v Petrus*, at 277.

a news report stating facts. As such, the article and its contents qualify as an assertive speech act with the illocutionary force of claiming, reporting and stating. The published article insinuated that the magistrate treated black offenders much harsher than white offenders. The implicature is that the magistrate is a racist and judicially unfair. Because the article reported incorrect facts, it infringed the Gricean maxim of quality (to be truthful) and so also infringed politeness maxims (for instance, Leech's tact maxim) by attacking the magistrate's positive face; his want to be socially accepted and respected. It is hard to imagine that a seasoned, senior journalist would publish contentious facts before verifying them. Therefore, we can pose the question whether he wrote the articles with a covert intention to deliberately attack the magistrate's positive face by misleading his readers on purpose. Because an audience follows the path of least resistance when they process new information, and because people use whatever context is most relevant at that point in time (a South African background of racial discrimination), an audience will likely accept the news report as a true reflection of events and accept that the white magistrate is a racist. Claiming that someone is a racist and that their racist ideology clouds their judgement and behaviour at work, could incite others to behave hatefully towards that individual and others in that person's group. Because the journalist could have been wilfully deceptive, a court could do well to consider to what extent the news reports qualify as aggravated impoliteness – a deliberate attempt at negatively affecting a particular individual's social identity. Though we do not have the contested news report for reference, a court would benefit by paying attention to the word choices used in the text. This will help to get an impression of the textual tone of the text and how it contributes towards the pragmatic meaning being conveyed.

Using a variety of pragmatic tools to conduct a brief linguistic analysis could help courts better understand the scope and nature of a contested (language related) transgression.

5.11. Conclusion

In this chapter, we shifted our attention from a semantic approach to a more pragmatic approach in meaning making. We started by looking at the various reasons courts experience different linguistic challenges. To understand this, we looked at what constitutes language variety and language contact. We speak the way we do because we move between different domains and often have to adapt our language use according to the situation we find ourselves in. This means that we switch between language varieties and due to close contact, we exchange words and expressions. In some situations, people are vernacular speakers of mixed varieties. In multilingual countries like South Africa, people depend on a language like English to communicate between different cultures and language communities. This is a product of language planning and policy. However, the level of communication skills in English strongly depends on the level of education, which is substandard in many areas and which may hamper processes in the justice system.

In this chapter, we realised once again how important context is for pragmatic inferences, both the linguistic and physical context of a speaker. We had a look at what constitutes spoken language and how speakers can perform a number of acts through language. We saw that there are different types of speech acts, some direct and others indirect. Speech acts showed us that people often say one thing but mean something else entirely. To understand how people are able to infer such messages, we reviewed Grice's Cooperative Principle and his ideas behind conversational implicatures. Here we saw that people implicate certain messages without saying them outright. Speakers understand implicated messages because they try to cooperate during conversations and trust that their conversational partners are doing the same. The extent of the conversational cooperation is visible in the relevance and politeness of messages. Receivers trust that a sender creates messages that contain the most relevant information that require as little effort as possible in deciphering. Senders produce these messages knowing that receivers will use whatever context is most obvious to them to decode the message. Messages are therefore clear and straightforward. However, when politeness is the main concern, clarity takes a backseat. In this chapter, we saw that people will generally try their best not to offend; instead, they will try to accommodate their conversational partners as much as possible. That said, some individuals design their words to hurt a particular person or group's dignity. This is considered impolite behaviour.

Hopefully, this chapter has also proven that many language-related problems cannot be solved simply by consulting a dictionary. In the next chapter, we take a much closer look at dictionaries: their purpose, target audiences, limitations and best practice for use in court cases.

6. Understanding Dictionaries

More than thirty years ago, Shuy (1986:296) observed that when we are confronted by a word in dispute, we tend to look it up in a dictionary. It is often the first thing we do. And, as he states, it is generally a wise move. The South African judiciary seems to agree. Dictionary use was sanctioned through case law on various occasions, most notably by *Association of Amusement and Novelty Machine Operators v Minister of Justice*, *S v Collop*, *Blue Circle Cement Ltd v Commissioner for Inland Revenue*, *Jowells Transport v South African Road Transportation Services*, *Fundstrust (Pty) Ltd v Van Deventer*, *Cargo Africa CC v Gilbeys Distillers and Vintners (Pty) Ltd* and *Online Lottery Service (Pty) Ltd v National Lotteries Board*.[1] Before and since, South African courts have used dictionaries to gain clarity when words or phrases cause problems. They remain important reference works for statutory interpretation, to say the least.

Unfortunately, studies of dictionary usage by presiding officers and those preparing heads of argument have revealed disturbing results. Judges sometimes use incorrect dictionaries and they use dictionaries incorrectly.[2] This is apparent when presiding officers are seen using bilingual, learner or even pocket dictionaries instead of standard descriptive dictionaries to define words (Carney and Bergh 2014:43). Similarly, presiding officers seem to prefer dictionaries published in foreign countries above locally produced reference works, and worse, they are seen using outdated dictionaries (Carney and Bergh 2014:42). More recently, the presiding officers of *Purveyors South Africa Mine Services (Pty) Ltd v Commissioner for the South African Revenue Services (Pty) Ltd* used a dictionary published in 1973.[3] The case was decided and reported in 2021, which means this particular dictionary was out of print

1 *Association of Amusement and Novelty Machine Operators v Minister of Justice* 1980 (2) SA 636 (A); *S v Collop* 1981 (1) SA 150 (A); *Blue Circle Cement Ltd v Commissioner for Inland Revenue* 1984 (2) SA 764 (A); *Jowells Transport v South African Road Transportation Services* 1986 (2) SA 252 (SWA); *Fundstrust (Pty) Ltd v Van Deventer* 1997 (1) SA 710 (A); *Cargo Africa CC v Gilbeys Distillers and Vintners (Pty) Ltd* 1998 (4) SA 355 (N); *Online Lottery Services (Pty) Ltd v National Lotteries Board* 2010 (5) SA 349 (SCA).

2 See the seminal work done by Solan (1993), Aprill (1998), Thumma & Kirchmeier (1999), Mourtisen (2010) as well as Carney & Bergh (2014) for a South African perspective.

3 *Purveyors South Africa Mine Services (Pty) Ltd v Commissioner for the South African Revenue Services (Pty) Ltd* (135/2021) [2021] ZASCA 170 (7 December 2021).

and almost fifty years old by the time they delivered their judgment. This creates the impression that the judiciary does not have access to more recent reference works, least of all an online dictionary.[4] It also implies that the judiciary does not take reference works like dictionaries too seriously either.

Jurists must bear two factors in mind: each dictionary has a specific target audience, and lexicographers cannot conceive of every possible context in which speakers could / will use a given word. In addition, every good dictionary has a user guide in the front, explaining how that particular dictionary should be used. The user guide is written based on the needs of the target audience and will therefore differ between dictionaries. So far, research has shown that most users are either unaware of the user guide, or they choose to ignore it (Svensén 1993:16; Mouritsen 1999:1929; Prinsloo 2013:376). This is ignorant, because this approach implies that people use instruments without considering what they are actually meant for of how they function. The making of dictionaries is difficult and time-consuming work. Lexicographers are almost always constrained by money, time and space. No dictionary is intended to contain all the words in a language, nor are any of them meant to contain definitions for every possible pragmatic scenario. That is simply impossible. It is vital that dictionary users know and understand this. What it means is that we cannot use just any dictionary for any query. And, we cannot accept that every dictionary definition will be sufficient in solving unique language problems.

Does it mean that dictionaries should be avoided when dealing with contested words of phrases? Not at all. However, dictionary users must be informed about the tools they intend on using. A butcher will not use a butter knife to cut meat from the bone and a barber will not use nail clippers to trim a man's beard. The best practice is to know how and why dictionaries are different and to determine which one is the best for the job.

Dictionary use by the judiciary is often met with negative criticism, but Hutton (2020:90) makes a valid counterargument – it would be better if dictionary use is integrated or 'domesticated' into the interpretative culture of law. This chapter aims at doing that by providing

4 During a conference hosted in 2022, a judge from the High Court admitted that the Department of Justice and Constitutional Development no longer funded resources like dictionaries and JutaStat for lower courts. This explains in part why presiding officers use antiquated resources.

the necessary information to help statutory interpreters select and use dictionaries wisely.

6.1. Defining 'dictionary'

Shuy (1986:296) touches on something very important when he says 'there is no such thing as *the* dictionary'. People in general are inclined to talk about dictionaries as if there is only one, big dictionary. With this assumption comes the belief that dictionaries are authoritative instruments. If 'the' dictionary defines a word in a certain way, then there is no point in arguing. The authority of dictionaries can partly be traced back to their role in codifying and standardising language. As such, they have gained status and authority; some dictionaries more so than others. Its status can be traced back to Samuel Johnson's English dictionary, which set the standard for more than 150 years. As Jackson (2002:21) points out, dictionaries form part of the cultural fabric of a society – along with religious scripture, every household is expected to own at least one copy. Children learn to use them at school, lecturers expect their students to consult them frequently, and professionals prepare their documents and discourses with the help of dictionaries. It is one of the most cited documents in history. That said, a dictionary's status and authority are arbitrary and believing that they are absolute would be naïve (Gouws 1989:49).

So, what exactly is a dictionary? Simply put, a dictionary is a reference work of words. Broadly speaking, we can distinguish two types: encyclopaedic and linguistic. An encyclopaedia features general facts about life and the world, whereas dictionaries contain linguistic data. Sometimes there is overlap, especially between encyclopaedias and comprehensive dictionaries, but for the most part they differ in their compilation, presentation and purpose. Dictionaries also serve as records of a language's lexicon. They often contain words that are no longer used or meanings that have changed.

In general, a dictionary encompasses a variety of linguistic information: grammatical detail like parts of speech, semantic detail like definitions and word relations, syntactic detail like limited contextual use and semantic roles as well as phonetic detail like pronunciation. Furthermore, a dictionary usually indicates if a word is irregular and it will label words according to their current status (taboo, archaic, pejorative), aiding a user in applying the word correctly (Jackson 1995:159).[5] As a

5 Of course, all of this make dictionaries prescriptive instead of descriptive. They tend to set a standard of use / best practice that many

reference work, it will often indicate style, etymology and figurative language use. In other words, it is a powerful resource packed with information that helps a user understand a particular society's vocabulary (Jackson 2002:74).

6.2. Dictionary limitations

Even though dictionaries can be wonderful resources, they can never be perfect. When we think of dictionaries, several problems come to mind, especially in developing countries like South Africa where the status of dictionaries remains rather authoritative, and where printed copies are a lot more popular than electronic or web-based sources (Carney and Bergh 2014:44-46).

Firstly, printed dictionaries get outdated very quickly and some only receive one print cycle, which means that the lexicography unit responsible for its compilation will not update it. In turn, this means that some dictionaries do not keep up with any semantic changes that occur.

Secondly, printed dictionaries have limited space. Even if the lexicographers assigned to that dictionary want to include as many words as possible, the publisher will ultimately decide what is cost effective. Dictionaries are expensive to make and equally expensive to buy, which impacts the number of headwords included in a dictionary. This implies that a dictionary's semantic reach is limited too. The fewer words a reference work contains the more incomplete it is, in effect limiting its semantic reach.

The price of dictionaries is a third issue in a developing country. It is not possible for a publisher to produce a dictionary at low cost. As a result, many people cannot afford one, specifically a standard descriptive dictionary. This means that when someone buys a dictionary, it must last a household or an office for life. Interestingly, dictionaries retain their status regardless of their age, which explains why South African jurists still use printed copies from the 1970s. The cost dilemma extends to electronic or web-based dictionaries. They are by far a much better alternative to printed copies, particularly regarding their size and currency. However, subscription fees might be too high for average users and internet access is required.[6] This makes it a running expense, whereas a printed copy is a once-off expense.

---

speakers interpret as the ways in which a language must be spoken and written.

6 At the time of writing, individuals could subscribe to Oxford's online English dictionary for £100 per year. Currently, that equates to approximately R2000. This is too expensive for most South African

The fourth problem is the fact that there are a number of dictionaries available, but they are not of equal standard. Some contain little useful information and their definitions are poorly formulated, leaving users either confused or helpless. Different dictionaries also define words differently, which might lead to less clarity.

As a fifth problem, dictionaries define words out of context and seldom indicate word relations or family resemblances. This is not necessarily a weakness within the dictionary itself, but poses a problem for a user like a jurist who wants precise, context-specific clarity. Dictionary definitions try to describe concepts, and concepts tend to be fuzzy at the margins (Solan 1993:52). As such, they have an 'imperfect relationship' to the statutory context (*Harvard Law Review* 1994:1449). Of course, general dictionaries are not made for statutory contexts; therefore, it cannot tell users what meaning a word in a given context must bear (Mouritsen 2010:1924; Shuy 1986:297). More issues include the fact that standard language reference works seldom cover colloquial language or include valuable collocations.

Today, many dictionaries are available online for free and will allow you to conduct simple searches. However, an online user will never have access to the full dictionary without subscribing. Without a full subscription, a user has access to very little. Also, many of the available online dictionaries are dubious and should not be used for more serious language problems.

A limitation that might seem surprising is dictionaries' propensity to provide too much information. 'They describe the universe of all possible meanings', says Solan (2010:19).[7] This is often a problem, because it begs a judge or legal practitioner to differentiate between the different possibilities listed under headwords, in effect making the task of deciphering more tedious and difficult.

Overall, users must know what the basic limitations of a dictionary are and consider them along with the query at hand. If a speaker simply wants to confirm the spelling or definition of a certain word in a crossword puzzle, then a pocket dictionary from 1982 might suffice well enough. But when a court of law must clarify *educational institution* for statutory purposes, a comprehensive online dictionary might be a better starting point.

households. Institutions pay different rates, and developing countries may qualify for reduced subscription fees.

7 The dictionary becomes a maze in which judges lose themselves (Posner in Hutton, 2020: 86).

6.3. Dictionary types and intended users

As pointed out earlier, jurists must take note of the fact that dictionaries are aimed at specific target users; consequently, they are made with a very particular purpose in mind. In fact, dictionaries are commercial products like any other. None of them are the same. Some dictionaries are aimed at young schoolchildren while others are aimed at people learning a foreign language. Some dictionaries are aimed at the 'average member of the speech community' (Gouws and Prinsloo 2005:14), you and I, while others are meant for people who need to understand a specialised field or who enjoy games and hobbies. The target user informs the purpose of the dictionary and it goes without saying that a dictionary for 'Baby's First Words' will not help a mathematics student clarify the word *polygon*.

We distinguish between general-purpose and restricted (specialist) dictionaries (Svensén 1993:17; Jackson 1995:159, 165; Gouws and Prinsloo 2005:47). A general-purpose dictionary is often monolingual and can be either comprehensive or a standard concise edition. Both types are descriptive, but a comprehensive reference work spans numerous volumes, like the *Oxford English Dictionary*, the German *Duden*, the Dutch *Van Dalen* and the Afrikaans *WAT*. Standard concise editions are limited to a single volume, like the *Oxford South African Concise Dictionary*. Subcategories include school, learner and multilingual dictionaries. Note that each of these subcategories has different target users. School and learner dictionaries are much smaller in scope and their definitions are simplified, whereas multilingual works assist in translation. The latter do not define words; instead, they offer equivalents between two or more languages. Very few hybrid dictionaries exist. So far, there is only one dictionary in South Africa that is both a bilingual and concise descriptive source text: the *ANNA* (Afrikaans-Nederlands, Nederlands-Afrikaans dictionary). Unless a speaker uses a hybrid text, it is impossible to use a bi- or multilingual dictionary to define words or to look up their various senses. Translation dictionaries contain limited grammatical and additional linguistic data. The publisher and lexicography team compiling multilingual dictionaries accept that the user already knows most of a searched word's details in the source language, but now has to confirm its equivalent in the target language. Look at the following two examples of the English word *bluff*. The first lemma is taken from *Pharos' Concise Afrikaans-English Dictionary* (Pheiffer 2007:846) and the second is taken from the online *Oxford English Dictionary* (Oxford University Press 2022).

6.1 **bluff**, ww. (oor)bluf, oordonder; uitoorlê; verbouereer, bangmaak; wysmaak.

6.2 **bluff**, v1. **3**. intransitive. To practise or attempt the imposition described in sense **2**; to assume a bold, big, or boastful demeanour, in order to inspire an opponent with an exaggerated notion of one's strength, determination to fight, etc.

The clear difference between the two entries is that the translation dictionary in 6.1 only provides the Afrikaans equivalents for *bluff*, but does not define the word or provide any useful context. The example taken from the online Oxford dictionary represents the third sense. However, it refers the user back to the second sense, which is a more detailed definition related to the card game, poker.

Headwords for general purpose reference texts are selected from approximately two million of a language's most frequently used words. Depending on the target user, that selection may be broadened to include more terminology or vocabulary that might be less familiar to average users (obsolete words, derivatives). For school and learner dictionaries, that selection is a lot smaller, limited to a frequency list of roughly two thousand words.[8] They too do not define words in any sophisticated way, because the target users do not have the necessary vocabulary to help them understand what they are reading.

Specialist dictionaries are restricted to a specified field or subject. They cover terminology like the *Dictionary of Economics* and the *Dictionary of Architecture and Construction*, but they include more specialised source texts like dictionaries for spelling, pronunciation and even reference works of names (for humans, places, terms of endearment). Some of these are very restricted in their scope and use. Obviously, you cannot use a dictionary of names to determine how many senses the word *catholic* has. However, a specialist dictionary like a thesaurus can be used a lot more broadly.

As summarised in Table 6.1 below, Atkins and Rundell (2008:24-29) offer the following properties of dictionaries. Table 6.1 helps to distinguish between the different types of reference works, their intended users and uses. The information in the table below helps us position the statutory interpreter. If a presiding officer or legal practitioner wants to look up a

8 All dictionaries of a language (for instance, English) share the same core vocabulary, regardless of their size and type. Deciding which words must be added to the core depends on many things. Apart from the purpose of the dictionary, lexicographers must also decide what new words to include or to reject. Inclusion hinges on criteria like the longevity of a word, its number of separate uses and its acceptance by the speech community. See Diamond (2015).

word like *abandon* or *lapse*, then he or she might consider a specialist dictionary of legal terms and definitions. In this instance, the statutory interpreter is a professional who uses a restricted source text compiled for a particular subject. The context is a lot more certain. However, if the interpreter wants to confirm the ordinary meaning of words like *building* or *relocate*, he or she will probably reach for a standard monolingual dictionary that encompasses general language information. The user will doubtless consider the headword from both a decoding and encoding perspective – not only what a word means, but how a word may be used. In principle, statutory interpreters will be both general and specialist users, both first and additional language speakers of English. Ideally, the selected dictionary will be monolingual (unless translation is necessary), comprehensive (but nothing less than concise), web-based (or very recent, if printed) and covering general language (which includes some terminology, cultural material and important linguistic data).

Table 6.1: Summary of dictionary types, target users and uses

Properties of dictionaries	**Dictionary users**	**Dictionary uses**
The dictionary's language: · monolingual · bilingual · multilingual	· Adults · Children (young and older) · Language learners (beginner, intermediate, advanced) · General users · Specialists	· General reference purpose (understanding words, checking spelling and pronunciation) · Studying a particular subject · Learning a language · Writing texts (in first and additional languages) · Translating texts
The dictionary's coverage: · general language · encyclopaedic and cultural material · terminology · specific area of language (spelling, collocations, idioms)		
The dictionary's size: · comprehensive · standard · concise · pocket		

Table 6.1: Summary of dictionary types, target users and uses		
Properties of dictionaries	**Dictionary users**	**Dictionary uses**
The dictionary's medium: · print · electronic (CD-Rom) · web-based		
The dictionary's organisation: · word to meaning · word to meaning to word		
The user's language: · users speak the same language · two distinct groups of language speakers · learners of the dictionary's language		
The user's skills: · linguists and language professionals · literate adults · school children · young children · language learners		
What the users use the dictionary for: · decoding (understanding meaning; translating from a foreign language into own language) · encoding (using a word correctly; translating from own language into a foreign language)		

6.4. Definitions

Like many people, statutory interpreters mostly consult a standard descriptive dictionary for the definitions contained therein.[9] After all, it is the job of a dictionary to tell us what a word (possibly) means. It must answer the question 'what is it?' and it must do so using simple language (Gouws and Prinsloo 2005:143). Definitions are essential. If they fail, so does most of the dictionary. A definition has the important task of explaining what a given headword means – within a limited number of words – and it must assist a user in recalling the applicable concept. Furthermore, definitions must be clear, accurate, consistent and objective (Gouws and Prinsloo 2005:147).

There are different kinds of definitions: paraphrases, synonym forms, **circular definitions** and definitions that distinguish conceptual features (to name only a few). Definitions that use synonyms to describe a word can lead to uncertainty, because a user might not be familiar with that particular word's synonyms either, which could prevent successful information retrieval. Also, absolute synonyms are rare, which means that the dictionary user might think the searched word means the same as the cited word (Atkins and Rundell 2008:421; Harris and Hutton 2007:11). Similarly, circular definitions are problematic, because they define a word partly in terms of itself. For instance, *forensic linguist* is described as *a linguist who works in forensic settings*. It provides the user with no clarity.[10] Words can also be defined either by intension or extension (Svensén 1993:120-121). This means that a word can be described in terms of its

9 Presiding officers use dictionaries for many reasons, not only to look up definitions. In *Lueven Metals (Pty) Ltd v CSARS* (31356/2021) [2022] ZAGPPHC 325 (19 May 2022), Davis J used a dictionary to look up grammatical information on the relative pronoun *which* and then proceeded to use that information for a brief syntactic analysis. In this instance, a single dictionary served Davis J well enough, even though a grammar reference work would have been a much better and trustworthier choice.

10 Circular definitions are problematic because it tells you nothing about the term being described. Surprisingly, they are quite common in both dictionaries and statutes. Consider the definition of *levy* in section 1 of the Financial Sector Regulation Act 9 of 2017: '*levy* means a levy imposed by a financial sector body in terms of legislation that empowers the imposition of a levy, and includes interest payable on an unpaid levy'. This definition fails to describe what a levy is; instead, it says when levies are charged and confirms that incurred interest is included in a levy. The fact that the word is included in section 1 implies that the word is used as a term, which in turn implies that it reaches beyond the ordinary meaning of *levy*. Yet, what the semantic features of *levy* are, remain unclear.

concept (what it is) or in terms of the range to which the concept belongs. For example, a dictionary can say what *motor vehicle* means (intension), or it can specify that it is a *car*, *motorcycle* or *truck* (extension).

At this point, it is useful to distinguish between the definitions found in statutes and the definitions found in standard monolingual dictionaries. Every Act of Parliament contains a list of definitions. In South Africa, they are included as the first section or chapter of a statute. This list of terms functions as a glossary, describing how a statutory interpreter must understand selected words in that particular act. Not all terms are explained in the lexicographic sense of the word. In some instances, the act simply confirms that the term represents a known entity. For example, '*Pension Funds Act* means the Pension Funds Act No. 24 of 1956'. This is done to prevent any unnecessary confusion and to ensure that everyone has the same cross reference in mind when using the statute. When Parliament needs to change the ordinary meaning of a word to fulfil a specific purpose, it does so by defining or describing that word in a certain way. Tiersma (2000:115) calls this a declaratory definition, because the legislature declares its own terms and their semantic criteria. In lexicography, this type of definition is known as a **stipulative definition**. Its purpose is to clearly express limits of use; 'to draw attention to a distinction that is blurred in the common usage' of a word (Harris and Hutton 2007:9). An example taken from the Financial Sector Regulation Act 9 of 2017 looks like this:

> 6.3 '**governing body**' means –
>
> (a) in relation to a financial institution, a person or body of persons, whether elected or not, that manages, controls, formulates the policy and strategy of the financial institution, directs its affairs or has the authority to exercise the powers and perform the functions of the financial institution, and includes –
>
> (i) the general partner of an *en commandite* partnership or the partners of any other partnership;
>
> (ii) the members of a close corporation;
>
> (iii) the trustees of a trust;
>
> (iv) the board of directors of a company; and
>
> (v) the board of a pension fund referred to in section 7A of the Pension Funds Act; and
>
> (b) in relation to an ombud scheme, the body of persons that oversees the affairs of the ombud scheme.

The definition of *governing body* makes it clear that it does not apply to similar standing committees in schools, churches, sectional title schemes or book clubs. If a particular governing body falls outside the listed criteria, the conditions of the Act do not apply to it. In contrast, a standard descriptive dictionary definition does not stipulate the limitations of a word. In its place, dictionaries provide general definitions that are more prototypical in order to satisfy many different queries. The online Collins dictionary defines the same word as:

> 6.4 **governing body**. noun. /ˈɡʌvənɪŋ ˈbɒdɪ/
>
> the group of officials who draw up the rules that govern the actions and conduct of a body such as a school, or a sport, and who ensures that these rules are followed (Collins English Dictionary, 2022).

The Collins dictionary's definition is a lot more prototypical, not only in its references to a school and sport, but also in its description. It is not limited to a group of officials in a financial institution specifically.

Because the Act specifies explicit limitations, *governing body* becomes a term and can no longer be used as an ordinary word in relation to financial institutions. The legislature clearly distinguishes it from a standard dictionary definition. This means that every other word in the Act that goes undefined must be read according to its ordinary or non-technical meaning. But this is not so simple. Sometimes parties insist that a word be given its ordinary meaning, yet they use it in a technical sense. In *SASRIA v Slabbert Burger Transport (Pty) Ltd*, the applicant insisted the word *strike* should carry an extended meaning to be more compatible with the context of the case.[11] The applicant argued that *strike* should include the semantic features of *riot* and *public disorder* to indicate the violent nature of some strikes and particularly the strike that caused damages to Slabbert Burger Transport's vehicle, which was indemnified by the applicant.[12] The court decided that the ordinary definition of *strike* suffices, indicating that the applicant only has itself to blame for failing to give *strike* its extended definition in its own policy document.[13] Similar behaviour is seen in the way SARS uses the words *voluntary* and *disclosure*

11 *SASRIA v Slabbert Burger Transport (Pty) Ltd* 2008 (5) SA 270 (SCA), para 6.

12 *SASRIA v Slabbert Burger Transport (Pty) Ltd* 2008 (5) SA 270 (SCA), para 8.

13 *SASRIA v Slabbert Burger Transport (Pty) Ltd* 2008 (5) SA 270 (SCA), paras 9 and 10.

in relation to their voluntary disclosure programme.[14] For instance, it is held that if information is disclosed to SARS *voluntarily* it is not done so out of fear. Suddenly, the lack of fear becomes a semantic feature of *voluntary*, which goes beyond its ordinary meaning (Van Zyl and Carney 2021:101-105). If SARS views the fear of being penalised as a constraint to voluntary disclosure, then *voluntary* must be stipulated in the Tax Administration Act 28 of 2011. The legislature must then describe how it wants people to understand words like *voluntary* and *disclosure*, because they are used as terms and not as ordinary words.

Lastly, the difference between statutory and dictionary definitions includes the difference between definitions for decoding and encoding (see Atkins and Rundell 2008:408-410). Definitions for decoding recall a speaker's passive lexicon, because this kind of definition is meant for understanding how a word was used within its context. Decoding definitions provide the necessary information to aid inference. At the opposite end, definitions for encoding are meant to turn passive vocabulary into active lexis. This means the definition helps a speaker use a word or expression productively. For this reason, encoding is more difficult than decoding. What is important is the realisation that standard monolingual dictionaries tasked with describing words in a general fashion encompass definitions for decoding. Standard dictionaries help users understand words; they very seldom help users to apply them. Therefore, when statutory interpreters claim that a dictionary indicates how we should use a word or expression, they are mistaken. Dictionaries will, at most, help the user understand a contested word in its broader context. Therefore, it is also advisable not to use dictionaries as reference works for grammar or syntax.

6.5. Using a thesaurus

A thesaurus is a specialist dictionary. It is often viewed as a dictionary of synonyms. Its uniqueness lies in its organisation – it is highly systematic, often presenting its information thematically as opposed to alphabetically. The information in a general thesaurus is organised in broad classes and those classes open up to subclasses. For instance, the category 'time' is subdivided into (among others) 'duration', 'period', 'day and night' and

14 See both *Purveyors South Africa Mine Service (Pty) Ltd v Commissioner for the South African Revenue Service* (611689/2019) [202] ZAGPPHC 409 (25 August 2020) and *Purveyors South Africa Mine Services (Pty) Ltd v Commissioner for the South African Revenue Services* (135/2021) [2021] ZASCA 170 (7 December 2021).

'relative time'. The subclass 'period' is further subdivided into 'year', 'a month', 'a week' and so on.

At its core, a thesaurus is organised in line with frame semantic and conceptual principles. Related words that express various aspects of a concept are grouped together into smaller subfields. Even though a thesaurus is not aimed at jurists in the same way as a dictionary of legal terms, it can add value when investigating disputed words and concepts, because it exposes common semantic relations between words (Shuy 1986:298). Take a look at the entry for *voluntary* in the online Oxford Historical Thesaurus:

6.5 the mind
- -mental capacity
- -attention and judgement
- -goodness and badness
- -emotion
  - -will
    - -free will
      - -of actions
      - -instances of
      - -one who holds the doctrine
      - -self-determination, etc.
      - -voluntarism
        - -volunteer
          - -of things
        - -occurrence due to voluntary action
      - -non-obligation
      - -act of own free will
      - -choice or choosing
    - -necessity
    - -wish or inclination
    - -intention
    - -decision
    - -motivation

In his printed thesaurus of 1991, Urdang (1992:166) lists *voluntary* as one of the senses under the headword *free*, grouping it with words like *unasked for*, *unbidden*, *spontaneous* and *unconditional*. It is also listed under the headwords *independent* and *wilful*. Urdang used an alphabetic layout for his thesaurus, but entries are still conceptual, recalling semantic frames. As can be seen from both examples, each indicates an unconstrained action. The online thesaurus does provide a much broader picture, which makes it a lot easier to notice semantic relations. For instance, the concept at the centre of *voluntary* is not only related to the idea of *free will*, but it is also connected to *motivation*, *intention* and *decision*. These are three important ideas. It says that a voluntary act is the result of an intended decision. An intended decision is not necessarily related to free will. Such a decision can be made under coercion as well. If a robber puts a gun against someone's head and tells them what to do, that person did not act in free will. Justice Fabricius made it clear that for SARS' voluntary disclosure programme to succeed, the voluntary act must be unconstrained.[15] An unconstrained act is related to the motivation behind it. Survival motivates a victim's cooperation with an armed robber. However, to disclose sensitive information to SARS, the taxpayer must be motivated to do so for different reasons, one being the opportunity to correct a mistake.[16]

Thesauri are helpful reference works, because they categorise information on the user's behalf. Noticing where a searched word is placed within the various layers of a concept, could assist statutory interpreters in understanding its broader conceptual reach as well as its limitations. A thesaurus is especially helpful when a jurist considers a contested word's semantic relations and features.

---

15 *Purveyors South Africa Mine Service (Pty) Ltd v Commissioner for the South African Revenue Service* (611689/2019) [202] ZAGPPHC 409 (25 August 2020) paras 9.7 and 12.

16 Interestingly, the word *non-obligation* is also listed here as an entry in the Historical Thesaurus. Usually, *obligation* denotes that a person is morally or legally bound to do something. It indicates a duty or commitment. If a voluntary act is also a non-obligatory act, then SARS really needs to define *voluntary* for its voluntary disclosure programme, because it is both morally and legally obligatory to disclose any past tax sins from SARS. Urdang's inclusion of synonyms like *unasked for* and *unconditional* are relevant here as well. For the voluntary disclosure programme to succeed, taxpayers have to comply with a set of criteria. This means the programme is conditional. There is also the possibility that SARS might catch you if you do not make use of the programme. This means you could face serious penalties. Once again, taking part in the programme is conditional and 'asked for'. SARS' disclosure programme does not seem that 'voluntary' after all. Once again, both jurists and legislative drafters must pay attention to the divide between terms and ordinary words and determine which words truly express ordinary meaning.

6.6. Best practice when using dictionaries for legal interpretation

In *Association of Amusement and Novelty Machine Operators v Minister of Justice*, Appellate Justice Kotze mentions that courts should refrain from making a fortress of a dictionary.[17] But then he proceeds to look up six words in sixteen different dictionaries. He also confirms that courts are allowed to consult *authoritative* dictionaries to clarify the language of the legislature, but fails to describe what the authoritative qualities of a dictionary are or which dictionaries are typically authoritative.[18] Appellate Justice Diemont points out that even though dictionary usage is allowed, it is not always helpful in solving problems of construction.[19] One of the reasons is that headwords often contain numerous entries, indicating different polysemous or homographic senses. Ultimately, this could lead to more confusion instead of less. A similar thought was expressed by Appellate Justice Hefer in *Fundstrust (Pty) Ltd v Van Deventer*. According to him, lexical research can be very helpful, but sometimes it is not.[20] Dictionaries also offer little guidance when it comes to colloquial language. Justice Levy came to this conclusion when consulting dictionaries on the meaning of *stock meal* and coming up short.[21] He correctly argues that there is little use in looking up local words in foreign published reference works.[22] Finally, Appellate Justice Heher reminds us that courts do not need linguistic expert advice, because dictionaries speak for themselves and courts are more than capable of reading a dictionary.[23] This might be true, but a little guidance could only be beneficial.

Thumma and Kirchmeier (1999:290) indicate that courts choose and use dictionaries inconsistently because there is an obvious lack of judicial guidelines for using dictionaries. As a means to counter this, they offer

17 *Association of Amusement and Novelty Machine Operators v Minister of Justice* 1980 (2) SA 636 (A) at 641.

18 *Association of Amusement and Novelty Machine Operators v Minister of Justice* 1980 (2) SA 636 (A) at 637.

19 *S v Collop* 1981 (1) SA 150 (A) at 161.

20 *Fundstrust (Pty) Ltd v Van Deventer* 1997 (1) SA 710 (A), para 9.

21 *Jowells Transport v South African Road Transportation Services* 1986 (2) SA 252 (SWA) at 254. The compound noun is still not recorded in any South African dictionary.

22 *Jowells Transport v South African Road Transportation Services* 1986 (2) SA 252 (SWA) at 257.

23 *Online Lottery Services (Pty) Ltd v National Lotteries Board* 2010 (5) SA 349 (SCA), para 21. After boasting about the court's ability to use dictionaries, Heher JA then proceeds to consult a pocket dictionary, of all things.

the following guidelines which could form part of a judicial best practice (Thumma and Kirchmeier 1999:264–276):

1. A court must determine which word really needs defining.
2. The proper type of dictionary must be selected.
3. Once the proper type is selected, a court must select the correct dictionary within that type.
4. The appropriate edition of the dictionary must be selected.
5. The appropriate definition must be selected.
6. A court must use dictionaries as a starting point and not as an end point.

The importance of context for statutory interpretation has been established several times. An interpreter must infer the meaning of a word, expression or phrase from the wider context, which includes the statute, its language and the context that lead to its existence.[24] If the context fails to clarify the interpretation dispute, then a court may consider consulting a dictionary in order to understand both the word and its context better. Furthermore, a court must ensure they look up the correct word. Thumma and Kirchmeier (1999:267) cite a case in which a majority bench looked up the word *damages* when the applicable statute used the word *damage*. In this specific context, *damages* described harm to persons whereas *damage* denoted harm to property.

When a court has decided to consult a dictionary, the correct dictionary must be selected. This approach must not be mistaken for Kotze JA's ideation of an *authoritative* dictionary. What is meant by *correct dictionary* is simply the appropriate dictionary for the job: if a court is dealing with a term of art, then a specialist dictionary is suitable; if an ordinary word is contested a standard or comprehensive descriptive dictionary is necessary. A court must first determine whether the word they are scrutinising is used in terms of common usage or in a technical sense before they select an appropriate dictionary.

Once a court has selected the appropriate dictionary (general or restricted dictionary), they must select the correct type of dictionary within that category.[25] For instance, if a court needs to clarify an ordinary word, they would have decided to use a general dictionary. Now they

24 Taken from *Endumeni* (para 18), this is now common knowledge.

25 It is doubtful that a pocket, illustrated, learner or translation dictionary will ever provide more or equal clarity than a standard or comprehensive monolingual dictionary. Of course, where a very specific need calls for such a dictionary, it is within a court's mandate to consult them. However, a court must always think of the dictionary's target audience and intended goal before reaching for it.

must decide which type of general dictionary is the most fitting. Either a comprehensive or standard desk copy of a monolingual dictionary would be suitable. It is always advisable to start with a locally published dictionary before considering any other country's reference work. Comprehensive dictionaries are by far the most complete works and will contain a great number of archival information too, which could be helpful in working out what a word might have meant at the time of an act's drafting. Comprehensive dictionaries are always being updated. Note however, that some indigenous languages do not have comprehensive dictionaries while others are still a work in progress.

After a court has selected the best dictionary for the enquiry, it is important to use the latest edition. It is simply unacceptable to consult a dictionary that is out of print or to use the first or second edition when newer editions exist. Not only may newer editions include more words, they sometimes define words differently. Compare the following two entries in the *Longman Dictionary of Contemporary English* of 1978 and 1995 (Atkins and Rundell 2008:419):

6.6 **raft**[2] v **1** [X9] to carry (something) on a raft (somewhere): *raft the stores over to the island* **2** [X9] to send (wood) in the form of a raft (somewhere): *raft the logs down the river* **3** [T1] to cross (water) on a raft: *They rafted the lake.* **4** [L9] to travel (somewhere) on a raft: *They rafted down the river to New Orleans.* (1978)

6.7 **raft**[2] v [I, T] to travel by raft or carry things by raft. (1995)

Understandably, it is expensive and even wasteful to continue collecting newer print editions, which is why the Department of Justice and Constitutional Development should subscribe to online dictionary services (if it does not already). Online dictionaries are user-friendly, large, and updated more frequently than printed copies. A court may consider older dictionaries if they want to get a sense of how a specific word was used when the relevant statute was written.

As Appellate Justice Diemont observes in *S v Collop*, dictionaries usually list a number of related senses for some headwords and this could potentially lead to confusion, or further difficulties.[26] A court must consider which of the senses listed applies to the case at hand. If a court seeks to clarify an ordinary word, it is a good idea to be guided by its prototypicality. For example, if the word *father* is contested in terms of his liability to pay school fees and the court decides to consult a dictionary,

26 *S v Collop* 1981 (1) SA 150 (A) at 161.

they could see the following lemma taken from the *Oxford South African Concise Dictionary* (DUSAE 2010:423):[27]

> 6.8 **father** n. **1** a man in relation to his natural child or children. • a male animal in relation to its offspring. • an important figure in the origin and early history of something. • a man who gives care and protection. • the oldest member or doyen of a society or other body. **2** (often as a title or form of address) a priest.

In the example above, the first sense is prototypical in relation to a parent liable to pay fees. Even though the remaining senses do indicate a polysemous relationship and offer insight into the word *father*, only the first sense applies directly.

In addition, if a court finds it necessary to consult a dictionary, it must be as a starting point or first step. A dictionary must only provide the necessary clarity to aid a jurist in the actual argument or investigation that follows. It should not form the base or final decision on meaning (the end point). In the end, a dictionary shows a user what a word could mean, but not what it actually does mean within its unique context (Thumma and Kirchmeier, 1999: 293). As a starting point, dictionaries should be used alongside other sources, either case law or alternative linguistic methods that assist in clarifying a word or phrase. Linguistic analysis (either superficial or in-depth) can potentially substitute dictionary usage or direct it to be more purpose-driven.

As a final thought, jurists should motivate why they selected and used a certain dictionary. Even though it is not common practice in South Africa for presiding officers and those who prepare heads of argument to explain why they chose specific dictionaries, this would help to establish the authority of that particular reference work in that case. It will also support any attempt at proving why a certain definition is airtight. If a jurist finds that he or she cannot motivate its use sufficiently, then that should suffice as a sign that the selected dictionary is not suitable.

6.7. A digital dictionary of statutory terms: an idea

The following idea might be a leap into the future and could be foreign to some. Nevertheless, it is something worth considering. The Department of Justice and Constitutional Development should contemplate creating an online dictionary of statutory terms that covers all of the words

27 See for instance *Fish Hoek Primary School v GW* 2010 (2) SA 141 (SCA).

and phrases that are defined in legislation.[28] Not only would an online dictionary be easily accessible by everyone (the judiciary, government, private and business sectors), it would make it that much easier for legislative drafters to add new words or rework existing definitions. Ideally, it would also contain words that were stipulated through case law.

In this envisaged digital dictionary, each headword would include hyperlinked cross-references to the applicable act or bylaw as well as any specific section within that act (or other legislation).[29] Each headword would be entered in line with lexicographic principles, in other words, indicating the necessary linguistic metadata such as parts of speech. Where a specific word is defined differently between two or more statutes for varied purposes, those differences can be disambiguated in the same way that polysemous and homographic senses are disambiguated.

As an illustration, let us take a look at the compound noun *tax period* in 6.9 below. The term is currently listed in section 1 of the Tax Administration Act 28 of 2011, but the section entry does a poor job of explaining what a tax period is. In reality, the item is simply an amalgamation of cross-references to the various tax acts that describe the period of assessment applicable to that specific tax situation.[30] A lemma in a centralised database could not only assist users in understanding what the term means, but it could also make it a lot easier to update whenever new legislation or amendments come into effect (like adding the Carbon Tax Act's definition).

6.9 **tax period** (noun) **1** ITO income tax, any period of twelve months (s1 Income Tax Act 58 of 1962) **2** ITO skills development levies, the period starting 1 April 2001 (s3 Skills Development Levies Act 9 of 1999) **3** ITO unemployment insurance, every month (s6 Unemployment Insurance Act 4 of 2002) **4** ITO value-added tax, (a) two months of a calendar year for Category A, ending on the last day of January, March,

28 In reality, anyone could attempt a project like this. It could be initiated and managed by a university, an NGO or a private law firm who wishes to create a useful repository for both academic and private use.

29 Cross-references already exist in statutory definitions. For example, the Tax Administration Act 28 of 2011 defines *taxpayer* as 'has the meaning assigned under section 151'. The same is visible in the Carbon Tax Act 15 of 2019. It defines *taxpayer* as 'a person liable for carbon tax in terms of section 3'.

30 Some of the cross-references are terrible. For example, the Tax Administration Act refers readers to section 1 of the Diamond Export Levy (Administration) Act, and section 1 merely refers readers to section 4(2) of the Act.

May, July, September and November; (b) two months of a calendar year for Category B, ending on the last day of February, April, June, August, October and December; (c) one month of a calendar year for Category C, ending on the last day of every month; (d) six months of a calendar year for Category D, ending on the last day of February and August (s27 Value Added Tax Act 89 of 1991) **5** ITO royalty payable on the transfer of mineral and petroleum resources by a natural person or trust, starting 1 March and ending on the last day of February of the following year; royalty payable by any other person starts on the first day of its financial year (or the first day of the first month) and ends on the last day of that financial year (s1 Mineral and Petroleum Resources Royalty (Administration) Act 29 of 2008) **6** ITO the levy on diamond exports by a natural person, the period starts 1 March and ends 31 August, and starts again 1 September and ends on the last day of February; for any other person the period starts the first day of the financial year and ends six months after that day, and starts again on the second day after the six month assessment period and ends on the last day of that financial year (s4(2) Diamond Export Levy (Administration) Act 14 of 2007) **7** ITO securities transfer tax of purchased and transferred listed securities, the period is the fourteenth day of the following month; securities transfer tax for other transfers of listed securities, the period is the fourteenth day of the following month; securities transfer tax for transfer of unlisted securities is payable within two months of the date of transfer (s3 Securities Transfer Tax Administration Act 26 of 2007); **8** ITO a jeopardy assessment, the period is decided in advance of the date on which a return is normally due (s94 Tax Administration Act 28 of 2011); **9** ITO carbon tax, the period starts 1 January of each year and ends on 31 December of that year (s16(2) Carbon Tax Act 15 of 2019).

Admittedly, the example in 6.9 can benefit from improvement, but the lemma helps users understand what is meant by *tax period* by providing a description for each identified tax situation.[31] It eliminates the present practice of having to consult different sections in different texts. If

31 I acknowledge that my proposed statutory definition is not entirely compatible with the current principles and protocols of legislative drafting, but I think this can at least inspire a creative middle ground or solution.

the lemma is digitised, users will have access to the relevant statutes through embedded hyperlinks. Interlinking cross-references provides direct access to the statutory context. In the end, the section or chapter of definitions in each statute will contain a single reference to the online dictionary, which could become the country's official statutory directory for legislative terms. This could potentially shorten statutes and improve legislative communication.

Attempting a project of this nature will claim considerable resources in time, money and expertise – creating an online dictionary of statutory terms must see legislative drafters and lexicographers working together – but the reward can be promising if executed correctly.

6.8. Conclusion

This chapter provided an overview of common facts about dictionaries to empower users who rely on them for statutory interpretation. It is safe to say that dictionaries are wonderful resources that often assist the judiciary to gain clarity when words and phrases cause confusion. They remain an important linguistic tool. To ensure that dictionaries contribute maximally, users must not only select the text that suits the query the best, but users must also know its purpose and how it functions. It is important to realise that dictionaries are dissimilar; consequently, they will not be able to do the same thing in exactly the same way or with the same ability. Choosing the best text for the task means that its user appreciates that each resource has a different target audience and that it is only meant to help a user understand the lexis of a speech community in general. It is unrealistic to assign authority to it. Instead, it should rather be used together with other tools of analysis.

7. Understanding Corpora

In many ways, corpus linguistics has changed the manner in which scholars study everyday language. It has become an important research tool and methodology within linguistics and, by extension, language-related studies. In particular, forensic linguists use it to solve both statutory enquiries and authorship identification. The use of corpus linguistic methods to clarify contested words or phrases for statutory purposes is therefore not new. The past two decades saw a number of scholars in linguistics and law argue either for or against it (Carney 2020:284, fn 82). As a methodology, it can be quite complex at times, but it works extremely well when combined with other methods or theories. As such, there is no reason why simple corpus searches cannot offer clarity and understanding when deciding cases. Good corpora offer something that dictionaries often cannot: insight into context. Corpora represent real-life language used in real-life contexts and they make it possible to study words and phrases from different angles, potentially revealing significant word relations.

This chapter provides a basic introduction to corpus linguistics and illustrates simple word searches. It also provides a guide to building one's own corpus.

7.1. What is a corpus?

A **corpus** is a collection of naturally occurring spoken or written texts (or a combination thereof) for the purpose of linguistic analysis.[1] Each corpus is collected and structured with a specific goal and scope in mind. For instance, a corpus can consist of South African English academic texts only, providing users with a view of that particular subset of language use.[2] Other corpora are more wide-ranging and may contain a variety of text types to reflect general language use.

When it comes to corpora, size matters. A corpus is usually very large, because they are supposed to function as a representative sample of a particular language variety (Baker 2010:6). Large corpora make it

1 The plural for *corpus* is *corpora*.

2 There is even a Corona Virus Corpus, which is more than 1.5 billion words strong, representative of English used in twenty countries across the world. It is a web-news corpus, which means it comprises news reports distributed on the web. Other large English corpora that represent very specific data include a TV corpus, a Wikipedia corpus and Hansard corpus, which is constructed of the British parliament's Hansard.

possible to notice patterns and pick up on usage frequency. This helps us determine whether certain occurrences form part of normative language behaviour or mark irregular language use. Even though a corpus cannot represent an entire language, they do make it a lot easier to claim that a certain phenomenon is significant within a language variety or speaker community. Dictionaries cannot do this (it is not what they are made for).

Some corpora are huge, like the News on the Web corpus, which spans more that fifteen billion words and keeps growing. The British National Corpus was collected between 1980 and 1993 and has a hundred million words. However, this does not mean that smaller corpora are useless. Depending on the topic of research, a small corpus can be more purpose-driven to expose answers to a more complex topic. For instance, Arntfield (2016) analysed a corpus consisting of 29 holdup notes collected over a period of twenty years within one Canadian city. These holdup notes were written by bank robbers and silently given to bank tellers with messages ranging from *This is a robbery* to *Gun. Money. Quickly* (Arntfield, 2016:246). Noticeably, his corpus is very small but Arntfield was still able to uncover the complexity of these notes and what they reveal about the perpetrator and the victim. It is important to note that smaller corpora are often specialised and only provide insight into very distinct queries. They are not meant for generalising about language occurrences.

Utilising a corpus depends on software and corpus tools. Online corpora like the Corpus of Contemporary American English already have the necessary software installed, but users who analyse corpora that they collected themselves need a separate corpus analysis software programme with toolkit and concordancer. Without it, analysis is impossible. We will take a closer look at the characteristics and tools of corpora in the following sections.

7.2. Types of corpora

We can differentiate between a number of different corpora; some have already been mentioned: *spoken* and *written* as well as *general* and *specialist* corpora. In some instances, there are also visual corpora that contain video material of gestures or sign language lexis as well as collections of symbols or icons that convey semiotic information. Potentially, spoken corpora provide the most authentic of language data because unlike written texts, there is seldom editing or cautioning involved. Before spoken data can be entered into a database, it must be transcribed into a written form and encoded into Unicode for software readability. If a corpus contains a variety of genres, we refer to it as a *mixed corpus*. Mixed corpora are usually balanced. This means the corpus comprises spoken and written texts in equal measure. If a corpus is constructed from written texts only, representing different genres (newspaper clippings, academic texts, political speeches, prose and so on), there should be balance between them as well.

We can also distinguish between *synchronic* and *diachronic* corpora. Synchronic corpora represent contemporary language whereas diachronic corpora contain texts that enable historical or comparative studies. The latter will typically include texts with old or archaic language (Weisser 2016:15). If a court wants to know what a word or phrase means today, then a synchronic corpus is ideal. Lately, American scholars are also advocating the use of diachronic corpora to understand how words were used or understood during the time that the constitution or a statute was written. This could be beneficial when interpreting acts that are quite old and have not been revised or amended extensively. This approach to statutory interpretation is known as *originalism* – determining statutory meaning in history. For such an approach to succeed, there must be a corpus representative of the language used at the time in question (like the Corpus of Historical American English). For more detail and illustrations on how such corpora could provide insight into history, please see Solan and Gales (2020), Lee and Mouritsen (2018) as well as Solan (2016).[3]

Another distinction is between *static* and *dynamic* corpora. The data for a static corpus is collected and finalised during a specific period (like the British National Corpus). This means the collection of texts remains the same and as time passes, the corpus ages. Other corpora are updated frequently (some even daily) to reflect the changing nature of language (Weisser 2016:25). We refer to dynamic corpora as **monitor corpora**, because they allow us to keep track of a language and any changes that come about. They are also an essential part of dictionary making.

In addition, corpora can be either *annotated* or *clean*. Most established corpora are annotated, which means that each text contains

3 An example of how investigations into historical language can be informative, is the South African word *dagga*. According to the *Dictionary of South African English*, the word was recorded as early as 1670 and it has the same denotation today that it had back then. This means it has undergone no significant semantic change in about 350 years. The Tobacco Products Control Amendment Act 12 of 1999 defines *smoke* in section 2(*j*) as the inhale and exhale of an ignited tobacco product, weed or plant. The word *weed* has been synonymous with cannabis for a very long time, which makes its inclusion in the Amendment Act peculiar, especially because its use was illegal when the Amendment Act was published. If the legislature had a completely different meaning in mind (other than cannabis), then a search in a historical language corpus could provide clues.

meta-textual information ranging from demographic data to the genre of the text, its register and intended audience. Annotation helps users to make in-depth analyses and to compare texts with one another. Specific linguistic annotation takes the form of tagging. Tagging involves attaching meta-linguistic data to each word, mostly reflecting semantic and grammatical information like parts of speech. This enables users to do more focused searches like the use of the verb *bat*, which will then exclude the noun within the same lexeme. If a person builds his or her own corpus, it will be clean. Any annotation must be added to the corpus. Software exists that automatically tags words with the necessary semantic information, but other types of annotation (like certain grammar or meta-textual etiquettes) must be added manually or through coding. It is also possible to create a unique tagging taxonomy if required.

So far, it must be obvious that a corpus is a carefully constructed resource and even though it is entirely possible to build a corpus by yourself, it must be done with care from the start. Creating a corpus for statutory purposes would fall into the category of specialised corpora. Apart from general corpora like the Corpus of Canadian English, which provides useful information on the ordinary meaning of contested words, a specialised corpus like the US Supreme Court Opinions corpus provides insight into the structured language of judges. This particular corpus allows usual language analysis, but also makes it a lot easier to search all the cases decided by a specific judge as well as looking up cases that dealt with the same word problem or legal issue.

7.3. South African limitations

One of the most glaring problems in South Africa is the availability of representative corpora. Although many people are working hard to create corpora and make these available to the public, it is a slow process. Most of the English corpora in South Africa are small or specialist corpora, which will not help much in general inquiries about the ordinary meaning of words.[4] For instance, the South African Centre for Digital Language Resources (SADiLAR) offers a range of resources including a corpus that is made up of different collections. Theoretically, their corpus could be an ideal place to start, but it fails easy tests. For example, when Minister Nkosazana Dlamini-Zuma notoriously advised South Africans not to share self-rolled cigarettes during the Covid 19 pandemic, she used the word

4 This does not mean that smaller specialist corpora have no role to play in statutory interpretation. A corpus of Black South African English or a corpus of South African slang could add value when it becomes clear a certain word is typical of a particular vernacular.

zol as a verb: 'When people zol, they put saliva on the paper...'. A South African corpus should be able to give an indication on how *zol* is primarily used. *Zol* is a common lexical item in South Africa, yet the SADiLAR corpus contains no entry for it.[5]

If we consider some of the other words discussed in this book and we compare it to an established corpus like the British National Corpus (BNC), SADiLAR's limitations are obvious. SADiLAR has no entry for *faggot* whereas BNC has 26 hits providing a wide range of its usage. In an attempt to verify the frequency with which *petrol* and *bomb* collocate, a search for *bomb* delivers only ten hits in the SADiLAR corpus, providing merely two significant compound nouns: time bomb and car bomb. The BNC delivers at least 1000 hits, providing a variety of compound nouns: atomic bomb, walking bomb, hydrogen bomb, mailbox bomb, car bomb, media bomb, radio bomb, spindle bomb and yes, a petrol bomb. Another aspect that is noticeable when the two corpora are compared, is that the SADiLAR corpus is not as balanced as the BNC. The BNC comprises many different texts. A search for *incidental* delivers hits from a compilation of personal letters, academic literature from the Humanities and Natural Sciences as well as texts taken from popular culture and commerce. The SADiLAR entries for the same word are taken mostly from legislative texts. This does not provide much clarity on a varied use of the word.

The purpose of this discussion is not to discourage users to employ any of the South African resources, neither is it meant to focus a harsh light on the good work that SADiLAR and similar institutions are doing. For now, it is purely meant to serve as a caution. Corpora can be wonderful aides, but they must be at an advanced stage if they are to deliver trustworthy and robust results for legal purposes. Even though the same rule that applies to dictionary usage (start local) must also apply to corpus usage, South African jurists would presently benefit more by consulting larger international corpora.[6]

Another, less serious, limitation is subscription fees. To gain full access to established international corpora, individuals or institutions must subscribe at an annual fee. Unfortunately, the difference between free corpora and those that are available through a licence is quite clear. Paid corpora tend to have better user interfaces and are also more

5 Dlamini-Zuma denoted tobacco cigarettes specifically (which is one of its senses), but it is prototypically associated with cannabis. This is very apparent when searched in slang databases like *Wat Kyk Jy?*

6 Corpora like *News on the Web* and *iWeb* contain entries from South African sources as well.

thoroughly constructed. Of course, a dearth of South African corpora should serve as a motivation to build and support our own.

7.4. The tools of a corpus

Using a corpus can seem daunting at first (even to linguists), because there are multiple tools. Further, a look at the back matter of some corpora would give most people nightmares. Luckily, we only need to know a few tools in order to conduct simple searches. Before we can illustrate straightforward searches, we must introduce the basic corpus tools and terms. These tools and terms will be the same for existing online corpora that have the necessary software embedded, as well as corpus analysis toolkits and concordancers that someone would use for a corpus stored in a computer file.

7.4.1 Concordancer and KWIC searches

The **concordancer** is one of the main tools within corpus analysis software. As the name suggests, the concordancer produces a list containing the word form or lexeme being investigated. Put differently, it is a collection of word occurrences in its textual environment (Sinclair in Tribble 2012:167). It presents every hit within its direct context. The concordancer is very important, because it allows the user to study a word in context, which makes it possible to note patterns (grammatical, semantic, pragmatic), frequency (how often a word occurs) and co-occurring relations (collocations). Many of the results of straightforward corpus searches is visible within the concordance window.

Results of a concordance search are displayed in KWIC format. KWIC is an acronym for *Keyword in Context* and means that the search term is presented in the middle of each concordance line, providing the reader with a better scope of the immediate context of the searched term. See figure 7.1 below for an example.

1	no proof that the dog was attacking or attempting to	**bite**	the plaintiff, and that the defendant was not guilty
2	Semble, that if the dog was attacking or attempting to	**bite**	the plaintiff, the defendant would be liable in damages
3	dogs. The charge further alleged that he let the dogs	**bite**	the complainant, Morleen Murimwa, though letting dogs bite someone
4	to be at large and that he let the dogs	**bite**	the complainant. He was sentenced to a fine of $50

5	to be at large unmuzzled ferocious dogs and letting them	**bite**	the complainant Dogs at large even though the farm
6	dog. In the case before us the dog did not	**bite**	the cycle or its rider, but got directly in
7	a dog rushed out and either bit or attempted to	**bite**	the horse; in consequence of this, the horse bolted
8	fence and thereby frighten the dog and cause it to	**bite**	the neighbour. The neighbour was in the circumstances negligent
9	dat Marais "wrongfully and unlawfully allowed the said dog to	**bite**	the plaintiff", en in para. 5 daarvan het hy beweer
10	satisfy me that the dog was attacking or attempting to	**bite**	the plaintiff at the time when the accident happened.

Figure 7.1: Example of a KWIC token search

The KWIC excerpt in figure 7.1 is taken from the Dog Case Law corpus. This corpus comprises 48 South African cases from 1927 to 2012 that address interactions with dogs. It contains more than 200 000 words at present.[7] A search for the word form *bite* delivered 48 hits; ten concordance lines are presented here, each containing the searched term in the middle. These ten lines already provide interesting information. The preceding words *attempting to*, *cause it to*, *let it* stand out and are semantically loaded. We will look at these types of associations again when discussing collocations.

7.4.2 Word forms, types, tokens and nodes

Talking about words in relation to corpus analysis can become confusing quite quickly. To help us understand what we are doing, we distinguish between a number of terms. The first distinction is between *lexemes* (also called *lemmas*) and *word forms*. As explained in Chapter 2, a lexeme is the base form of a word. If we say *run*, we refer to each of the various instances of that word: run, runs, running and ran. Each of the instances within a lexeme is called the **word form**. So, the lexeme *run* has at least four word forms. *Bed* and its plural *beds* are two word forms of the lexeme *bed*. When we study a corpus, we do not observe lexemes directly; rather, we observe their word forms and make inferences about the lexeme based on what we

7 The source texts have not yet been cleaned for proper corpus analysis. This means the actual token size falls below 200 000. The importance of cleaning a corpus is addressed in the section about building one's own.

see happening to the word forms. Users can conduct searches for both. If you choose to search a lexeme like *relocate*, it will isolate all the relevant word forms in one concordance (*relocate*, *relocates*, *relocating*, *relocated*, *relocation*). If the word form *relocate* occurs 12 times and *relocating* occurs 18 times, it means the corpus has 30 hits for the lexeme *relocate*. However, if you choose to search the singular noun *relocation* only, your results will include no other word form.

Figure 7.2 below reflects a lexeme search for *bite*, which means that all the word forms of the word *bite* are included. Two word forms are isolated here, *bite* and *bites*. In the previous examples (fig. 7.1), *bite* occurs 48 times but a lexeme search casts a wider net (it tallies both word forms), which results in 59 hits in the Dog Case Law corpus.

1	a mischievous; propensity, as, for instance, a dog accustomed to	**bite,**	or a horse accustomed to kick, or the like,
2	of the contra naturam requirement suggests that 'a dog which	**bites**	or barks can never be said to act against
3	animal (feram bestiam) which has caused damage to, or actually	**bites**	or hurts another person, then the owner should be
4	his dog or horse in a place where he cannot	**bite**	or kick. If, on the other hand, the owner
5	such dog or other dogs the property were liable to	**bite**	and injure persons who entered the property. Since E

Figure 7.2: Example of lexemes and word forms

Our second distinction concerns the difference between word *types* and word *tokens*. Each word form that occurs in a text is a **word token**. If a corpus comprises 100 words, then it also contains 100 tokens. When we scrutinise the 100 tokens, we notice that many of the word forms repeat throughout the text. We do not consider every repetition a different word. To differentiate from tokens, we refer to each different word as a **word type**. If the word *run* occurs 22 times, then we have 22 tokens but only one type. If *run*, *runs* and *ran* each occurred 11 times, we would have 33 tokens but 3 types.

Using the example in figure 7.2 once again, we see that our Dog Case Law corpus has 59 tokens (*bite*) but only two types (*bite*, *bites*).[8]

Lastly, we use the term **node** when we talk about the lexeme (or one of its word forms) that we are investigating. To determine co-occurrence patterns, we look at words that appear on the left and right of a node word. In our two examples above, the node word is both *bite* and *bites*.

7.4.3 Frequency, wordlists and keywords

Baker (2010:19) describes **frequency** as the 'bedrock of corpus linguistics', because it plays such an important role in arguments and conclusions based on corpus data. Simply put, frequency refers to the number of times an item occurs in a corpus. However, knowing how regularly a specific word occurs within a corpus says very little unless a user wants to know how dominant a certain word or expression really is or when the frequency tally is compared to other data. In our earlier example of *faggot / fagott*, a corpus study revealed that the pejorative *faggot* occurred far less among speakers than we initially predicted. Knowing this provides us with an opportunity to speculate about conventional habits of refraining from using taboo words. Another example is the difference between eating and drinking. A corpus comprising scripts of the American television series 'Looking' offers some insight. A corpus of the second series (ten episodes) sees 11 hits for the token *eat*. It is rather insignificant and uninteresting considering the sum of tokens is more than 40 000. Interestingly, the token *drink* delivers 23 hits. It is also not very significant in terms of statistics, but the word occurs more frequently than *eat*. When we take a closer look, the word form *drink* has 18 hits and 15 of them are nouns that refer to alcoholic beverages. In relation, the token *drunk* occurs 12 times. Even though frequency is low for both tokens, it still says something about the characters' approach to the rituals of eating and drinking in fictional Western narratives. Drinking and getting drunk is sometimes portrayed as more common.

It is very common for linguists to compare results from different corpora. If a certain word occurs quite frequently (or not at all) in more than one corpus, it could be revealing of its prototypicality (or lack thereof). However, keep in mind that different corpora constitute different sizes. For this reason, it is useful to recalculate frequencies to a frequency

8 The corpus actually yields five types: *bite*, *bites*, *bit*, *bitten* and *biting* within 172 tokens.

of 1000 000. This is known as normalisation.[9] The calculation looks like this (Baker 2010:20):

$$\frac{\text{Total number of occurrences of lexical item}}{\text{Total words in corpus}} \times 1000\,000$$

If we compare our results for *eat* and *drink* in the 'Looking' corpus with results in the Brown corpus,[10] we must normalise the results, because the Brown Corpus is significantly larger.

Table 7.1: Standardised frequencies for *eat* and *drink*

	Total tokens	Total hits	Frequency per million words
'Looking' corpus	40 547	eat: 11 drink: 23	eat: 271 drink: 567
Brown corpus	1 026 010	eat: 116 drink: 163	eat: 113 drink: 159

So, what does it mean to normalise the frequency between different corpora? Because we calculate frequency to a number out of a million, it makes it easier to compare results. For instance, from table 7.1 we see that drinking of alcohol is a lot more common in a television series depicting everyday life than it is in the reporting of actual everyday life. *Drinking* occurs 400 times more frequently in the 'Looking' corpus than the Brown corpus. Of course, in this specific situation we should also consider external factors like the age difference between the two corpora. The Brown corpus was established in 1961 whereas the second series of 'Looking' was televised in 2015.

Many corpus analysis software can generate a *wordlist*. It offers a list of words according to different sorting criteria like frequency, part of speech, or lexeme. If a list is sorted by frequency, it will register tokens from most to least frequent, meaning that the words that occur the most often in a corpus will be at the top. Grammar words like articles and prepositions are almost always at the top, because they are the words that speakers use the most. In the 'Looking' corpus, the personal pronouns

9 Normalisation can also be done per 1000 words, instead of a million. See Evison (2012:126).

10 The Brown corpus is one of the first English language corpora built for corpus linguistic research. It was compiled in 1961 by American scholars at Brown University. The corpus is balanced by different texts across 15 genres.

you and *I* are at the top, which is typical of dialogue. Many linguists use wordlists to see which lexical words stand out due to frequency, and then proceed to scrutinise those twenty or thirty words in detail. When we study the wordlist of the Brown corpus for interesting lexical words based on frequency, it is noticeable that *man* is cited a lot more at 1364 hits than *woman* at 247 hits.

It is not sufficient to draw conclusions on what a user sees in a wordlist. If a statutory interpreter wishes to employ a wordlist, it is advisable to do so at the start of an investigation as an exploration. A wordlist could provide insight into the frequency of a contested word as well as its ranking compared to the rest of the words in the corpus. Ultimately, what is gained from the wordlist must be transferred to what is seen in the concordance.

Another powerful display is possible through the *keyword tool*. The keyword tool shows a user which words are the most prominent in a corpus by comparing the entire body of texts with another corpus. The words that stand out are called keywords and their frequency is determined by chi-squared or log-likelihood tests. To calculate keywords, a user must load the target corpus as well as a reference corpus. For instance, if we want to know what the keywords in the Lancaster-Oslo/Bergen (LOB) corpus is, we can use the Brown corpus as reference.[11] Keywords that stand out include *london*, *britain* and *commonwealth*. This might not be too surprising for a British corpus. What might be surprising is the words *colour* (ranked 6th), *aluminium* (ranked 36) and *africa* (ranked 56). If we swap the two corpora, we see words like *states* (ranked 3rd) and *federal* (ranked 11th), which is to be expected from a general corpus on American English. Surprises include *jazz* (ranked 25th) and *railroad* (ranked 38th). The strongest keyword in the LOB corpus is *labour* (ranked 1st). Similar to the British vocabulary, *labor* is ranked in 8th position and *color* in 9th. A comparison between the two might say something about the cultural proximity of American and British speakers.

A keyword search could be useful for statutory purposes if an investigator suspects a certain word is (un)common in a speaker community's lexicon and wants to determine its saliency. For this, the user must have access to corpora representative of two different speaker communities, say South African English and British English. Keyword searches could also be useful when a person wants to determine how legislation citing marriage is worded. A target corpus of national

11 The LOB corpus is the British equivalent of the Brown corpus. They are almost the same size and contain the same sample sets. It is a balanced corpus.

legislation compared against a reference corpus of provincial legislation could yield interesting results. So could an investigation into the language used in labour relations cases compared to criminal cases.

7.4.4 Collocations and n-grams

In Chapter 3, we said that a collocation is two or more words that co-occur quite frequently, to the extent that repetitive use creates obvious semantic patterns. They are very common in corpus linguistic analysis and can communicate valuable semantic information used to construct semantic frames. Stubbs (2002:117) mentions that commonly recurring events involve typical actors, equipment and activities. For instance, going to the dentist involves appointments, fillings, extractions, dentist chairs, drills and the like. As people living in the world, we accept that doors open, the sun shines and dogs bark. These co-occurring words reveal a lot about our world and our perspectives. Of equal importance is the fact that collocation provides context for the searched word.

A search for collocates of *dog* in the Corpus of Contemporary American English (COCA),[12] delivers associations with the nouns *cat*, *food*, *owner*, *park* and *puppy* as the most regular co-occurrences. It co-occurs with the adjectives *hot*, *mad*, *top*, *wild* and *stray* the most and with the verbs *walk*, *bark*, *eat*, *train* and *feed*. These collocates reveal information about both the behaviour of (domesticated) dogs and the humans that interact with them.

How do we search collocates? Firstly, collocates are usually calculated in terms of a word span. Preferably, for collocates to be significant they must occur close to one another within the same sentence in order to claim that there is a reliable pattern. The standard is three to four words on either side of the node word. See the example extracted from COCA:

7.1 #**Cats** aren't like **dogs**, he said.
the big **cats**, the top **dog**
videos that show **cats** that act like **dogs**
lots of rats and **cats**, but no **dogs**
about a **cat** who stole a **dog's** bed

If we want to study words that regularly co-occur in sequence (words that follow each other directly), we select **n-grams**. N-grams are usually

12 The Corpus of Contemporary American English was collected between 1990 and 2019 and comprises about 1 billion words spread across eight genres. It is a balanced corpus.

studied in bi- and tri-grams (two or three word sequences), for instance the bi-grams *hot dog*, *old dog* and *family dog*. Tri-grams include *cats and dogs*, *get a dog* and *dogs do not*. In the event that a larger string of words co-occur, we refer to them as **clusters** like *boy and his dog* and *dog ate my homework*.

Let us apply this to the Dog Case Law corpus. Before we search the word *dog*, we have to set the minimum frequency. Because this corpus is small, it is set at a minimum of 5. In other words, collocates must occur at least five times throughout the corpus to qualify as a pattern. Larger corpora like the COCA would be set at a higher minimum (20). For this search, we also set the span at four words either side of the node word. The first five semantic words indicated by the results are *owner*, *bitten*, *eating*, *large* and *scab*. The tokens *attack* and *vicious* form part of the top ten words. Seeing as the corpus is constructed from cases that deal with dog bites, it is telling that *dog* is associated with these words. What is especially interesting is the word *eating*, because it provides a window into the potential cause for dog bites. After all, it is common knowledge that a person should not come between a hungry dog and its food; something that is often taught to children.

When we do an n-gram search, we can start by setting the size at 2, followed by a minimum frequency of 5. The results reveal mostly grammatical patterns: *dog was*, *dog which*, *dog would*. If we increase the n-gram to a tri-gram and we focus on sequences containing lexical words, we see *dog was eating*, *dog in question*, *dog by pulling* and *dog found trespassing*. Once more, a larger string provides us with interesting results. Trespassing and eating seem to be common causes for bite incidences.

Considering larger clusters, we can experiment and set the cluster size at 6 words that co-occur as a string at least 4 times throughout the corpus. The most interesting result is the cluster *dog by pulling a scab off*.[13] When we select that particular phrase and we study it in its concordance, we see that someone antagonised a dog by pulling a scab from its nose while the dog was eating.

13 It is important to keep in mind that this specific corpus is small and used for illustrative purposes only. This means that repetition of any kind can be limited to a single text but it could look like it is significant based on frequency alone. The cluster *dog by pulling a scab off* occurs five times throughout the corpus, but repeats in a single court case. Obviously, this presents one example (one reason) for dog bites and is not a significant cause for dog bites in South Africa in general. Because the cluster contains an unusual combination of words, it begs scrutiny to make sure that it is representative and an actual linguistic pattern.

Lastly, some corpus software allows users to set the minimum *range* for collocate, n-gram and cluster searches. Range indicates the number of occurrences across texts in the corpus. If the range is set at a minimum of 1, it means that the node and its collocates have to appear at least in one text throughout the corpus. The larger the minimum range, the wider the search, spanning a greater number of texts. If a corpus is small, it will not deliver much if the range is set at a high minimum. When we set the cluster size at 4, its minimum frequency at 4 and the minimum range at 1, the search delivers 11 hits for clusters containing the token *dog*. Three of those clusters occur in a single text each. When the range minimum is increased to 4, we are left with three hits: *dog to be at*, *dog under proper control*, *dog will be liable*. The cluster *dog will be liable* is more significant than *dog by pulling a scab off*, because it occurs in more than one court case, which means that a dog owner's liability is a much more common issue in case law than someone antagonising a dog by picking at its wounds.

Ultimately, paying attention to words that form patterns because they co-occur regularly could communicate valuable information about a contested word and its semantic relation to other words and concepts.

7.5. Simple word searches for legal interpretation

If a statutory interpreter decides to use a corpus to help clarify the meaning of a contested word or phrase, he or she will probably do so to decide either its ordinary or technical meaning. Even though a more thorough corpus analysis could provide insight into more complex word problems, it is unlikely the aim of such an interpreter to launch a linguistic study of discovery. A statutory interpreter must be guided here by the prototypicality of the searched term. The more common it is, the greater the chances of it being an ordinary word with a widely accepted meaning; the further away from the prototypical radius, the less likely it is to be a word with common usage. The following search illustrations are based on this principle.

As mentioned before in this chapter, online corpora have user-friendly software interfaces, which means that a corpus user does not need a separate software programme to search those corpora. However, if a user employs a corpus stored in a computer file or central database, he or she will need a software programme to carry out analysis. Two well-known software packages are WordSmith Tools and AntConc. WordSmith Tools is licenced and requires payment in British pounds, whereas AntConc is free to download. Both packages are updated every few years and many tutorial videos and user guides exist to assist users with tools and troubleshooting. AntConc was used when non-web based corpora were consulted.

7.5.1 Search methods

How should we attempt a KWIC search? If a corpus is very large, it can (and will) provide hundreds or thousands of concordance lines. Reading through all of them for clues is not only time consuming, but it can also be very daunting. Scholars suggest different approaches (Baker 2010:21):

1. study 100 concordance lines for general linguistic patterns and 30 lines for detailed patterns;[14]
2. select 30 lines at random to record patterns, followed by another 30 lines until no new patterns are noticed;
3. select the first 30 lines to make a hypothesis and then carry out a more refined search based on the hypothesis.

Stubbs (2002:45) further suggests three principles:

1. study words in collocations;
2. check the findings from one corpus against another, independent corpus;
3. if there are any counter-examples, they must be checked carefully.

Generally, we can use a combination of these approaches depending on the word and the nature of the disagreement. If we suspect that a word has many nuanced senses, we could study more than 100 concordance lines and conduct additional searches of isolated hits.

When we do searches, we can use a **wildcard** to list various word forms simultaneously. The wildcard itself is an asterisk attached to the end of the lexeme, word stem or affix.[15] For example, searching *laugh** in the LOB corpus delivers hits for *laugh*, *laughter*, *laughing* and *laughed*. See figure 7.3 below.

1	to be plunged in at random ? He 'd learned to	**laugh**	when something went wrong or the situation became ludicrous ,

14 When we talk about *patterns*, we are referring to repetition. Repetition often occurs naturally in language and it is these repetitions that may reveal something about both the speaker, the speech community and the meaning being conveyed. See Hunston (2012).

15 It can also be attached to the front of a lexical item. For example, **gin* will deliver hits for *origin* as well as *begin*.

2	swamped with aid or blown OFF the map . Love and	**laughter,**	he feels , engender more happiness than politics or philanthropy .
3	muffet " — " Miss Muffet and the spider " he had explained and	**laughed**	at her . " What are you going to do ? " she
4	in a great glass house ; shadows moving with music and	**laughter.**	Now a brighter rectangle of light appeared in the
5	when she was young . " Come on ! " she called , nervous and	**laughing. "**	He 's shy . Poor Mark . " Perhaps he sensed that

Figure 7.3: Example of a wildcard

Some software programmes include a feature called *regex*, which stands for *regular expressions.* It works the same as a wildcard, but is a lot more powerful. For instance, if we use regex to search *laugh*, it will provide all the word forms that uses it as a stem: *laughter*, *laughingly* and *laughable.* But it will include words like *slaughter*, *onslaught* and even the name *Laughton* as well.

The *sorting* tool is another useful feature. Once concordance results are displayed, we can sort the lines in a number of ways to find regularities a lot easier. We can sort the same results for *laugh** (or *laugh* in regex) by selecting *center to right*, which will list the same word forms together, followed by sorting the first and second words on the node's right. This will expose patterns. See figure 7.4 below.

1	not depends entirely on my efforts — alone and unaided ! " He	**laughed**	**at her** crestfallen expression . " I love to tease you
2	muffet " — " Miss Muffet and the spider " he had explained and	**laughed**	**at her** . " What are you going to do ? " she
3	Lois was in the room . She heaved a sigh , then	**laughed**	**at herself** for being so silly and self-pitying .
4	Jimmy brought two lobsters , dressed ready for the table . Nan	**laughed**	**when she** saw them . " I saw you out on

5	cattle to be the cause of an accident . Gloria had	**laughed**	**when she** told him how she had accounted for
6	as he saved to appease the hunger and they both	**laughed**	**when the** false economy dawned on them . She bought
7	provided that it ‘s short , sharp and rewarding . “ They both	**laughed**	**and felt** relaxed . Then Ormston frowned and went on , “
8	that ‘s your country , why are you here ? “ His lips	**laughed**	**and the** rashness in him glowed hot again and
9	ca n’t withhold permission once we ‘re determined . “ She	**laughed**	**softly against** his ear . “ It ‘s remotely possible that
10	bargain just because you ca n’t hold her . “ Gregory	**laughed**	**softly and** smoothed his brown wavy hair . “ I can

Figure 7.4: Example of sorting center to the right

As we can see in figure 7.4, sorting displays patterns that allow us to make inferences. For instance, we see that laughing is usually directed at someone or something (the preposition *at*), laughter is often an affect caused by something else (the relative pronoun *when*) and it is something that has a measurable audibility, which connotes semantic information (the adverb *softly*). If we sort the lines to the left, we find another pattern. See figure 7.5 below.

1	as he saved to appease the hunger and **they both**	**laughed**	when the false economy dawned on them . She bought
2	going to be all that bad ? If it **is — “ she**	**laughed**	uncertainly — “you can have your ring back . “ She loosened
3	same kind . “ “You read the wrong sort of **newspapers , Cedric , “**	**laughed**	Tarrant , but he felt less confident than he sounded .
4	bargain just because you ca n’t hold **her . “ Gregory**	**laughed**	softly and smoothed his brown wavy hair . “ I can
5	not depends entirely on my efforts — alone and **unaided ! “ He**	**laughed**	at her crestfallen expression . “ I love to tease you

Figure 7.5: Example of sorting center to the left

Figure 7.5 shows that the act of laughing is preceded by a subject, which is primarily a person. (Although see line 3, where the subject follows the verb.) It seems to be a human reaction.

Before we continue, a friendly word of caution: guard against *confirmation bias* (McEnery and Hardie 2012:14–16). It is easy to approach a corpus with your mind made up. This implies that the user already has a theory in mind or has already decided what the answer is and now seeks confirmation in the corpus. The problem is that you will never be able to prove the theory wrong, because the corpus will probably give you what you want. One way to prevent confirmation bias as far as possible is to use the entire corpus and not to start selecting only those corpus samples that benefit the theory.[16] Another way of approaching a query is merely to be as objective as possible. Use a corpus to see what results come up; corpora almost always offer a few surprises and nuances that a user did not expect. It will also be helpful for a user to briefly explain how he or she conducted a search. This will ensure that anyone else will be able to replicate the search and come to the same findings. Consequently, replicability shows that the user has nothing to hide and did not try to manipulate the data.

7.5.2 Case study: *incidental* and *money*

At the start of this book, we looked at the word *incidental* and ABC Mining's argument that their purchase of prospecting rights were incidental costs.[17] We saw that *incidental* means something is an irregular manifestation. However, another sense of the word denotes that something happens as a result of something else – a cause and effect. This might have been the argument the applicant was trying to make: before they can start prospecting, they need prospecting rights. When we use a wildcard to search the LOB corpus, we see 27 hits reflecting two word types: *incidental* and *incidentally*. The latter is used as a discourse marker throughout the concordance and does not provide any semantic information related to our query. When we isolate *incidental*, we are left with three hits. Although the results are very infrequent, all three hits refer to the first sense: namely, an extra of some kind, not a necessity. Following Stubbs' advice to pay attention to collocates and to compare our results with that of another corpus, our three hits are validated by the BNC. When we sort the concordance lines center and to the right, it offers the following collocates:

16 Of course, as McEnery and Hardie (2012:15) point out, a balanced corpus is itself a pre-selection of samples and it is scientifically sound to conduct studies on isolated samples. Nevertheless, it is about the way an investigator uses or manipulates the data to satisfy a language query.

17 *ABC Mining (Pty) Ltd v Commissioner for the South African Revenue Service* (IT24606) [2021] ZATC (25 February 2021), paras 2 and 61.

7.2 incidental adjustments; incidental benefit; incidental boxes; incidental by-products; incidental catch(es).

The results become even more interesting when collocates include multiword units like

7.3 incidental and consequential orders; incidental and irrelevant consideration; incidental and unplanned smoking education.

In addition, the BNC offers collocates with *cost* and *expenses*:

7.4 miscellaneous incidental costs including vet's fees; incidental expenses like buying carpets; incidental expenses of the committee – phone bills.

Studying less than a hundred concordance lines provides natural occurring evidence that confirms our initial suspicion that *incidental* signifies something extra.

In *Feldman v Midgin*, the Supreme Court of Appeal had to decide whether the word *money* included *cheques* or were restricted to cash and coins; the court *a quo* decided it was inclusive but the SCA disagreed.[18] Searching either *money* or *cheque* by themselves does not offer much clarity about any superordinate relationship between *money* and its potential inclusion of *cheque.* Back in the day, when cheques were a lot more common, people were usually given a choice to pay cash or by cheque. The phrase *cash or cheque* is a regular expression. Conducting a search for collocates should therefore provide better results. The BNC cites 63 instances in which *cash* and *cheque* collocate; sometimes together with *credit card*: 'pay either by cheque or credit card (no coins)'; 'move away from cash transactions to cheque and credit card'. The results also show that a cheque is something you can cash. Still, the collocation of *cash or cheque* provides little evidence that *money* excludes cheques. One hit actually says 'cash includes cheque payments, bank transfers and credit card payments' (which looks like a very specific definition). In order to understand the collocation of *cash or cheque* better, we must change our question somewhat: is *cash* a synonym for *money*? If it is, then it means that a cheque is considered something else.

When we search *cash* and *money* as collocates, the BNC reveals 79 hits that imply a synonymous relation between the two words. Here are some of the most common results:

18 *Feldman v Midgin* 2006 (6) SA 12 (SCA) para 1. In addition, see Carney (2020: 295–296).

7.5 ...got the money to pay for cash on delivery...; ...cash money...; ...shares for cash and invest that money...; ...discount if they pay, and that money...; ...money was withdrawn in cash...; ... draw money from a cash machine...; ...cash, commission-free foreign money...; ...savings include cash, money in the bank...; ...money, preferably cash...; ...cash machines sweep money from your Current Account...; ...cash position in the money market...

Theoretically speaking, a cheque is probably a form of money in terms of a medium of exchange. However, in common usage the word *money* is prototypically associated with *cash*, which is something separate from a cheque. When we confirm the results in the Corpus of Canadian English,[19] we see 31 hits that verify cash is often considered a physical form of money:

7.6 ...money in the cash register...; ...money missing from the cash register...; ...you haven't brought any cash money...; ...pick up cash at a Money Mart location...; ...up to $20 cash – for pocket money...; ...money from the cash drawer...; ...enough money in its cash reserves...; ...you wire the money by cash off to a third country...; ...after failing to cash the money...

The concordance lines include one reference to 'cash money orders or cheques for more money'. This points toward the possibility that a cheque is perceived as a form of money, but the fact that it only appears once in the 31 hits is indicative that it is not prototypical.

7.5.3 Case study: *which* and *remarriage*

In *Lueven Metals (Pty) Ltd v CSARS*,[20] the court was approached for a declaratory order to clarify the conditions for the sale of gold levied at a zero VAT rating. Section 11(1)(*f*) of the Value Added Tax Act 89 of 1991 states:

> (f) the supply is to the South African Reserve Bank, the South African Mint Company (Proprietary) Limited or any deposit-taking institution registered under the Deposit-taking Institutions Act, 1990 (Act No. 94 of 1990), of gold in the form of bars, ingots,

19 The Canadian corpus, also known as the Strathy Corpus of Canadian English, comprises 50 million words and was collected between 1920 and 2010; it is a balanced corpus.

20 *Lueven Metals (Pty) Ltd v CSARS* (31356/2021) [2022] ZAGPPHC 325 (19 May 2022).

> buttons, wire, plate or granules or in solution, which has not undergone any manufacturing process other than the refining thereof or the manufacture or production of such bars, ingots, buttons, wire, plate, granules or solution.

Justice Davis highlights the fact that paragraph (*f*) contains a relative clause that starts with the pronoun *which*.[21] To be more precise, this is a restrictive relative clause. Generally, it has two functions: it describes the noun or noun phrase preceding the clause and it limits the description to the preceding noun or noun phrase. It does the same work as an adjective, but it is quite essential to the complex sentence and cannot be left out without affecting the entire sentence.

If necessary, a corpus could be used to confirm this grammatical feature and its ordinary meaning by comparing corpus examples with the legislative text. The sentence in paragraph (*f*) is *gold ... which has not undergone any manufacturing process other than the refining thereof...* Using the Brown corpus, we see many restrictive relative clauses that share the same syntactic structure as the legislative draft.

The pronoun *which* occurs 3561 times in the corpus. If we sort hits center to the left, the concordance lines show many examples where *which* is preceded by a preposition (in which, through which, under which). Even though restrictive relative clauses may contain prepositions, we want to match the clause in the Act as much as possible. See figure 7.6, where the pronoun follows the noun immediately.

1	ratings were made on the basis of a **point system**	**which**	was developed after studying the distributions of actual behaviors
2	to be sorted out and handled within a **political system**	**which**	moves by consent in relation to an external environment
3	The **transportation system**	**which**	serves the National Forests is a complex of highways
4	During all his busy life he had only **done things**	**which**	had to be done . This habit had become so
5	to fear in this age of nuclear weapons, **dreadful things**	**which**	are too horrible to contemplate. I doubt that "fear

21 *Lueven Metals (Pty) Ltd v CSARS* (31356/2021) [2022] ZAGPPHC 325 (19 May 2022), paras 5.2–5.3.

6	a metropolitan area are related in different ways **from those**	**which**	are characteristic of the comprehensive high school described in
7	elements which capture his liberal and humanistic imagination **are those**	**which**	make the English story worth telling and worth remembering .
8	is fully competent to deal with any element **of experience**	**which**	arises from an object in space and time . When ,
9	of a home rule charter was cited as **a factor**	**which**	has caused the Citizens Group to obtain signatures under
10	He supervised the cleanups and handled the shipments of **raw gold**	**which**	each week went out to San Francisco . Hague

Figure 7.6: Example of restrictive relative clause starting with *which*

Figure 7.6 shows that each noun in the main clause is modified by a relative clause. If we were to delete the additional description, the noun or noun phrase would communicate an incomplete thought. Take lines 1 and 6 as examples. Line 1 says that ratings were made according to a point system. Without the relative clause, we do not know much about the point system in use. Line 6 is even more unclear without the relative clause. It says that the identified metropolitan area is different from other areas, but without the relative clause the specified differences remain unknown.

In *CB v HB*,[22] the court considered the meaning of *remarriage* and had to determine whether cohabitation and a religious ceremony meant a couple remarried. Writing for the majority, Appellate Justice Mocumie found that the wedding ceremony did not satisfy any of the requirements set by section 29A of the Marriage Act; therefore, the situation did not constitute a remarriage.[23] Dissenting, Appellate Justice Makgoka argued that there were plenty of examples in South Africa where cohabitation qualified as common-law marriages, which means that this particular situation qualified as a remarriage as well.[24] Does a corpus search provide any clarity?

When we attempt a KWIC search in the BNC, it becomes apparent that *divorce* and *remarriage* co-occur quite often. This indicates that both are recognised rituals. *Cohabitation* and *remarriage* also collocate, but

22 *CB v HB* 2021 (6) SA 332 (SCA).
23 *CB v HB* 2021 (6) SA 332 (SCA), paras 14–17; Marriage Act 25 of 1961.
24 *CB v HB* 2021 (6) SA 332 (SCA), paras 29, 31–34.

not nearly as frequently. From these preliminary results, we can tell that cohabitation is not commonly seen as remarriage; instead, cohabitation, divorce and remarriage are separate states of events. Below are some examples taken from concordance lines:

7.7 ...cohabitation prior to remarriage has also increased...; ...keep their pensions on remarriage and operates no cohabitation rules...; ...does not actually forbid remarriage for those whose partner has died...; ...one in three marriages in 1986 was a remarriage for one or both partners...; ...the frequency of remarriage after divorce...; ...the rate of remarriage among divorced women...; ...the death of his mother, the remarriage of his father...; ...or on the happening of a specified event (such as remarriage of the wife) if earlier rather than have repayment of his...; ...and 4% involved the remarriage of two divorcees...; ...a widow on the death of her husband, her remarriage or prospects of remarriage should not be taken into account...

Using the COCA to confirm results, we see once more that *divorce* and *remarriage* collocate frequently, whereas *remarriage* co-occurs infrequently with *cohabitation*. Once again, preliminary results imply that cohabitation is something separate to (re)marriage in common parlance. It is often indicated as one *or* the other. See examples taken form concordance lines:

7.8 ...separation, divorce or bereavement, and may arise through cohabitation, marriage or remarriage...; ...legal marital status without including information about cohabitation or remarriage...; ...private sector schemes are increasingly permitting widows to keep their pensions on remarriage and operate no cohabitation rules...; ...The period of cohabitation prior to remarriage has also increased in the 1980s, from 28 months in 1979 to 34 months...; ...live with a natural mother and stepfather in a reconstituted family formed by cohabitation or remarriage...; ...similarly, a one parent family may become a two parent family through marriage or remarriage, reconciliation or cohabitation...; ...he interrupted their remarriage ceremony to convince her not to take him back...; ...use the medallion in their remarriage ceremony...; ...unless participants have had an annulment, their remarriage can't be sanctioned...; ...divorce rate after remarriage is declining...; ...the process of a remarriage licence is the same

> as for a marriage licence...; ...after her father's death and mother's remarriage...

As Appellate Justice Makgoka pointed out in his dissent, the ex-wife wanted to create the impression that she was a newly married Christian woman who did not live in sin, but she did not want to register the marriage for fear of losing her monthly maintenance from her ex-husband. That said, her cohabitation does not constitute a marriage under South African law.

The following section provides guidelines on how to build a corpus.

7.6. Building and designing your own corpus

Nelson (2012:54) reminds us that many corpora already exist; as such we must ask ourselves why a new corpus would be necessary. Building a new corpus will partly depend on the needs of its user. Reasons may vary from access to existing corpora to motivations for specialist corpora. Building a corpus can therefore be a worthwhile venture. With legal practice and scholarship in mind, a corpus of legal texts like legislation, judgments, court transcripts and / or textbooks can benefit various statutory and / or case-related queries like searching all the cases decided by a specific judge, searching the use of a word across several cases, or studying the way a concept is defined or debated either within a single sample (genre) or throughout the entire corpus. It will allow a user to scrutinise the way legislative drafters use words in different acts and bylaws. Corpora like these make language enquiries into specific legal texts that much easier.

That said, because corpora are well-structured databases of linguistic data, a corpus builder must keep several factors in mind when planning and designing a corpus. The subsections that follow will briefly discuss each of these factors in terms of building a legal corpus primarily for statutory interpretation and comprising case decisions only (a Case Law corpus). However, other corpora can be built on the same principles.

7.6.1 Size, sampling and balance

Building a corpus to conduct statutory interpretation searches, means that it should be of a considerable size. The main motivation behind a large corpus (as opposed to a smaller, specialised corpus) is for the statutory interpreter to be able to identify prototypicality and to see whether a searched word is used as an ordinary word or a term. For a corpus to do this and for search results to carry any weight or provide any trustworthy insight, it has to be large. Keep in mind that such a corpus is supposed to represent the legal fraternity's use and understanding of both technical and ordinary language. A large corpus would enable users to conduct searches that cover a much wider range; this will prevent language phenomena from looking noteworthy but in fact only occur in a single text. Considering how many judgments are produced per year, it would not be difficult to reach a large size rather quickly.

To ensure that a corpus is representative, its builder must pay close attention to both sampling and balance. Remember that a corpus is itself a sample of a language variety, in this particular instance, case law (statutory interpretation and the language of judges) (Nelson 2012:56-57). Generally, a sample represents one text. The corpus creator must decide which texts to include in the corpus, and how many. Selecting samples can be tricky. The COCA comprises samples from at least eight sample categories:

- TV/Movie subtitles,
- spoken texts,
- fiction,
- popular magazines,
- newspapers,
- academic journals,
- blogs, and
- web pages.

Each of these categories contain samples taken from different sources. The category for fiction contains samples from short stories, plays, movie scripts and the first chapters of books. Short stories were taken from various sources like magazines. Together, this sample set tallies 120 million words. In the event of a Case Law corpus, a builder can employ opportunistic sampling, which means that samples are taken from where they can be found (Nelson 2012:58). However, sample categories can be divided between:

- magistrates courts,
- high courts;
- specialist courts (labour, tax, equality),
- supreme court of appeal, and
- the constitutional court.

Because this corpus could be a monitor corpus and can essentially be updated regularly, it would be better to set a minimum sample size (and not a target size).

There is also the issue of inclusiveness. Should a Case Law corpus include cases that were decided before a certain year or era? There are clear historical periods that can easily be divided by prominent dates like 1910, 1961 and 1994. The corpus builder must decide how inclusive the corpus should be, or whether it would be better to have two separate corpora – a contemporary and a historical corpus.

Another issue to consider is language. Many judgements were written in Afrikaans and some in isiXhosa and Sepedi. For purely practical reasons, it is advisable to limit a corpus to one language and to rather create a separate sub-corpus of Case Law in additional languages and to label each accordingly.

For general language corpora to be representative, the sampling must be balanced. This means that the corpus should contain more or less the same number of samples per genre. This does not necessarily apply to a specialist corpus in the same way (Weisser 2016:32). An opportunistic corpus makes no claims of following rigorous sampling techniques; instead, they represent nothing more than the data collected for its purpose (McEnery and Hardie 2012:11). Take the Corpus of US Supreme Court Opinions as an example. It is built solely out of one sample type, namely Supreme Court decisions. It contains texts from the 1790s to the 2010s and its collection is divided into decades. None of the decades has the same number of texts. It is balanced by the type of text and the type of corpus itself.

7.6.2 Chosen data

Data can be gathered from different places. Some information is available in the public domain (with or without a creative commons licence) while other data is private. It goes without saying that a corpus builder needs the necessary copyright permission and ethical clearance for any data that is not freely available. Creating a corpus is not merely a matter of collecting what you want. Available online corpora have already gone the extra mile to negotiate the necessary copyright allowances and to ask the required permission to include any data collected from human participants. Because law reports are published to the public domain, it should be permissible to compile them into a corpus that is either used privately or made available to the greater public. However, a corpus creator must ensure that he or she does not include any texts that are protected by copyright laws or have any ethical implications. Consider the fact that law reports often contain names of people and that their privacy could be affected. What are the legal and ethical implications, even when the texts are taken from the public domain?[25]

25 McEnery and Hardie (2012:62) cite examples of ethical issues regarding spoken texts. Some of these texts not only contain personal identifiers

7.6.3 Preparing data for entry

A document like a judgment contains all kinds of meta-data, which provide necessary information related to the actual body of the text. Some of the information appears at the top and some at the bottom of the document, enveloping the main text. Let us take the SCA's recent decision in *Qurashi v S* as an example; see figure 7.7.[26]

THE SUPREME COURT OF APPEAL OF SOUTH AFRICA
JUDGMENT

Reportable
Case No: 1166/2018

In the matter between:

SALEEM QURASHI	**FIRST APPELLANT**
FARHAN ULLAH	**SECOND APPELLANT**
SHABBIR GULLAM	**THIRD APPELLANT**

and

THE STATE	**RESPONDENT**

Neutral citation:	*Qurashi and Others v The State* (Case no 1166/2018) [2022] ZASCA 118 (22 August 2022)
Coram:	PONNAN, VAN DER MERWE, and CARELSE JJA and MAKAULA and PHATSHOANE AJJA
Heard:	10 May 2022
Delivered:	22 August 2022
Summary:	Criminal law and procedure – admission of evidence pursuant to

search and seizure allegedly in violation of constitutional right to privacy and fair trial – distinction between real and self-incriminatory or conscriptive testimonial evidence

Figure 7.7: Example of meta-data in a judgment

Weisser (2016:34–35) uses the terms *header* and *footer* to differentiate between the meta-data at the top and the information at the bottom. In figure 7.7, the header contains the national coat of arms and the name of the court. It states that the case is reportable and cites the case number.

like names but they often also enclose private data like credit card numbers. Personal information must be anonymized before they can be included in a corpus.

26 *Qurashi v S* (1166/2018) [2022] ZASCA 118 (22 August 2022).

All the parties involved are listed as well as the presiding officers who attended to the case. A neutral citation is provided along with the hearing date, the report date and a summary of the facts and decision. Some judgments also contain a list of all the cases cited. This particular case contains two main headings separating the order from the judgment. The footer includes the details of the relevant law firms and the public prosecutor as well as the names of two judges. In addition, the footer contains footnotes.

When reading a judgment as a law report, the meta-data are important for the overall interpretation of the judgement, which includes its organisation and layout. However, it does not contribute to what Weisser (2016: 34) calls the *meaning potential* of the text. The meaning potential is the part of a text that provides the most salient linguistic data. If we leave the meta-data in the text and use the entire document as it is, it will influence the search results. Currently, the text contains unnecessary repetition that function as an organisational summary but contribute almost nothing linguistically for general assumption. For instance, if a corpus holds 50 law reports that deal with unlawful property searches, header information like *reportable* or *case number* contribute nothing linguistically to any potential semantic or pragmatic queries. The same applies to the phrase *in the matter between*. Meta-data like this are the same for every law report. To prevent redundancy from occurring, it is necessary to cut the meta-data that cause linguistic noise.

Take note that it is not necessary to discard the meta-data entirely. This information is usually stored in a different file or as part of the annotation of the corpus text. If the corpus is constructed as an online resource, the meta-data will probably be embedded into an HTML tag of some kind. The user would still need this information in order to cite the cases as evidence or justification. If a user wants to scrutinise a particular case in more detail, the meta-data will enable him or her to do so.

Before a document can be scrubbed for corpus use, it must be converted from its existing file format (often PDF) to plain text format (TXT) to make it easier for software programmes to read and for web designers to encode.[27] Some meta-data such as visual information does not convert to plain text and is therefore not readable in software programmes. The coat of arms in the header of figure 7.7 is a good

27 Working within Windows, once a document has been converted to plain text format, the document will open in Notepad (or similar versions like Notepad++). This is the ideal text editor to make changes to a corpus document. For Mac, consider TextWrangler. See Weisser (2016:46–48) for more detail.

example. Also, the coat of arms contributes nothing to any future linguistic searches. See figure 7.8 for an example of a plain text version of *Qurashi v S.*

```
THE SUPREME COURT OF APPEAL OF SOUTH AFRICA
JUDGMENT
Reportable
Case No: 1166/2018
FIRST APPELLANT
SECOND APPELLANT
THIRD APPELLANT
RESPONDENT
In the matter between:
SALEEM QURASHI
FARHAN ULLAH
SHABBIR GULLAM
and
THE STATE
Neutral citation: Qurashi and Others v The State (Case no 1166/2018)
[2022]
Coram:
Heard:
Delivered:
Summary:
ZASCA 118 (22 August 2022)
PONNAN, VAN DER MERWE, and CARELSE JJA and
MAKAULA and PHATSHOANE AJJA
10 May 2022
22 August 2022
Criminal law and procedure - admission of evidence pursuant to
search and seizure allegedly in violation of constitutional right
to privacy and fair trial
- distinction between real and self-incriminatory or conscriptive
testimonial evidence
- hearsay evidence - admissibility of extra-curial statements by
a non-testifying
```

Figure 7.8: Example of a plain text conversion

As can be seen from figure 7.8, the converter extracted the information from the PDF document to a plain text format. However, the information in the header is not in the correct place. The information that is supposed to be next to *coram*, *heard* and *delivered* have shifted to the summary section. This happens often, which means that the corpus creator must continue to edit a text to ensure that it is ready for inclusion. Figure 7.9 below provides another perspective on the necessity to comb a text for conversion problems. From this example, it is clear that there is unnecessary white space and that sentences are separated by artificial line breaks. The white spaces and the line breaks have to be corrected otherwise it will 'interfere with the processing of the text later and even create a number of problems that could affect the meaningfulness of at least part of your data for linguistic analysis' (Weisser 2016:56). The converted text in figure 7.9 includes the first footnote, which has inserted itself in the middle of paragraph 2. Following the footnote, we see an upwards pointing arrow next to a 3. Why are they there? The arrow and the 3 represent the page number. The footnote and page number must be scrubbed from the text.[28]

```
[2]

Count 1 relates to the alleged participation of the accused in
organised criminal

gang activity in contravention of s 9 of POCA. And, that as part
of a pattern of such

1 The fact that the accused and several of the witnesses were
Pakistani nationals would appear to have

resulted in names not always being consistently spelt. For example,
whilst the name of appellant 3 is

reflected in the indictment as Shabir Gullam, the evidence seems to
suggest that he is known as

Shabber Ghulam.

↑3

activity, the accused either individually or collectively committed
the various offences

set out in the indictment. The prosecution alleged that in November
2007, the four

deceased in counts 10 to 13, Malik Yasser Awan, Amanullah Nusrullam,
Shabodien

Hussein and Majid Saleem, who were also Pakistani nationals, were
lured to Clocolan

in the Free State, were they were robbed of a BMW sedan motor
vehicle, four Nokia
```

28 Of course, the corpus builder can decide what information must be included in a sample and what must be deleted. If it is believed that footnotes / endnotes provide valuable linguistic data, they can be included. Even so, the corpus builder (more specifically, the text editor) must create a protocol indicating which footnotes / endnotes to keep and where to place them within a sample. It is not advisable to edit samples without keeping track of serious changes or being consistent.

```
cellphones and two firearms (count 9). They were then murdered and
buried in a

shallow grave (counts 10, 11, 12 and 13).
```

Figure 7.9: Example of necessary editing in converted text

Figure 7.10 represents a text that has been scrubbed clean and which can be used for corpus analysis or be encoded for online use. The example in figure 7.10 no longer contains line breaks, white space, page numbers (or arrows) or the footnote visible in figure 7.9.

```
[2] Count 1 relates to the alleged participation of the accused in organised criminal gang activity in contravention of s 9 of POCA. And, that as part of a pattern of such activity, the accused either individually or collectively committed the various offences set out in the indictment. The prosecution alleged that in November 2007, the four deceased in counts 10 to 13, Malik Yasser Awan, Amanullah Nusrullam, Shabodien Hussein and Majid Saleem, who were also Pakistani nationals, were lured to Clocolan in the Free State, were they were robbed of a BMW sedan motor vehicle,four Nokia cellphones and two firearms (count 9). They were then murdered and buried in a shallow grave (counts 10, 11, 12 and 13).
```

Figure 7.10: Example of a clean copy

Thorough editing is a necessary requirement, whether a corpus builder adapts material in electronic format, converts text by optical scanning, or transfers it by keyboarding.[29] It is also possible to use web-based software programmes to build a corpus. Web-based corpus creators can build a corpus in minutes. Depending on the parameters set by its user, they collect the necessary texts from all over the web and compile them into a corpus (called *web-as-corpus*). However, these programmes are often subject to subscription fees and the user must still spend time in appraising the corpus to make sure each sample is clean, which is seldom the case. There is also the issue of copyright and ethical behaviour.

29 Optical scanning entails the conversion of printed material that is not available in electronic format. For this to work, the user needs Optical Character Recognition software. Keyboarding involves the transferring of a printed text by hand (more specifically, by keyboard) and is a lot more time consuming and expensive. If a corpus builder finds it necessary to include old cases that are available in print only, or that has been scanned using an ordinary scanner, such a text might have to be converted using one of these two methods. See Nelson (2012: 62).

Cleaning a sample text is time-consuming work, even more so when a corpus comprises thousands of texts. Yet it is a necessary step in building a reliable corpus.

7.6.4 Annotation

As mentioned before, some corpora are annotated. We also differentiated between two types of information included as annotations: meta-data and linguistic data. Meta-data would typically include header information (information signifying details about the case), whereas linguistic data would typically include parts of speech tagging (also known as *POS-tagging*).

A corpus builder can decide to annotate a corpus if annotation is believed to contribute to the corpus. It is not a requirement. Some linguists feel it is better to leave a corpus as unprocessed as possible, while others argue for both tagged and untagged versions. If a corpus builder requires a more complex tagging inventory, it must be added manually or by using special software or algorithms. Essentially, tagging involves the insertion of an identifier at the end of a chosen token. It will look something like this: house_NN or house_NOUN, which indicates that *house* is a singular noun. Figure 7.11 shows what *Qurashi v S* looks like once the sample has been tagged using the TagAnt software programme.

Annotation is a scientific method of classifying data and systematically analysing results. Not only can it aid semantic and grammar analysis, but POS-tagging also goes a long way to help clarify ambiguous words, especially grammatical polysemy (Weisser 2016:102). The word *house* is both a noun and a verb just as *that* is simultaneously a relative pronoun and a determiner. Tagging helps to indicate the difference. A few established tag sets exist and form the basis for most tagging conventions in corpus linguistics. Once a corpus builder has tagged the corpus, it is a good idea to run a few tests to ensure that the tags transferred correctly.

```
Count_PROPN 1_NUM relates_VERB to_ADP the_DET alleged_ADJ
participation_NOUN of_ADP the_DET accused_VERB in_ADP organised_
ADJ criminal_NOUN gang_NOUN activity_NOUN in_ADP contravention_
NOUN of_ADP s_NOUN 9_NUM of_ADP POCA_NOUN ._PUNCT And_CCONJ ,_
PUNCT that_SCONJ as_ADP part_NOUN of_ADP a_DET pattern_NOUN of_ADP
such_ADJ activity_NOUN ,_PUNCT the_PRON accused_VERB either_CCONJ
individually_ADV or_CCONJ collectively_ADV committed_VERB the_DET
various_ADJ offences_NOUN set_VERB _SPACE out_ADP _SPACE in_ADP _
SPACE the_DET _SPACE indictment_NOUN ._PUNCT
```

Figure 7.11: Example of a tagged text

Apart from solving ambiguity, tagging may help by isolating certain data faster. For elementary searches, we can use tags to limit our query to very specific word types like the simple past tense verb *manufactured*. Let us take another example: if we want to determine whether the phrase *dispose of* co-occurs with the noun *bodies* among other nouns, we can conduct a search in the Corpus of US Supreme Court Opinions where we combine our search term with a noun tag. The results will isolate all the nouns in the corpus that cluster with *dispose of*, making it easy to check for its co-occurrence with *bodies* and all other nouns. In this instance, the results indicate that most people dispose of *property*, *land*, *income* and *claims*. Because the US Supreme Court does not often deal with murder cases, it should not be strange that the corpus results do not mention *bodies* (or other references to human remains).

Lastly, the naming convention of samples must enjoy the required attention. Corpus software is designed in such a way that a user can access individual texts for further scrutiny. For this to be possible, the name of each text must be visible. The best naming convention for a Case Law corpus is simply to use the full citation of the law report as the file name. That way users have immediate access to crucial information, which will allow users to search related information regarding the case.

Even though annotation can aid complex searches and provide rich data, ordinary searches based on lexemes (tokens and types) will suffice for statutory interpretation. Yet, seeing as tagging software makes annotation a lot easier, a corpus builder may consider having both tagged and untagged versions.[30]

7.6.5 Data storage and retrieval

An important consideration when planning a corpus is where to store it and how to retrieve corpus data once it is built. This depends largely on who the corpus is meant for. If an independent researcher chooses to create a Case Law or Legislation corpus for his or her own use, that corpus can be stored in a computer file of some kind. Whenever the user needs it, he or she can load it into a chosen software package and analyse the data.

If the corpus is meant for more than one individual, it can still be archived and shared as a computer file (like a ZIP file), or uploaded onto a storage cloud that provides identified users access. Both standard computer files and cloud storage options make it easy for users to add new

30 Many corpus analysis software programmes have the option to hide tags, which means that ordinary searches remain possible without seeing the tags in the concordance window.

files to the corpus, often through a drag-and-drop action. So far, these options are the most cost effective.

At this point, a juvenile corpus will probably consist of hundreds or thousands of separate documents, each representing individual samples. It is possible to combine a number of samples (say, 100) into a single plain text document. This will reduce the number of individual documents and make it a lot easier to load corpus files into the software package.[31] It is also possible to create a corpus database using software packages like AntConc. This allows you to load all the plain text corpus documents and then to create a single database, which the user can archive under a chosen name. Whenever he or she needs the corpus, they can just select the database file within the software programme and start their investigation. This database file can be shared as a computer file as well.

If the corpus is meant for more people or even the general public, it is best to host the corpus on the web. In this case, the online corpus would have the necessary software and code language embedded. The creator can build its own web platform or the corpus can be handed over to existing platforms like SADiLAR. Of course, a creator can restrict access to the online portal and only allow a particular group of users like the judiciary, or legal practitioners and scholars, to use it. Some South African corpora are available to the public through online portals (like the ViVA corpus), but expect users to pay a fee or register for free if they are academic researchers.

7.7. Conclusion

Corpora are useful resources, especially when they are combined with other types of analysis like investigations into word relations and conceptual mapping. Even though corpora can be used in the place of dictionaries, the two work well together. A statutory interpreter can start by consulting a dictionary and follow up with a corpus search to see how the dictionary data compares to real-life usage. Corpora are useful because they offer a window into pragmatic context and this helps to establish to what extent an ordinary word really is *ordinary* and prototypical.

It is also entirely possible for anyone to build a corpus. The fact that the Corpus of US Supreme Court Opinions was published to the web in 2017 is a sign that there is a need for specialised law corpora. Building a

31 It is important to indicate the number of sample texts present in a single corpus document, in order to keep track of the number of samples that comprise the corpus. This kind of information is included in the non-linguistic meta-data.

Case Law or Legislation corpus could be beneficial to the legal fraternity at large. However, for such a corpus to be truly effective, it has to be big. The American Case Law corpus contains 32 000 decisions, spanning 130 million words and more than 200 years – and it is updated regularly. A large corpus project requires a team to build it. It needs resources like people, money and time. The initial build is very time consuming, but once the corpus exists it will be much easier to update it by adding new law reports to the collection. As with the proposed digital dictionary of statutory terms, a law corpus can be built by any number of institutions: private law firms, university research programmes or the Department of Justice and Constitutional Development. There is no reason why such a project cannot be a shared, interdisciplinary venture.

8. Conclusion

Describing the relationship between law and linguistics, Kaplan (2020: 205) aptly says:

> I sometimes think of law as a giant ship proceeding ponderously through waves, difficult to turn, and linguistics as a solitary little tugboat trying to nudge the giant ship, a little, toward a better direction.

One of the reasons for this, Kaplan suggests, is that linguistics is not a field most people know much about. Even though law needs language to function, it does not depend on linguistics to be understood. He points out that linguistics is irrelevant to most areas of law, and where it does prove to be relevant most legal practitioners do not consider it important (Kaplan 2020:205). Linguistics plays a vital role in areas such as contracts, wills, legislative drafting and the interpretation of statutes. This is apparent in the language investigations and debates present in case law. South Africa, at least, is still a long way from seeing regular professional consultation between lawyers and linguists, partly because there is a tradition of ignoring or doubting linguistic expert reports when deciding cases. Also, there might be a belief that the legal practitioner is capable of employing linguistic analysis by him- or herself (which is often true). Furthermore, the two disciplines tend to keep to their own; they read their own journals and they attend their own conferences.[1] It makes interdisciplinary interaction difficult, to say the least. This book is a means to bridge the gap, or to nudge the ship ever so slightly.

As a language resource for law, the book was always meant as a basic exposure to linguistics and how it may assist legal interpretation. It was never meant as a comprehensive text on either linguistics or legal interpretation. Ultimately, the reader is encouraged to move beyond this text onto specialist works. That said, the book contributes to law in a number of important ways, I believe. Firstly, the book tries to provide readers with a new perspective on the concept of *meaning*, with a realisation that the task of assigning meaning is a lot more varied, and that the application of context and grammar is significantly more nuanced. The tugboat helps to direct the giant ship by shining a light on the various

1 There is a very small group of active forensic linguists in Southern Africa (currently fewer than 10), who are usually the only linguists present at law conferences. My attendance is usually met with surprise and confusion.

existing relations between words and phrases. This approach is actually already familiar in law, because the *eiusdem generis* canon concerns itself with words and the company they keep. Legal interpreters' understanding and experience with the canon merely needs some adjustment to extend the vast networks of word relations beyond the statutory context. Hopefully, readers will find what they need here, to make that adjustment.

Secondly, the book focuses attention on the value of non-verbal and stylistic communication. Admittedly, more research needs to be done on the admissibility of non-verbal evidence, which could pave the way for its inclusion in the interpretation effort. To me, however, this is an important caveat in legal interpretation because non-verbal and stylistic communication potentially contribute a lot toward the semantics and pragmatics of what is said and written. Its absence from investigations into equality and personality infringement cases, as well as language crimes like incitement and threats, is obvious. Without considering the non-verbal facts of a case, the interpretation will lack depth and sometimes even accuracy.

The book also aims at explaining why speakers often say one thing but mean something entirely different. This not only helps us understand the intention behind someone's words (what did someone really say?), but it also helps us to look out for any potential pitfalls in our own communication output. This is helpful to anyone responsible for writing any legal document, ranging from letters (containing warnings and the like) to contracts and statutes. What is the message behind the words? Speech acts and maxims for communication help us comprehend why misunderstandings occur and how to prevent them in future.

Furthermore, the book highlights the importance of dictionaries and corpora as linguistic resources for legal interpretation. The inclusion of these two linguistic tools stem from my own critical perspective of dictionaries as well as requests from legal practitioners to teach them how to use corpora. Regarding dictionaries, I agree with Christopher Hutton, who believes that judges should not be discouraged from using dictionaries. Instead, linguists can contribute to existing practice by providing guidelines on how to use dictionaries better. As for corpus application, a number of courts in the United States have already experimented with the use of corpora to gain better insight into ordinary meaning. Admittedly, using corpora can be tricky. But they can yield wonderful results even for elementary searches. And that is the point. Chapter 7 is not meant to train corpus linguists. In the end, being aware of limitations and knowing how to use both dictionaries and corpora goes a long way towards their successful application. They have the potential to contribute a lot when they are employed together with any of the other tools offered here.

Throughout the book, I have tried to do at least two things: I have illustrated the various ways that a legal interpreter can use basic linguistic tools to help clarify language related interpretation challenges, and I have provided linguistic background information to some of the reasons why courts are exposed to certain language related problems. The purpose of this book was to facilitate linguistic comprehension. Ultimately, understanding why something is a problem will help to solve it. Knowing which tools are available and how they work should also contribute to problem solving. I do not expect users of this book to apply every single tool to every situation. Rather, a number of tools are provided in order for readers to choose freely, depending on the problem that they face. It is possible to combine various tools, but it is not a requirement. Some language challenges are easily solved while others might necessitate a bit more effort.

Regardless of an investigator's chosen instrument, I wish to contribute towards a realisation that elementary linguistic analysis can assist those tasked with language inquiries to reach interesting and fulfilling clarification. Lastly, I hope this book inspires curiosity for language related research in law. Apart from questions concerning the admissibility of language evidence, so much more research in Southern Africa must be done: language, literacy and the law; language and legislative drafting; language and ordinary meaning; language and court interpreting services; language, trademarks and copyright; language and police interviews; and so on. The list is long and fascinating.

Glossary

Adjacency pairs: two utterances by two speakers, the one eliciting the other. During turn-taking, one speaker will say something which leads to a response. For example, if person A says *hello*, it will evoke a similar response from the interlocutor.

Ambiguity: the possibility of interpreting a word in more than one way; inexactness. For example, it is not clear who is wearing the pyjamas in the sentence *I walked the dog in striped pyjamas.*

Antonym: a lexical relation that expresses opposition. For example, hot x cold, student x teacher.

Body language: the body as message transmitter; communicating meaning by using different parts of the body. For example, the use of the facial cue *frowning*. See also *non-verbal communication.*

Circular definition: a description of a word in which the word itself or a derivative is used to describe it. This leads to circularity, which expects speakers to know the key term in the definition. For example, when *cellular phone* is defined as 'a phone that is cellular'.

Cluster: a cluster is an n-gram that features four or more words in sequence. For instance, if the phrase *God bless Africa and all its people* repeats regularly across different sample texts, this could be considered a cluster. See also *n-gram*.

Code-mixing: the use of two language varieties simultaneously. For example, in the mixing of German and English in one utterance: *Ach so, I didn't realise.*

Code-switching: the switch between two or more language varieties as a speaker's communication needs dictate. For example, when a speaker communicates with a friend in Setswana but then switches to isiZulu when he / she buys a bus ticket from a vendor.

Cognitive principle of relevance: a theory that states that speakers try to make their utterances as relevant as possible. Speakers do this, because they generally spend as little effort as possible in decoding messages. To ensure a message is relevant, speakers only include information that is easy to process.

Collocation: a relation between words that frequently co-occur together. For example, *financial interest, government policy.*

Communicative principle of relevance: a theory that states that a speaker produces optimally relevant information. In other words, a speaker's utterance is worth the listener's processing effort.

Concept: an abstract idea that is fundamental to thoughts and beliefs, often expressed through words and phrases. For example, *government* is a concept of an organisation used to administer a country's affairs, both internally and externally. See also *lexicalisation*.

Concordancer: a computer programme that can produce a concordance from a corpus. A concordance is a list of words in which a specified word is presented in its immediate context.

Connotation: the social, cultural or emotional association that speakers make when they hear or read a word or phrase; added meaning. For example, referring to someone as a *pig*, recalls negative association with the farm animal like filth, obesity and laziness.

Context (linguistic): the words of an utterance or written text that surround a contested word or phrase. For instance, the relevant section in a statute that a contested word belongs to, as well as the entire statute.

Context (physical): the time and space (the when and where) in which an utterance occurs or a written text exists. For instance, a written notice on a notice board at the door of a community supermarket.

Context: both the physical and linguistic situation in which communication takes place, either written or spoken; the verbal and non-verbal signals that help speakers process and decode messages. For example, in the utterance *What is the time of arrival?* information related to airports, flights and international travel contribute to the relevant context.

Convention: a way of acting or speaking agreed upon by a community and that manifests through frequent use. For example, the maxim that whoever arrives lasts must be the first to greet is a communication principle that was entrenched by communal agreement and through repetitive usage.

Conventional meaning: the meaning a speech community assigns to words and phrases and that might differ from a dictionary meaning or that of a different speech community. For example, the word *robot* signifies a traffic light in different South African vernaculars, but only refers to *computerised machines* in other varieties of English.

Cooperative Principle: a principle that aims at effective communication between speakers, based on four Gricean maxims. For example, when speakers talk, they must be as informative and honest as possible. See also *maxims*.

Corpus: a collection of language data comprising real-world texts that reflect actual language use. A corpus can consist of written and spoken data. For example, the British National Corpus, which contains 100 million words based on British English taken from various written and spoken texts.

Corpus (monitor): a corpus that is updated regularly in order to keep track of all the potential changes taking place in a language variety. The iWeb corpus is an example of a monitor corpus, because it collects English language data from across the web, which is added to the corpus on a daily basis.

Deixis: words or phrases used by speakers to point towards time, space and people is called deixis or deictic expressions. For example *his*, *there* and *today*.

Dialect: a variety of a language. It is often used to describe non-standard varieties of language that can be distinguished based on vocabulary, grammar, accent and geographical area. For example, Sepitori, a Sepedi-Setswana dialect spoken in the City of Tshwane and parts of the North-West Province.

Diglossia: the existence of two domains within one language; the higher domain is more formal and codified whereas the lower domain is less formal and less codified. Each domain has a communication function. For example, speakers use the higher domain for academic, religious and legal matters, and the lower domain for conversation, social interactions and instructions to servants.

Discourse marker: a word or phrase that helps to maintain both the cohesion and coherence of a text or discourse. In general, they vary between conjunctions, particles and words that express hierarchy and causality like *because*, *first*, *consequently*.

Entailment: an expression of logical consequence, used to test the truthfulness of statements. If P is true, then Q must be true as well. For example, if we say *John is completely bald* and *John is a man*, then the implication would be that all men are bald. But we know this is not true, which means that Q is not equal to P.

Expression: any physical form that represents a linguistic unit. It can range from words and phrases to full sentences, either written, spoken or signed. For example, the utterance *wow* and the sentence *come and get it* are both expressions in English.

Face: a person's social value when interacting with other people. When speaking, a person must pay attention to his or her own face as well as that of the interlocutors. Speakers attempt various strategies to ensure their face remains intact by reducing face-threatening acts. For example, when person A deliberately insults person B, B's face is affected negatively.

Face-saving strategies: communicative strategies aimed at minimising any potential damage to a person's face. For example, instead of imposing, provide a person with more than one option to respond. Hedging and attempts at making people feel good about themselves are additional strategies.

Face-threatening acts: an utterance or deed that has the potential of affecting either the speaker or the listener's face in a negative way. For example, criticising someone could affect that person's positive face (his/her positive self-image) in such a way that they might think less of themselves.

Felicity conditions: the conditions that determine whether an utterance is well-formed and successful. If an utterance meets the necessary pragmatic conditions, it is felicitous. When the opposite is true, the utterance is infelicitous. Utterances that are self-contradictory, irrelevant or pragmatically impossible are infelicitous, like when a judge sentences someone to death but formulates his sentencing as a question.

Field relation: a semantic field comprising a group of lexical items that refer to a particular subject or concept. For example, the word *pet* belongs to the field of *domestic animals*, ranging from house pets to exotic and farm animals. See also *semantic frame*.

Filler: a sound or word that a speaker uses during a conversation to signal a pause. It communicates to interlocutors that he or she is not done speaking and that they are not giving up their turn. Common examples include *um*, *ah* and *uh*.

Flouting and violating: when a cooperative speaker intentionally disobeys a maxim and the context provides enough clues for the listener to realise it, this is referred to as flouting a maxim. A speaker flouts a maxim in order to convey information indirectly. If he/she sarcastically says *I adore John*, the speaker is flouting the maxim of quality to express a dislike. When a speaker has no intention to adhere to any of the maxims but instead lies or deliberately misleads the listener, he/she violates the maxim of quality.

Frequency: a measurement used in corpus linguistic research, indicating how often a lexical item occurs in a corpus. Based on (in)frequency, a researcher may speculate about the lexical item's normative, conventional or prototypical use in a speech community.

Gesture: a form of non-verbal communication in both spoken and signed languages in which the body is used to communicate additional information, either accompanying speech (or signing) or independently.

For example, using hand signals to flag a minibus taxi in South Africa. See also *body language*.

Grammar word: words with little lexical meaning that express grammatical relationship among words; functional words. For example, prepositions, conjunctions, pronouns, articles and auxiliary verbs are grammar words.

Hedge: a word or phrase used to express ambiguity, uncertainty, caution or probability about the proposition communicated. This is often used as a means to escape commitment to what is being said, or to protect sensitive information. Hedges include words like *might*, *loosely speaking*, *someone told me that…*.

Homonym: words that look and sound the same, but have unrelated meanings. Can be distinguished between homographs (words that look the same) and homophones (words that sound the same). For example, the word *ring* refers both to a band on someone's finger and the sound a telephone or bell makes.

Hyponym: a lexical relation that expresses inclusion within a broader semantic field, often displayed in hierarchical form. A hyponym refers to a *type*. For example, *apple* is a type of *fruit* and therefore inclusive to the broader category *fruit*. A *Fuji apple* is a specific type or *apple*.

Idiolect: each individual speaker's unique language use, characterised by each speaker's grammar, vocabulary and accent. For example, when a speaker refers to a second ex-partner solely as *mistake twice removed*.

Illocutionary act: a speech act that has taken place through an utterance. For example, when a speaker says *I will pick up the kids after school*, the speaker makes a promise. See also *speech act*.

Illocutionary force: a speaker's intention in producing an utterance. It may take the form of a promise, a warning, an instruction, and so on. For example, when someone says *People caught eating on the train might have to pay a fine*, he/she expresses an assertive speech act, but his/her intention is a (friendly) warning.

Implicature: something a speaker suggests or implies indirectly through an utterance. For example, if speaker A says *I'm out of cash*, speaker B might reply *There's an ATM around the corner*. The implicature of speaker B's utterance is that there really is an ATM and that it is in a working condition. See also *cooperative principle*.

Impoliteness: intentional behaviour aimed at affecting another person's face negatively, also known as deliberate face-attack. Verbal abuse and personality infringements are examples of linguistic impoliteness.

Indirect speech act: performing illocutionary acts indirectly for various reasons like politeness and flirting. Speakers often communicate by way of indirect speech acts. For instance, when someone says *A cup of coffee would be great right now*, he/she is actually requesting the listener to go and make coffee.

Intercultural communication: communication between people of different cultural and language backgrounds; the effect of culture on communication between various groups. For example, a South African Indian woman speaking to an isiXhosa man.

Intonation: the use of spoken pitch to communicate the attitude and emotion of a speaker, often accompanied by other prosodic features like stress, loudness, tone and rhythm. For example, when a speaker makes a factual statement, he/she uses a falling pitch, but uses a rising pitch when asking a question. See also *prosody.*

Jargon: technical or specialised vocabulary used by a particular group or discipline, expressing precise meaning within that group or discipline. For example, both linguists and engineers use the term *prototype*, though they define it very differently.

Language contact: when speakers of different languages and varieties interact closely and influence one another linguistically. This can lead to lexical borrowing, language shift and even the creation of new language variations. For example, the Afrikaans grammar and vocabulary was strongly influenced by close contact with both Khoikhoin and exposure to Bahasa speaking slaves.

Language death: a language no longer exists when its last native speaker dies and there are no additional language speakers left. Language death is usually a result of language shift. For example, the Native American language, Wichita, died in 2016.

Language maintenance: the persistent use of a language despite competition from other varieties. Speakers often achieve language maintenance through institutions like church and school as well as cultural practice. For example, the use of German in South Africa.

Language planning: a conscious effort to change the language behaviour of a speech community, often through policy. For example, the Namibian government changed the medium of instruction in all state-sponsored schools to English in an effort to shift the *lingua franca* toward its newly adopted government language. See also *language policy.*

Language policy: official directive by governments and private institutions that outlines their implementation of language in their daily activity. For example, when a university publishes a document outlining how they use two selected languages as their medium of instruction, but three languages as their medium of communication.

Language shift: the process whereby a speech community changes from one language to another as their main medium of communication. For example, after forced removals during Apartheid, many speakers shifted from the Afrikaans-based Tsotsitaal to the isiZulu-based Scamto (Brookes and Lekgoro, 2014).

Language variety: the different forms of a language, ranging between dialects, sociolects, registers, styles as well as a standard variety. For example, Cape Flats English is a variety of South African English mostly spoken in and around Cape Town.

Lemma: the headword in a dictionary entry, containing the definition and grammatical information relevant to the headword; the canonical form of a lexeme. For example, *swim* will be a lemma for the lexeme *swims, swam* and *swimming* in a dictionary or similar sourcebook.

Lexeme: the set of all the forms of a word that express the same meaning through inflection. For example, *eat*, *eats*, *ate*, *eaten* and *eating* are all forms of the same lexeme represented by the base form, *eat*.

Lexical borrowing: the incorporation of words from source languages into recipient languages. Lent lexical items become part of the recipient language's lexicon and may reflect differences in spelling, pronunciation and sometimes meaning. For example, the English word *chivalry* was borrowed from French and is related to the French word, *cheval*, meaning *horse.*

Lexical item: a single word, a part of a word or a chain of words that form the base of a language's vocabulary (lexicon) and express a single semantic meaning. For example, *apple*, *apple puree* and *the apple doesn't fall far from the tree* are lexical items of English.

Lexical semantics: the study of word meaning, predominantly the meaning of nouns, verbs and adjectives. It includes the classification and composition of lexical words, their role in grammar and relation between words. More precisely, it concerns the meaning of lexical units (lexical items), which consist of smaller units like affixes, larger units like standalone words and multiword units.

Lexical word: also known as a content word, lexical words consist mostly of nouns, verbs and adjectives. Lexical words have the potential to carry the most meaning, which may also change or vary over time. Lexical words belong to an open class, which allows new words and new meanings to be added.

Lexicalization: to put concepts, ideation or notions into words. In doing so, a speaker adds new lexis to his/her and the language's lexicon. Lexicalisation can take many forms, for example through lexical borrowing, compounding and new word creation (neologisms).

Lexicon: the vocabulary of a language and therefore an inventory of its available lexemes. A lexicon includes a speaker's knowledge of the world as well as information about the language.

Lingua franca: a language or language variety that speakers from different linguistic backgrounds use to communicate with one another. The *lingua franca* may be a speaker's native or additional language and he/she may be able to use it both for low and high domain functions or only limited communicative purposes. For example, English is a common *lingua franca* in South Africa, for South Africans and foreign nationals alike.

Linguistic fingerprint: the unique characteristics in a speaker's spoken (and written) language use that differentiate him or her from every other speaker. See also *idiolect*.

Linguistic variation: the regional, social and individual differences in the way a particular language variety is used. Speakers from different areas and social cultures show differences when communicating the same thing. This is also present in each individual's speech. Typical variation differences include accents and vocabulary.

Locutionary act: the performance of a meaningful utterance by a speaker. For example, when a real-life speaker says something like *Please leave the room!* he/she is performing a locutionary act.

Maxim of manner: a principle in communication that expects a speaker to be clear. This means he/she must avoid ambiguity and obscurity. The utterance must also be brief and orderly. For example, if someone enquires about the price of an item and you respond with *The price remains the same.*

Maxim of quality: a principle in communication that expects a speaker to say what is true. He/she must be able to support what is said. For example, do not lie if someone asks a question.

Maxim of quantity: a principle in communication that expects a speaker not to provide more information than is necessary. For example, only provide the route to the destinations if someone asks for directions. Do not elaborate on the neighbourhood or the road conditions.

Maxim of relevance: a principle in communication that expects a speaker only to provide information that is relevant to the communication situation. For example, if someone asks for the time there is no point in providing them with restaurant recommendations too.

Meronym: a lexical relation that expresses a part-whole relationship. A meronym identifies the particle that belongs to a larger unit. For example, *finger* is the meronym for *hand.*

Metonym: a lexical relation that expresses meaning through association. A metonym is a word or name of something that is closely associated with that thing or concept. For example, *the crown* is a metonym for the British government just as *Buckingham Palace* is a metonym for the British monarch.

Multiword unit: a lexical item that consist of more than one word that together conveys a single semantic sense. Multiword units may contain different lexical and grammar words and may take the form of noun phrases, collocations or compounds and idioms. For example, *luxury goods*, *bank statement* and *the devil is in the detail.*

N-gram: a sequence of words that usually co-occur, mostly studied as bi- or trigrams. They are important when searching for the presence of collocations in corpora. The words *hot dog* collocate frequently and are therefore an example of a bi-gram.

Node word: when studying concordance lines, a node word is the searched term, which is usually centred. Sorting is done either on the left or right of a node and when a collocation search is conducted, the investigator studies co-occurrence patterns on either side of the node.

Non-verbal communication: a speaker's use of his/her body, non-verbal sounds, physical proximity, clothing, facial cues and the like to communicate information or to add to what is being said verbally. A listener may use all of his/her senses (sight, sound, touch, smell, taste) to read or decode messages. For example, when a speaker leans into the listener and whispers close to his/her ear, the speaker is clearly communicating something private.

Ordinary meaning: the commonsense meaning associated with both a dictionary definition and the meaning understood by most speakers. Ordinary meaning does not represent any technical meaning. For example, the ordinary meaning of *relocate* denotes to move to a new place and to establish a new home. See also *prototype.*

Performative verb: in speech act theory, it is the verb that conveys the speech act being performed. For instance, when a priest says *I declare you husband and wife*, the verb *declare* performs the speech act. Other examples include *recommend*, *promise*, *advise*, *ask* and so on.

Perlocutionary act: the effect an utterance has on the addressee or audience. For example, when a speaker makes the statement *I can't find my car keys*, he/she is requesting information from the addressee: *Do you know* *where my car keys are?* If the addressee helps the speaker to look for the keys, or if the addressee replies with *I haven't seen it*, the perlocution was successful. The effect of the speaker's utterance led to either cooperation or an honest reply.

Perlocutionary effect: the outcome of an illocutionary act. It is not automatically the intended outcome of the speaker. Sometimes the listener reacts in a different or unsuspecting way, causing a different perlocutionary effect. For instance, if person A shouts to person B *Help me!* the intention is to acquire assistance from person B. If person B refuses, the perlocutionary effect causes a disconnect. See also *perlocutionary act.*

Phrase: a group of words that act together and express meaning as a unit. A phrase may have lexical or grammatical function. For example, *my fellow South Africans* is a noun phrase used to focus listeners' attention and muster unity as a way to initiate a speech.

Pitch: the sound quality that makes it possible perceptually to distinguish between higher and lower sounds. Speakers use pitch to express emotion and other linguistic information when they speak. For example, when the pitch lowers at the end of a sentence, it often indicates a statement of fact. *That's what he said!* (*said* pronounced with a lower pitch; [sɛd]). See also *tone.*

Politeness: the use of good manners to ensure that interlocutors' face remains unthreatened and to maintain successful communication. Speakers may achieve politeness through various linguistic devices, like the use of honorifics, indirect speech acts, hedging, euphemisms and words that express politeness. For example, *honourable colleague, would you mind assisting me?*

Polyseme: a lexical word that has more than one possible interpretation, all of them related to a central concept or notion. For example, *man* refers to adult males but also to the human race. To *man* a ship or machine means to operate it. All three senses are related to the central concept *human species.*

Presupposition: an implicit assumption about the facts related to an utterance; the assumption must be shared by both the speaker and the listener. A presupposition is not altered by negation. For example, if we say *John hates the taste of whiskey*, the presupposition is that John has tasted whiskey before. Negating the statement, makes no difference to the presupposition – *John does not hate the taste of whiskey*, presupposes that John tasted whiskey before.

Prosody: involves larger units of speech like syllables and include functions like intonation, stress and rhythm to express additional information that contribute to semantic and pragmatic meaning. For example, the word *manage* is stressed and could be meant sarcastically: *No worries, I MANAGED.*

Prototype: the best/typical example within a category. Prototypes mostly correspond with basic-level words and are the words that speakers acquire first and use the most often. For example, *clipa* is the prototypical reference for *R100* in the City of Tshwane area.

Refer: the use of words or phrases to identify someone or something in the real (or imaginary) world. For example, the word *mother* in *My mother is mad at me* identifies an actual person who exists.

Reference: the linguistic act of identifying someone or something in the real (or imaginary) world. For example, using the words *John* and *apples* in 'John hates apples' to identify entities in the world qualifies as the act of referencing.

Referent: the word that identifies someone or something in the real (or imaginary) world is called the referent. The phrase *a puppy* is the referent in the following utterance: *I bought a puppy!*

Register: a variety of language used in specific conditions by a certain social or professional group of people. It sometimes involves style, vocabulary and prescriptive norms set by grammar (either implementing or ignoring rules). For example, *legalese* is a legal register.

Relevance theory: a theory which states that the communication process involves more than speaking and listening, and includes making inferences based on contextual factors. At its core is the idea of optimal relevance, which means that a speaker only transmits the necessary information for comprehension to occur. Once a listener thinks he or she understands, they stop processing the remaining information.

Semantic features: properties or components that speakers associate with lexical items used to express a concept or ideation. They are usually expressed in binary: positive or negative values and placed between square brackets. For example, *dog* is [+animal], [+domesticated], [-feline].

Semantic frame: a coherent structure of related concepts that provide essential information that makes it possible to understand a word or phrase. Frames are based on reoccurrences, convention and encyclopaedic knowledge. For example, the *parenthood* frame includes the concepts *tiredness, little sleep, expenses, joy, education*, and *tradition.*

Sense: one of the potential meanings of a word, either related or unrelated. For example, the two related senses of *foot* are evident in *John's foot is broken* and *I saw him at the foot of the mountain*. See also *polysemy*.

Sentence: a string of words that express meaning as a unit. It contains a subject and a verb and is often broken into clauses (either independent or dependent). For example, *John ate a salami sandwich before he left for work* is a complex sentence consisting of two independent clauses.

Sociolect: a language variety associated with a certain group's social background, which is usually characteristic of a particular age group, profession or social class. For example, the words *shade* and *reading* are lexical items associated with drag culture.

Speech act: an act performed through language such as asserting, apologising, warning, requesting, inviting, refusing and congratulating. It is analysed on different levels, namely locutionary, illocutionary and perlocutionary acts. For example, the utterance *The movie starts at 20h00* is both an assertion of facts but also a request or invitation, depending on the context.

Standardisation: the elevation and development of a dialect to be used as a language of culture and government. Standardisation involves vocabulary development (corpus planning), social prestige and a highly codified grammar and language norms. For example, Sepedi is a standard variety of the many Northern Sotho dialects.

Stipulative definition: a definition that sets the limits in the way a word will be used in a specific context. It usually includes a qualifier of some kind, tying the defined term to its context. For instance, *For this discussion, I understand 'taxes' to mean 'emotional expenditure'.*

Stress: the emphasis placed on a specific syllable of a word when speaking and involves loudness, vowel length and other changes in tone of voice. For example, the stress in *You never seem to LISTEN* suggests that the addressee has been warned before.

Synonym: a lexical relation in which words have similar meanings but express contextual differences. For example, *pretty* and *beautiful* are synonyms in describing a flower.

Text stylistics: the study of language style markers in a text. It involves the language choices a speaker (author) makes and the linguistic variation as a result. The stylistics of a text can reveal many aspects about an author, including his/her background, attitude, emotion and the probability of his/her identity. For example, referring to someone as a *filthy pig* conveys the author's opinion of and attitude toward the referent.

Thesaurus: a type of dictionary that classifies words according to interrelated concepts and semantic fields. For example, the lemma for *abduct* in the Oxford Thesaurus of 1991 (Urdang, 1992: 1) includes the related synonyms *kidnap*, *carry off*, *snatch*, *seize* and *grab*.

Tone of voice: the use of pitch to distinguish lexical or grammatical meaning (especially in tonal languages) but including prosodic features.

For example, when someone says *I'd expect you to know this*, the tone is harsh and reprimanding.

Tone of writing (textual tone): the use of language variation and lexical choices to give a voice to the author in written texts. His/her attitude and opinion of the subject and/or the addressee comes across in the writing. For example, when someone refers to Parliament as *a waste of taxpayers' money*, the author clearly expresses his/her disdain through word choice.

Transcription: a visual representation of spoken text, sometimes featuring phonetic symbols and indications of time, pronunciation phenomena and other phonetic or phonological data present during the speech event or recording. For instance, *Then...(0.3) then he...(0.1) uh... (0.4) then he said where's the boss?* ([weəz də bɒs]).

Turn-taking: the order in which a conversation takes place. Each speaker taking part in a conversation, has a turn to speak. To know when a speaker might take a turn, he/she must listen carefully for the necessary cues. Similarly, if a speaker does not want to give up a turn just yet, he/she must communicate this either verbally or non-verbally.

Utterance: a unit of speech of any size, beginning and ending with a clearly observable pause. It usually accompanies other linguistic features like non-verbal communication and prosody. For example, when a speaker audibly says *Good morning* to someone else.

Vagueness: when it is not obvious what a speaker means by one or more words, because the meaning of the words are unclear. Vagueness sets in because the meaning conveyed is fuzzy. For example, the word *tall* is vague, because it is unclear what exactly constitutes tall height.

Vernacular: the language variety a speaker grows up speaking natively. Speakers may have more than one vernacular in multilingual households or countries, and it could consist of any language variety, ranging from a standardised language to dialects and sociolects. For example, about 2% of South Africans speak Tshivenda as a vernacular.

Wildcard: an asterisk or similar character appended to a word stem or affix as a means to search various word forms of a lexeme. The asterisk represents the missing character in a word form. For example, searching **ness* will produce a concordance list containing all words in the corpus ending with this suffix (*happiness, loneliness, sadness*).

Word form: one instance of a lexeme (or base word). For example, the lexeme *sleep* has many word forms: *sleep, sleeps, sleeping, slept.* See also *lexeme.*

Word token: each word form that occurs in a corpus is called a token. A corpus comprises several different tokens. If the word *house* occurs 7 times in a corpus, then it means we have 7 tokens for the searched term. See also *word form* and *lexeme*.

Word type: when different word forms can be identified in a corpus, we refer to them as types. If the word *house* occurs 7 times in a corpus, we have 7 tokens but 1 type. A corpus that delivers hits for *house*, *houses* and *housing* delivers 3 types of the token *house*.

Bibliography

Sources cited

Abdelaziz S. 2014. Teen arrested for tweeting airline terror threat. *CNN Travel*. Available Online: https://edition.cnn.com/2014/04/14/travel/dutch-teen-arrest-american-airlines-terror-threat-tweet/index.html (accessed 3 May 2022).

Álvarez-Mosquera P, Bornman E & Ditsele T. 2018. Residents' perception on Sepitori, a mixed language spoken in greater Pretoria, South Africa. *Sociolinguistic Studies*, 12(3–4):439–459. https://doi.org/10.1558/sols.33643

Anthony L. 2022. AntConc (Version 4.1.1). Computer software. Tokyo: Waseda University. Available online: https://www.laurenceanthony.net/software.

Anthony L. 2022. TagAnt (Version 2.0.4). Computer software. Tokyo: Waseda University. Available online: https://www.laurenceanthony.net/software.

Anthony L. 2022. AntFileConverter (Version 2.0.2). Computer software. Tokyo: Waseda University. Available online: https://www.laurenceanthony.net/software.

Aprill, EP. 1998. The law of the word: Dictionary shopping in the Supreme Court. *Arizona State Law Journal*, 30(2):275–336.

Arntfield M. 2016. 'Money. Armed. Quietly': An analysis of criminogenic prose in institutional holdup notes. *Semiotica*, 2016(208):237–257. https://doi.org/10.1515/sem-2015-0119

Atkins BTS & Rundell M. 2008. *The Oxford guide to practical lexicography*. Oxford: Oxford University Press.

Austin JL. 1962. *How to do things with words*. Oxford: Oxford University Press.

Baker P. 2010. *Sociolinguistics and corpus linguistics*. Edinburgh: Edinburg University Press. https://doi.org/10.1075/z.199

Baker A, Van den Bogaerde B, Pfau R & Schermer T. 2016. *The linguistics of sign language*. Amsterdam: John Benjamins Publishing Company.

Bauer L. 2012. *Beginning linguistics*. London: Palgrave MacMillan. https://doi.org/10.1007/978-0-230-39031-7

Bavelas J, Gerwing J & Healing S. 2014. Hand and facial gestures in conversational interaction. In Holtgraves TM (ed.) *The Oxford handbook of language and social psychology*. Oxford: Oxford University Press. 112–130.

Bell J & Engle G. 1995. *Cross' statutory interpretation*. London: Butterworths.

Berlin B & Kay P. 1969. *Basic colour terms: Their universality and evolution*. Berkeley: University of California Press.

BNC Consortium. 2007. *The British National Corpus*. Available online: http://www.english-corpora.org/bnc/.

Bosman N & Pienaar M. 2014. Afrikaanse semantiek. In Carstens WAM & Bosman N (eds.) *Kontemporêre Afrikaanse taalkunde*. Pretoria: Van Schaik. 245–274.

Bradley ED. 2020. The influence of linguistic and social attitudes on grammaticality judgments of singular 'they'. *Language Sciences*, 78:1-11. https://doi.org/10.1016/j.langsci.2020.101272

Brandford W & Claughton JS. 2002. Mutual lexical borrowings among some languages of Southern Africa: Xhosa, Afrikaans and English. In Mesthrie R (ed.) *Language in South Africa*. Cape Town: Cambridge University Press. 199–215. https://doi.org/10.1017/CBO9780511486692.011

Brookes H. 2004. A repertoire of South African quotable gestures. *Journal of Linguistic Anthropology*, 14(2):186–224. https://doi.org/10.1525/jlin.2004.14.2.186

Brookes H. 2005. What gestures do: Some communicative functions of quotable gestures in conversations among black urban South Africans. *Journal of Pragmatics*, 37:2044–2085. https://doi.org/10.1016/j.pragma.2005.03.006

Brookes H & Lekgoro T. 2014. A social history of urban male youth varieties in Stirtonville and Vosloorus, South Africa. *Southern African Linguistics and Applied Language Studies*, 32(2):149–159. https://doi.org/10.2989/16073614.2014.992642

Brown P. 2017. Politeness and impoliteness. In Huang Y (ed.) *The Oxford handbook of pragmatics*. Oxford University Press. 383–399.

Brown P & Levinson SC. 1987. *Politeness. Some universals in language usage*. Cambridge: Cambridge University Press. https://doi.org/10.1017/CBO9780511813085

Brown-Blake C. 2019. Judges as language referees for Caribbean English vernacular speakers: How do they score? In Ralarala MK, Kaschula RH & Heydon G (eds.) *New frontiers in forensic linguistics. Themes and perspectives in language and law in Africa and beyond*. Stellenbosch: Sun Press. 149–174.

Carney T. 2014. Being (Im)polite: A forensic linguistic approach to interpreting a hate speech case. *Language Matters*, 45(3):325–341. https://doi.org/10.1080/10228195.2014.959545

Carney TR & Bergh L. 2014. 'n Taalkundige perspektief op woordeboekgebruik in die hof: die woordeboek as toevlugsoord. *LitNet Akademies (Regte)* 11(2):23–64.

Carney TR & Bergh L. 2016. Using prototype theory to determine the ordinary meaning of words. *Tydskrif vir Hedendaagse Romeins-Hollandse Reg*, 79(3):486–495.

Carney TR. 2018. Disposing of bodies, semantically: Notes on the meaning of 'disposal' in *S v Molefe*. *Potchefstroom Electronic Law Journal* 21:1–20. https://doi.org/10.17159/1727-3781/2018/v21i0a4220

Carney TR. 2020. A legal fallacy? Testing the ordinariness of 'ordinary meaning'. *South African Law Journal*, 137(2):269–304.

Carney TR. 2021. Understanding one's rights when arrested and detained: An assessment of language barriers that affect comprehension. *South African Journal of Criminal Justice*, 34(1):1–30. https://doi.org/10.47348/SACJ/v34/i1a1

Carney TR. 2022. Sintaktiese uitleg van die BTW-wet bepaal wanneer goud teen die nulkoers verkoop mag word. 'n Besinning van 'n positiewe taalkundige benadering. *LitNet Akademies (Regte)* 19(3):834–846. https://doi.org/10.56273/1995-5928/2022/j19n3e1

Carney TR, Grundlingh L & Knobel J. 2023. The use of linguistics to determine meaning in cases of personality infringement. *Stellenbosch Law Review*, (forthcoming).

Carston R & Powell G. 2008. Relevance theory – new directions and developments. In Lepore E & Smith BC (eds.) *The Oxford handbook of philosophy of language*. Oxford: Oxford University Press. 341–360. https://doi.org/10.1093/oxfordhb/9780199552238.003.0016

Cele S. 2021. Zuma's daughter faces allegations of inciting South Africa riots. *Bloomberg*. Available Onine: https://www.bloomberg.com/news/articles/2021-07-14/zuma-s-daughter-faces-allegations-of-inciting-south-africa-riots (accessed 3 May 2022).

Chapman S. 2011. *Pragmatics*. London: Palgrave Macmillan. https://doi.org/10.1007/978-0-230-34519-5

Chick JK. 2002. Intercultural miscommunication in South Africa. In Mesthrie R (ed.) *Language in South Africa*. Cape Town: Cambridge University Press. 258–275. https://doi.org/10.1017/CBO9780511486692.014

Christensen R & Kübbeler C. 2011. Wortlautgrenze und Wörterbuch. *Zeitschrift für Europäischen Rechtslinguistik*, 2011:1–15.

Chokshi N & Taub EA. 2019. Elon Musk's defence: 'pedo guy' tweet was a generic insult. *The New York Times*. Available Online: https://www.nytimes.com/2019/12/03/business/elon-musk-defamation-trial.html (accessed 3 May 2022).

Clark HH. 1979. Responding to indirect speech acts. *Cognitive Psychology*, 11(4):430–477. https://doi.org/10.1016/0010-0285(79)90020-3

Conradie J & Groenewald G. 2014. Die ontstaan en vestiging van Afrikaans. In Carstens WAM & Bosman N (eds.) *Kontemporêre Afrikaanse taalkunde*. Pretoria: Van Schaik. 27–60.

Cooper RL. 1989. *Language planning and social change*. Cambridge: Cambridge University Press.

Cruse A. 2015. *Meaning in language. An introduction to semantics and pragmatics*. Oxford: Oxford University Press.

Culpeper J, Bousfield D & Wichmann A. 2003. Impoliteness revisited: With special reference to dynamic and prosodic aspects. *Journal of Pragmatics*, 35(10):1545–1579. https://doi.org/10.1016/S0378-2166(02)00118-2

Culpeper J. 2011. *Impoliteness: using language to cause offence*. Cambridge: Cambridge University Press. https://doi.org/10.1017/CBO9780511975752

Culpeper J. 2021. Impoliteness and hate speech: Compare and contrast. *Journal of Pragmatics*, 179:4–11. https://doi.org/10.1016/j.pragma.2021.04.019

Davies M. 2008. The Corpus of Contemporary American English. Available online: https://www.english-corpora.org/coca/.

Davies M. 2017. The Corpus of US Supreme Court Opinions. Available online: https://www.english-corpora.org/scotus/.

De Gelder B & Huis In 'T Veld EMJ. 2015. Cultural differences in emotional expressions and body language. In Chiao JY, Li S, Seligman R & Turner R (eds.) *The Oxford handbook of cultural neuroscience*. Oxford: Oxford University Press. 224–234. https://doi.org/10.1093/oxfordhb/9780199357376.013.16

Deumert A. 2011. Language planning and policy. In Mesthrie R, Swann J, Deumert A & Leap WL *Introducing sociolinguistics*. Edinburgh: Edinburgh University Press. 371–406.

De Vries A & Docrat Z. 2019. Multilingualism in the South African legal system. Attorney's experiences. In Ralarala MK, Kaschula RH & Heydon G (eds.) *New frontiers in forensic linguistics. Themes and perspectives in language and law in Africa and beyond*. Stellenbosch: Sun Press. 89–112.

Diamond G. 2015. Making decisions about inclusion and exclusion. In Durkin P (ed.) *The Oxford handbook of lexicography*. Oxford: Oxford University Press. 533–545. https://doi.org/10.1093/oxfordhb/9780199691630.013.38

Dictionary Unit of South African English. 2010. *Oxford South African concise dictionary*. Cape Town: Oxford University Press Southern Africa.

Dictionary Unit of South African English. 2022. 'Dagga, n.' Entry 2. DSAE Online. August 2022. https://dsae.co.za/entry/dagga/e01888 (accessed 15 August 2022).

Ditsele T. 2014. Why not use Sepitori to enrich the vocabularies of Setswana and Sepedi? *Southern African Linguistics and Applied Language Studies*, 32(2):215–228. https://doi.org/10.2989/16073614.2014.992652

Docrat Z, Kaschula RH & Ralarala MK. 2017. The exclusion of South African sign language speakers in the criminal justice system: A case based approach. In Ralarala MK, Barris K, Ivala E & Siyepu S (eds.) *African languages and language practice research in the 21st century: Interdisciplinary themes and perspectives*. Cape Town: CASAS. 261–278.

Docrat Z & Kaschula RH. 2019. Monolingual language of record. A critique of South Africa's new policy directives. In Ralarala MK, Kaschula RH & Heydon G (eds.) *New frontiers in forensic linguistics. Themes and perspectives in language and law in Africa and beyond*. Stellenbosch: Sun Press. 71–88.

Docrat Z, Kaschula RH & Ralarala MK. 2021. *A handbook on legal language and the quest for linguistic equality in South Africa and Beyond*. Stellenbosch: Sun Press. https://doi.org/10.52779/9781991201270

Du Plessis LM. 1986. *The interpretation of statutes*. Durban: Butterworths.

Du Plessis C. 2021. Stoking the flames: ANC condemns looting and violence, 'concerned' about tweets from Zuma's daughter. *Daily Maverick*. Available Online: https://www.dailymaverick.co.za/article/2021-07-13-stoking-the-flames-anc-condemns-looting-and-violence-concerned-about-tweets-from-zumas-daughter/ (accessed 3 May 2022).

Eades D. 2012a. Intercultural communication in law. In Bratt Paulston C, Kiesling SF & Rangel ES (eds.) *The handbook of intercultural discourse and communication*. Malden: Wiley-Blackwell. 408–429. https://doi.org/10.1002/9781118247273.ch20

Eades D. 2012b. Communication with aboriginal speakers of English in the legal process. *Australian Journal of Linguistics*, 32(4):473–489. https://doi.org/10.1080/07268602.2012.744268

Evans V. 2010. *How words mean. Lexical concepts, cognitive models and meaning construction*. Oxford: Oxford University Press. https://doi.org/10.1093/acprof:oso/9780199234660.001.0001

Evison J. 2012. What are the basics of analysing a corpus? In O'Keeffe A & McCarthy M (eds.) *The Routledge handbook of corpus linguistics*. New York: Routledge. 122–135. https://doi.org/10.4324/9780203856949-10

Fellbaum C. 2017. Lexical relations. In Talyor JR (ed.) *The word*. Oxford: Oxford University Press. 350–363.

Ferguson C. 2003. Diglossia. In Bratt Paulston C & Tucker GR (eds.) *Sociolinguistics. The essential readings*. Malden: Blackwell Publishing. 345–366.

Fillmore C. 1982. Towards a descriptive framework for spatial deixis. In Jarvella RJ & Klein W (eds.) *Speech, place and action. Studies in deixis and related topics*. New York: John Wiley & Sons. 31–59.

Fillmore C. 1985. Frames and the semantics of understanding. *Quaderni di Semantica*, 6(2):222–254.

Fillmore C. 2007. Frame semantics. In Evans V, Bergen BK & Zinken J (eds.) *The cognitive linguistics reader*. London: Equinox. 238–262.

Fiske J. 2011. *Introduction to communication studies*. New York: Routledge. https://doi.org/10.4324/9780203837382

Francke R. 2018. Don't call me mandjie. *Daily Voice*. Available Online: https://www.dailyvoice.co.za/news/national/watch-dont-call-me-mandjie-16818289 (Accessed 31 March 2022).

Francis WN & Kučera H. 1979. *Brown Corpus Manual*. Revised edition. Providence, Rhode Island: Department of Linguistics, Brown University. Available online: http://icame.uib.no/brown/bcm.html.

Fraser B. 2009. An approach to discourse markers. *Journal of Pragmatics*, 1:293–320. https://doi.org/10.1163/187730909X12538045489818

Fraser H. 2014. What did Oscar Pistorius really say? Forensic Transcription Australia. Available Online: https://forensictranscription.net.au/what-is-oscar-pistorius-saying/ (accessed 21 April 2022).

Gales T & Solan LM. 2020. Revisiting a classic problem in statutory interpretation: Is a minister a laborer? *Georgia State University Law Review*, 36(5):491–534.

Geeraerts D. 2010. *Theories of lexical semantics*. Oxford: Oxford University Press. https://doi.org/10.1093/acprof:oso/9780198700302.001.0001

Germishuys W. 2016. Religion above the law? Universal Church of the Kingdom of God v Myeni (DA 3/14) [2015] ZALAC 31 (28 July 2015). *South African Mercantile Law Journal*, 28(2):360–373.

Goffman E. 1967. *Interaction ritual: Essays on face-to-face behaviour.* Harmondsworth: Penguin Books.

Goldin-Meadow S. 2021. Gesture is an intrinsic part of modern-day human communication and may always have been so. In Gontier N, Lock N & Sinha C (eds.) *The Oxford handbook of human symbolic evolution*. Oxford: Oxford University Press. https://doi.org/10.1093/oxfordhb/9780198813781.013.12

Goodrich P. 1988. Modalities of annunciation. An introduction to courtroom speech. In Kevelson R (ed.) *Law and semiotics*. New York: Plenum Press. 143–165. https://doi.org/10.1007/978-1-4613-0771-6_9

Gouws RH. 1989. *Leksikografie*. Cape Town: Academica.

Gouws RH & Prinsloo DJ. 2005. *Principles and practice of South African lexicography*. Stellenbosch: Sun Press.

Grice HP. 1991a. Utterer's meaning, sentence-meaning, and word-meaning. In Davis S (ed.). *Pragmatics. A reader*. New York: Oxford University Press. 65–76.

Grice HP. 1991b. Logic and conversation. In Davis S (ed.). *Pragmatics. A reader.* New York: Oxford University Press. 305–315.

Grundlingh L. 2016. Interpreting 'PJ Powers': A relevance-theoretic approach. *Language Matters*, 47(2):246–268. https://doi.org/10.1080/10228195.2016.1190779

Gumperz JJ. 1992. Contextualisation and understanding. In Duranti A & C Goodwin (eds.) *Rethinking context: Language as an interactive phenomenon*. Cambridge: Cambridge University Press. 229–252.

Gumperz JJ. 2003. Contextualisation conventions. In Bratt Paulston C & Tucker GR (eds.) *Sociolinguistics. The essential readings*. Malden: Blackwell Publishing. 139–155.

Hale S. 2013. Court interpreting. The need to raise the bar: court interpreters as specialized experts. In Coulthard M & Johnson A (eds.) *The Routledge handbook of forensic linguistics*. New York: Routledge. 440–454.

Hardaker C. 2020. Pranksters, provocateurs, propagandists. Using forensic corpus linguistics to identify and understand trolling. In Coulthard M, May A & Sousa-Silva R (eds.) *The Routledge handbook of forensic linguistics*. London: Taylor & Francis Group. 694–708. https://doi.org/10.4324/9780429030581-52

Harding S & Ralarala MK. 2017. 'Tell me the story is and do not leave out anything'. Social responsibility and ethical practices in the translation of complainants' narratives: The potential for change. *The Translator*, 23(2):158–176. https://doi.org/10.1080/13556509.2017.1327792

HarperCollins Publishers. 2022. 'governing body'. Collins English Dictionary Online. August 2022. https://www.collinsdictionary.com/dictionary/english/governing-body (accessed 10 August 2022).

Harris R & Hutton C. 2007. *Definition in theory and practice*. London: Bloomsbury.

Harvard Law Review. 1994. Looking it up: dictionaries and statutory interpretation. *Harvard Law Review*, 107(6):1437–1454. https://doi.org/10.2307/1341851

Helmenstine AM. 2021. What is a Molotov cocktail? Definition and explanation. *ThoughtCo*, 29 July. Available Online: https://www.thoughtco.com/what-is-a-molotov-cocktail-607312 (accessed on 7 March 2022).

Heydon G. 2005. *The Language of police interviewing: A critical analysis*. New York: Palgrave Macmillan. https://doi.org/10.1057/9780230502932

Heydon G. 2019. *Researching forensic linguistics: Approaches and applications*. New York: Routledge. https://doi.org/10.4324/9780429290640

Hirschberg J. 2017. Pragmatics and prosody. In Huang Y (ed.) *The Oxford handbook of pragmatics*. Oxford: Oxford University Press. 532–549.

Hornberger NH. 2003. Literacy and language planning. In Bratt Paulston C & Tucker GR (eds.) *Sociolinguistics. The essential readings*. Malden: Blackwell Publishing. 449–460.

Hua Z. 2013. *Exploring intercultural communication. Language in action*. London: Routledge.

Huang Y. 2013. *Pragmatics*. Oxford: Oxford University Press.

Hübner Barcelos R, Dantas DC & Sénécal S. 2017. Watch your tone: How a brand's tone of voice on social media influences consumer responses. *Journal of Interactive Marketing*, 41:60–80. https://doi.org/10.1016/j.intmar.2017.10.001

Hunston S. 2012. How can a corpus be used to explore patterns? In O'Keeffe A & McCarthy M (eds.) *The Routledge handbook of corpus linguistics*. New York: Routledge. 152–166. https://doi.org/10.4324/9780203856949-12

Hutton C. 2014. *Word meaning and legal interpretation: An introductory guide*. London: Palgrave MacMillan. https://doi.org/10.1007/978-1-137-01616-4

Hutton C. 2020. Legal interpretation. The category of 'ordinary meaning' and its role in legal interpretation. In Coulthard M, May A & Sousa-Silva R (eds.) *The Routledge handbook of forensic linguistics*. London: Taylor & Francis Group. 79–92. https://doi.org/10.4324/9780429030581-8

Jackson H. 1995. *Words and their meaning*. London: Longman.

Jackson H. 2002. *Lexicography. An introduction*. London: Routledge.

Johansson S, Leech G & Goodluck H. 1978. *Lancaster-Oslo/Bergen Corpus Manual*. Oslo: Department of English, University of Oslo. Available online: http://khnt.hit.uib.no/icame/manuals/lob/INDEX.HTM

Kaplan JP. 2020. *Linguistics and law*. New York: Routledge. https://doi.org/10.4324/9780429450020

Kaschula RH & Maseko P. 2012. Intercultural communication and vocational language learning in South Africa: Law and healthcare. In Bratt Paulston C, Kiesling SF & Rangel ES (eds.) *The Handbook of intercultural discourse and communication*. Malden: Wiley-Blackwell. 313–336. https://doi.org/10.1002/9781118247273.ch16

Kidwell M. 2013. Framing, grounding, and coordinating conversational interaction: Posture, gaze, facial expression, and movement in space. In Müller C, Cienki A, Fricke E, Ladewig S, McNeill D & Tessendorf S (eds.) *Body – Language – Communication. Volume 1. An international handbook on multimodality in human interaction*. Berlin: De Gruyter. 100–113. https://doi.org/10.1515/9783110261318.100

Kurzon D. 1986. *It is hereby preformed... Explorations in legal speech acts*. Amsterdam: John Benjamins BV. https://doi.org/10.1075/pb.vii.6

Labov W. 1973. The boundaries of words and their meaning. In Fasold RW (ed.) *Variation in the form and use of language*. Washington DC: Georgetown University Press.

Lakoff R. 1973. The logic of politeness; or Minding your P's and Q's. In Corum C, Smith-Stark CT & Weiser A (eds.) *Papers from the 9th regional meeting of the Chicago Linguistics Society*. Chicago: Chicago Linguistics Society. 292–305.

Lakoff G. 1987. *Women, fire, and dangerous things*. Chicago: University of Chicago Press. https://doi.org/10.7208/chicago/9780226471013.001.0001

Laplante D & Ambady N. 2003. On how things are said: Voice tone, voice intensity, verbal content, and perceptions of politeness. *Journal of Language and Social Psychology*, 22(4):434–441. https://doi.org/10.1177/0261927X03258084

Lebese S. 2011. A pilot study on the undefined role of court interpreters in South Africa. *Southern African Linguistics and Applied Language Studies*, 29(3):343–357. https://doi.org/10.2989/16073614.2011.647498

Lebese S. 2014. Do justice to court interpreters in South Africa. *Stellenbosch Papers in Linguistics Plus*, 43:183–208. https://doi.org/10.5842/43-0-179

Lee TR & Mouritsen SC. 2018. Judging ordinary meaning. *The Yale Law Journal*, 127:788–879. https://doi.org/10.2139/ssrn.2937468

Leech G. 1983. *The principles of pragmatics*. London: Longman Group.

Legal Aid South Africa. 2016. Annexure C: Applicant language survey data. Language policy. Available Online: https://legal-aid.co.za/3d-flip-book/language-policy-680-kb-pdf/ (accessed on 24 March 2022).

Looking 2015. Series 2. HBO, January-March.

Löbner S. 2003. *Semantik: Ein Einfürung*. Berlin: Walter de Gruyter. https://doi.org/10.1515/9783110904260

Lyons J. 1979. *Semantics*. Volume 1. Cambridge: Cambridge University Press.

Mabasso E. 2019. Tell us the story in your Portuguese, we can understand you. The Mozambican justice system's dilemma in enforcement of the sole official language policy. In Ralarala MK, Kaschula RH & Heydon G (eds.) *New frontiers in forensic linguistics. Themes and perspectives in language and law in Africa and beyond*. Stellenbosch: Sun Press. 33–50.

Matoesian GM. 1993. *Reproducing rape: Domination through talk in the courtroom*. Chicago: Chicago University Press.

Matoesian GM. 2013. Multimodality and forensic linguistics. Multimodal aspects of victim's narrative in direct examination. In Coulthard M & Johnson A (eds.) *The Routledge handbook of forensic linguistics*. New York: Routledge. 541–557.

May A, Holt E, Al Saeed N & Ahmad Sani N. 2020. Legal talk: Socio-pragmatic aspects of legal questioning. Police interviews, prosecutorial discourse and trial discourse. In Coulthard M, May A & Sousa-Silva R (eds.) *The Routledge handbook of forensic linguistics*. New York: Routledge. 13–31. https://doi.org/10.4324/9780429030581-4

McEnery T & Hardie A. 2012. *Corpus linguistics*. Cambridge: Cambridge University Press. https://doi.org/10.1093/oxfordhb/9780199276349.013.0024

McMenamin GR. 2002. *Forensic linguistics. Advances in forensic stylistics*. Boca Raton: CRC Press. https://doi.org/10.1201/9781420041170.ch9

Mesthrie R & Leap WL. 2011. Language contact 1: Maintenance, shift and death. In Mesthrie R, Swann J, Deumert A & Leap WL *Introducing sociolinguistics*. Edinburgh: Edinburgh University Press. 242–270.

Mesthrie R. 2014. English Tsotsitaals? An analysis of two written texts in surfspeak and South African Indian English slang. *Southern African Linguistics and Applied Language Studies*, 32(2):173–183. https://doi.org/10.2989/16073614.2014.992637

Moeketsi RH. 2000. The do's and don'ts in court interpreting: A functional approach to a professional code. *Language Matters*, 31(1):222–242. https://doi.org/10.1080/10228190008566166

Mohlahlo AL & Ditsele T. 2022. Exploring multilingualism at the national department levels in South Africa post the Use of Official Languages Act of 2012. *Literator*, 43(1):1–9. https://doi.org/10.4102/lit.v43i1.1819

Moll M. 2012. *The quintessence of intercultural business communication*. New York: Springer. https://doi.org/10.1007/978-3-642-28238-6

Motau P. 2018. Kingdom of Eswatini change now official. *Times of Swaziland*. Available Online: http://www.times.co.sz/news/118373-kingdom-of-eswatini-change-now-official.html (accessed on 28 April 2022).

Mouritsen SC. 2010. The dictionary is not a fortress: Definitional fallacies and a corpus-based approach to plain meaning. *Brigham Young University Law Review*, 2010(5):1915–1980.

Murphy ML. 2012. *Lexical semantics*. Cambridge: Cambridge University Press.

Mzansi Taal. 2022. Kleva or cleva. Available Online: https://www.mzansitaal.co.za/terms/kleva-or-cleva/ (accessed on 28 March 2022).

Neethling J, Potgieter JM & Roos A. 2019. *Neethling on personality rights*. Durban: LexisNexis.

Nelson M. 2012. Building a written corpus. What are the basics? In O'Keeffe A & McCarthy M (eds.) *The Routledge handbook of corpus linguistics*. New York: Routledge. 53–65.

Nygaard LC & Lunders ER. 2002. Resolution of lexical ambiguity by emotional tone of voice. *Memory & Cognition*, 30(4):583–593. https://doi.org/10.3758/BF03194959

Nyoni J. 2021. Criticalities of non-verbal reading competencies: An Afrocentric ethnological approach to qualitative research. *KOERS*, 86(1):1–12. https://doi.org/10.19108/KOERS.86.1.2486

Odendal FF & Gouws RH. 2010. *Handwoordeboek van die Afrikaanse taal*. Cape Town: Pearson Education South Africa.

Oxford University Press. 2022. 'bluff, v.1'. OED Online. June 2022. https://0-www-oed-com.oasis.unisa.ac.za/view/Entry/20629?rskey=g2t01R&result=4&isAdvanced=false (accessed 3 August 2022).

Oxford University Press. 2022. 'voluntary'. Historical thesaurus online. August 2022. https://0-www-oed-com.oasis.unisa.ac.za/view/th/class/142938 (accessed 10 August 2022).

Özyürek A. 2018. Role of gesture in language processing: Toward a unified account for production and comprehension. In Rueschemeyer S & Gaskell MG (eds.) *The Oxford handbook of psycholinguistics*. Oxford: Oxford University Press. 592–607. https://doi.org/10.1093/oxfordhb/9780198786825.013.25

Parrott M. 2016. *Grammar for English language teachers*. Cambridge: Cambridge University Press.

Patrick Malone Associates. 2022. Oscar Pistorius cross-examination. Available Online: https://www.patrickmalonelaw.com/useful-information/legal-resources/attorneys/legal-resources-attorneys-injured-clients/cross-examination-transcripts/oscar-pistorius-cross-examination/ (accessed 3 May 2022).

Perry T. 2004. The case of the toothless watchdog: Language rights and ethnic mobilization in South Africa. *Ethnicities*, 4(4):501–521. https://doi.org/10.1177/1468796804047471

Pheiffer F. 2007. *Pharos kernwoordeboek / concise dictionary*. Cape Town: NB Publishers.

Poscher R. 2012. Ambiguity and vagueness in legal interpretation. In Tiersma PM & Solan LM (eds.) *The Oxford handbook of language and law*. Oxford: Oxford University Press. https://doi.org/10.1093/oxfordhb/9780199572120.013.0010

Prieto P & Espinal MT. 2020. Negation, prosody, and gesture. In Déprez V & Espinal MT (eds.) *The Oxford handbook of negation*. Oxford: Oxford University Press. 677–693. https://doi.org/10.1093/oxfordhb/9780198830528.013.34

Prinsloo DJ. 2013. 'n Kritiese beskouing van woordeboeke met geamalgameerde lemmalyste. *Lexikos*, 23:371–393. https://doi.org/10.5788/23-1-1220

Ralarala MK. 2014. Transpreters' translations of complainants' narratives as evidence: Whose version goes to court? *The Translator*, 20(3):377–395. https://doi.org/10.1080/13556509.2014.934002

Rock F. 2012. The caution in England and Wales. In Tiersma PM & Solan LM (eds.) *The Oxford handbook of language and law*. Oxford: Oxford University Press. 312–325. https://doi.org/10.1093/oxfordhb/9780199572120.013.0023

Rosch EH. 1973. Natural categories. *Cognitive Psychology*, 4:328–350. https://doi.org/10.1016/0010-0285(73)90017-0

Rosch E & Mervis CB. 1975. Family resemblances: Studies in the internal structure categories. *Cognitive Psychology*, 7:573–605. https://doi.org/10.1016/0010-0285(75)90024-9

Rosch E, Mervis CB, Gray WD, Johnson DM & Boyes-Braem P. 1976. Basic objects in natural categories. *Cognitive Psychology*, 8:382–439. https://doi.org/10.1016/0010-0285(76)90013-X

Rosch E. 1978. Principles of categorisation. In Margolis E & Laurence S (eds.) *Concepts: Core readings*. Cambridge, Mass.: MIT Press. 189–206.

Ross R. 2000. *A concise history of South Africa*. Cambridge: Cambridge University Press.

Rudanko J. 2006. Aggravated impoliteness and two types of speaker intention in an episode in Shakespeare's *Timon of Athens*. *Journal of Pragmatics*, 38(6):829–841. https://doi.org/10.1016/j.pragma.2005.11.006

Ruigendijk E, De Belder M & Schippers A. 2021. *Inleiding Nederlandse taalkunde. Voor aankomende neerlandici intra en extra muros*. Amsterdam: Amsterdam University Press.

Saeed JI. 2009. *Semantics*. Oxford: Wiley-Blackwell.

Savage C. 2021. Incitement to riot? What trump told supporters before mob stormed capitol. *The New York Times*. Available Online: https://www.nytimes.com/2021/01/10/us/trump-speech-riot.html (accessed 3 May 2022).

Schmidt CWH & Rademeyer H. 2021. *Law of evidence*. Cape Town: LexisNexis South Africa.

Searle JR. 1965. What is a speech act? In Black M (ed.) *Philosophy in America*. Ithaca: Cornell University Press. 221–239.

Searle JR. 1975. Indirect speech acts. In Cole P & Morgan JL (eds.) *Syntax and semantics*, vol. 3. New York: Academic Press. 59–82. https://doi.org/10.1163/9789004368811_004

Sendén MG, Renström E & Lindqvist A. 2021. Pronouns beyond the binary. The change of attitudes and use over time. *Gender & Society*, 35(4):588-615. https://doi.org/10.1177/08912432211029226

Sibiya N. 2018. Clicks woman must come forward – police. *Pretoria Record.* Available Online: https://rekord.co.za/183471/update-clicks-woman-must-come-forward-police/ (accessed 31 March 2022).

Shohamy E. 2005. *Language policy. Hidden agendas and new approaches.* London: Routledge. https://doi.org/10.4324/9780203387962

Shuy RW. 1986. Context as the highest standard of semantics: A lawsuit involving the meaning of 'accuracy' in Accounting. *Journal of English Language*, 19(2):295–303. https://doi.org/10.1177/007542428601900210

Shuy RW. 1990. Warning labels: Language, law, and comprehension. *American Speech*, 65(4):291–303. https://doi.org/10.2307/455505

Shuy RW. 2008. *Fighting over words. Language and civil law cases.* New York: Oxford University Press. https://doi.org/10.1093/acprof:oso/9780195328837.001.0001

Shuy RW. 2020. Terrorism and forensic linguistics. Linguistics in terrorism cases. In Coulthard M; May A & Sousa-Silva R (eds.) *The Routledge handbook of forensic linguistics.* London: Taylor & Francis Group. 445–462. https://doi.org/10.4324/9780429030581-35

Slabbert S & Finlayson R. 2002. Code-switching in South African townships. In Mesthrie R (ed.) *Language in South Africa.* Cape Town: Cambridge University Press. 235–257. https://doi.org/10.1017/CBO9780511486692.013

Solan L. 1993. When judges use the dictionary. *American Speech*, 68(1):50–57. https://doi.org/10.2307/455835

Solan LM. 1995. Judicial decisions and linguistic analysis: Is there a linguist in the court? *Washington University Law Quarterly*, 73:1069–1080.

Solan LM. 2010. *The language of statutes. Laws and their interpretation.* Chicago: University of Chicago Press. https://doi.org/10.7208/chicago/9780226767987.001.0001

Solan LM. 2016. Can corpus linguistics help make originalism scientific? *The Yale Law Journal Forum*, 126:57–64.

Solan LM & Tiersma PM. 2005. *Speaking of crime. The language of criminal justice.* Chicago: University of Chicago Press. https://doi.org/10.7208/chicago/9780226767871.001.0001

Speer S & Blodgett A. 2006. Prosody. In Traxler MJ & Gernsbacher MA (eds.) *Handbook of psycholinguistics.* Boston: Elsevier. 505–538. https://doi.org/10.1016/B978-012369374-7/50014-6

Sporer SL. 2014. Bodily communication and deception. In Müller C, Cienki A, Fricke E, Ladewig S, McNeill D & Tessendorf S (eds.). *Body – Language – Communication. Volume 1. An international handbook on multimodality in human interaction*. Berlin: De Gruyter. 1913–1921.

Statistics South Africa. 2012. Key results. Available Online: http://www.statssa.gov.za/census/census_2011/census_products/Census_2011_Key_results.pdf (accessed 29 March 2022).

Strathy Language Unit. 2010. *The Strathy Corpus of Canadian English*. Available online: http://www.english-corpora.org/can/.

Stubbs M. 2002. *Words and phrases. Corpus studies of lexical semantics*. Oxford: Blackwell Publishing.

Sukumane JB. 2000. Issues in language policy and planning: The case of Namibia. *Studies in the Linguistic Sciences*, 30(2):199–208.

Svensén B. 1993. *Practical lexicography. Principles and methods of dictionary-making*. Oxford: Oxford University Press.

The Guardian. 2012. Twitter joke trial: Paul Chambers wins high court appeal against conviction. Available Online: https://www.theguardian.com/law/2012/jul/27/twitter-joke-trial-high-court (accessed 3 May 2022).

Thetela PH. 2002. Sex discourse and gender construction in Southern Sotho: A case of police interviews of rape / sexual assault victims. *Southern African Linguistics and Applied Language Studies*, 20(3):177–189. https://doi.org/10.2989/16073610209486309

Thompson L. 1995. *A history of South Africa*. London: Yale University Press.

Thumma SA & Kirchmeier JL. 1999. The lexicon has become a fortress: The United States Supreme Court's use of dictionaries. *Buffalo Law Review*, 47(1):227–562.

Tiersma PM. 2000. *Legal language*. Chicago: Chicago University Press.

Tonhauser J. 2019. Prosody and meaning. In Cummins C & Katsos N (eds.) *The Oxford handbook of experimental semantics and pragmatics*. Oxford: Oxford University Press. 494–511. https://doi.org/10.1093/oxfordhb/9780198791768.013.30

Tribble C. 2012. What are concordances and how are they used? In O'Keeffe A & McCarthy M (eds.) *The Routledge handbook of corpus linguistics*. New York: Routledge. 167–183. https://doi.org/10.4324/9780203856949-13

Urdang L. 1992. *The Oxford thesaurus. An A–Z dictionary of synonyms*. London: BCA.

Usadolo SE & Kotzé E. 2014. Some interlingual communicative challenges for foreign African interpreters in South African courtrooms. *Stellenbosch Papers in Linguistics Plus*, 43:345–357. https://doi.org/10.5842/43-0-184

Van der Walt C & Evans R. 2018. Is English the lingua franca of South Africa? In Jenkins J, Baker W & Dewey M (eds.) *The Routledge handbook of English as a lingua franca*. New York: Routledge. 186–198. https://doi.org/10.4324/9781315717173-16

vannie.kaap. 2022. Skud with brasse who are not afraid to wys you that you are catching on kak. Instagram. 19 February. Available Online: www.instagram.com/p/CaJIN1MKKIA/?utm_medium. (accessed on 24 March 2022).

Van den Berg K. 2019. A case of crying wolf? A linguistic approach to evaluating hate speech allegations as linguistic acts of violence. In Ralarala MK, Kaschula RH & Heydon G (eds.) *New frontiers in forensic linguistics. Themes and perspectives in language and law in Africa and beyond*. Stellenbosch: Sun Press. 301–326.

Van den Berg K & Surmon M. 2019. The act of threatening. Applying speech act theory to threat texts. In Ralarala MK, Kaschula RH & Heydon G (eds.) *New frontiers in forensic linguistics. Themes and perspectives in language and law in Africa and beyond*. Stellenbosch: Sun Press. 255–278.

Van Zyl SP & Carney TR. 2021. Just how voluntary is 'voluntary' for purpose of a voluntary disclosure application in terms of section 226 of the Tax Administration Act 28 of 2011? Purveyors South Africa Mine Service (Pty) Ltd v Commissioner: South African Revenue Service (61689/2019) [2020] ZAGPPHC 404 (25 August 2020). *Tydskrif vir Hedendaagse Romeins-Hollandse Reg*, 84(1):95–110.

Wachsmuth I & Salem M. 2014. Body movements in robotics. In Müller C, Cienki A, Fricke E, Ladewig S, McNeill D & Tessendorf S (eds.). *Body – Language – Communication. Volume 2. An international handbook on multimodality in human interaction*. Berlin: De Gruyter. 1943–1948.

Wallis M. 2019. Interpretation before and after *Natal Joint Municipal Pension Fund v Endumeni Municipality* 2012 4 SA 593 (SCA). *Potchefstroom Elektroniese Regsjoernaal*, 22:1–29. https://doi.org/10.17159/1727-3781/2019/v22i0a7416

Wardhaugh R & Fuller JM. 2015. *An introduction to sociolinguistics*. Malden: Wiley Blackwell.

Webb V. 2010. The politics of standardising Bantu languages in South Africa. *Language Matters*, 41(2):157–174. https://doi.org/10.1080/10228195.2010.500674

Wilson D. 2017. Relevance theory. In Huang Y (ed.) *The Oxford handbook of pragmatics*. Oxford: Oxford University Press. 79–101. https://doi.org/10.1093/oxfordhb/9780199697960.013.25

Winn P. 1996. Legal ritual. In Grimes RL (ed.) *Readings in ritual studies*. Upper Saddle River: Prentice-Hall. 552–565.

Yeung P. 2020. Why Sweden's gender neutral pronoun is a model to follow. *apolitical*, 19 June. Available online: https://apolitical.co/solution-articles/en/why-swedens-gender-neutral-pronoun-is-a-model-to-follow (accessed 25 Augustus 2022).

Yule G. 2020. *The study of language*. Cambridge: Cambridge University Press.

Yus F. 2015. Relevance theory. In Heine B & Narrog H (eds.) *The Oxford handbook of linguistic analysis*. Oxford: Oxford University Press. 641–663.

Zuckerman M, Amidon MD, Bishop SE & Pomerantz SD. 1982. Face and tone of voice in the communication of deception. *Journal of Personality and Social Psychology*, 43(2):347–357. https://doi.org/10.1037/0022-3514.43.2.347

Legislation cited

18 US Code Nr 924.

Arms and Ammunition Act 75 of 1969.

Cannabis for Private Purposes Bill B19 of 2020.

Carbon Tax Act 15 of 2019.

Children's Act 38 of 2005.

Constitution of the Republic of South Africa Act 108 of 1996.

Criminal Procedure Act 51 of 1977.

Customs and Excise Act 91 of 1964.

Diamond Export Levy (Administration) Act 14 of 2007.

Drugs and Drug Trafficking Act 140 of 1992.

Explosives Act 26 of 1956.

Extension of Security of Tenure Act 62 of 1997.

Financial Sector Regulation Act 9 of 2017.

Genetically Modified Organisms Act 15 of 1997.

Income Tax Act 58 of 1962.

Labour Relations Act 66 of 1995.

Marriage Act 25 of 1961.

Mineral and Petroleum Resources Royalty (Administration) Act 29 of 2008.

Prevention and Combating of Hate Crimes and Hate Speech Bill 9 of 2018.

Promotion of Equality and Prevention of Unfair Discrimination Act 4 of 2000.

Road Accident Fund Act 56 of 1996.

Road Traffic Act 7 of 1973.

Road Transportation Act 74 of 1977.

Securities Transfer Tax Administration Act 26 of 2007.

Skills Development Levies Act 9 of 1999.

Tax Administration Act 28 of 2011.

Tobacco Products Control Amendment Act 12 of 1999.

Trespass Act 6 of 1959.

Unemployment Insurance Act 4 of 2002.

Use of Official Languages Act 12 of 2012.

Value Added Tax Act 89 of 1991.

Witchcraft Suppression Act 3 of 1957.

Cases cited

ABC Mining (Pty) Ltd v Commissioner for the South African Revenue Service (IT24606) [2021] ZATC (25 February 2021).

Afriforum v Malema (18172/2010) [2010] ZAGPPHC 39.

ANC v Sparrow (01/16) [2016] ZAEQC 1 (10 June 2016). https://doi.org/10.1055/s-0035-1563914

Association of Amusement and Novelty Machine Operators v Minister of Justice 1980 (2) SA 636 (A).

Blue Circle Cement Ltd v Commissioner for Inland Revenue 1984 (2) SA 764 (A).

Cape Killarney Property Investments (Pty) Ltd v Mahamba 2000 (2) SA 67 (C).

Cargo Africa CC v Gilbeys Distillers and Vintners (Pty) Ltd 1998 (4) SA 355 (N).

CB v HB 2021 (6) SA 332 (SCA).

Commissioner for the South African Revenue Services v Daikin Air Conditioning South Africa (Pty) Ltd (185/2017) [2018] ZASCA 66 (25 May 2018).

Economic Freedom Fighters v Minister of Justice and Constitutional Development (87638/2016) [2019] ZAGPPHC 253.

Feldman v Midgin 2006 (6) SA 12 (SCA). https://doi.org/10.1016/S1365-6937(06)71108-X

Fish Hoek Primary School v GW 2010 (2) SA 141 (SCA).

Fundstrust (Pty) Ltd v Van Deventer 1997 (1) SA 710 (A).

Gordhan v Malema 2020 (1) SA 587 (GJ). https://doi.org/10.4236/oalib.1105971

Heroldt v Wills 2014 JOL 31479 (GSJ).

Herselman v Geleba (231/2009) [2011] ZAECGHC 108 (1 September 2011).

Isparta v Richter 2013 (6) SA 529 (GNP). https://doi.org/10.1007/978-3-642-20691-7_44

Jacobs v Waks 1992 (1) SA 521 (A).

Jonker v Davis 1953 (2) SA 726 (GW). https://doi.org/10.5694/j.1326-5377.1953.tb100415.x

Jowells Transport v South African Road Transportation Services 1986 (2) SA 252 (SWA).

Kiepersol Poultry Farm (Pty) Ltd v Phasiya 2010 (3) SA 152 (SCA).

Le Roux v Dey 2011 3 SA 274 (CC).

Lourens v President van die Republiek van Suid-Afrika (49807/09) [2010] ZAGPPHC 19.

Lueven Metals (Pty) Ltd v Commissioner for the South African Revenue Service (31356/2021) [2022] ZAGPPHC 325 (19 May 2022).

Manuel v Economic Freedom Fighters 2019 (5) SA 210 (GJ).

Masuku v South African Human Rights Commission 2019 (2) SA 194 (SCA).

Minister of Justice and Constitutional Development v Prince; National Director of Public Prosecutions v Rubin; National Director of Public Prosecutions v Acton [2018] ZACC 30.

Minister of Safety and Security v Xaba 2004 (1) SACR 149.

Natal Joint Municipal Pension Fund v Endumeni Municipality 2012 (4) SA 593 (SCA).

OLG Bamberg NJW 2008.

OLG Nürnberg NJW 2010.

Online Lottery Services (Pty) Ltd v National Lotteries Board 2010 (5) SA 349 (SCA).

Pieterse v Clicks Group Ltd 2015 (5) SA 317 (GJ).

Purveyors South Africa Mine Service (Pty) Ltd v Commissioner for the South African Revenue Service (611689/2019) [202] ZAGPPHC 409 (25 August 2020).

Purveyors South Africa Mine Services (Pty) Ltd v Commissioner for the South African Revenue Services (135/2021) [2021] ZASCA 170 (7 December 2021).

Qurashi v S (1166/2018) [2022] ZASCA 118 (22 August 2022).

Rustenburg Platinum Mine v SAEWA obo Bester [2016] ZALCJHB 75.

Rustenburg Platinum Mine v SAEWA obo Bester [2018] ZACC 13.

Ryan v Petrus 2010 (1) SACR 274 (ECG).

R v Dema 1947 (1) SA 599 (E).

R v Lucas [1998] 1 SCR 439 ((1998) 50 CRR (2nd) 69 (SCC)). https://doi.org/10.1023/A:1019042329841

S v Abrahams 2001 (2) SACR 266 (C). https://doi.org/10.1079/BJN19480047

S v Bresler 2002 (2) SACR 18 (C).

S v Collop 1981 (1) SA 150 (A).

S v Hoho 2009 (1) SACR 276 (SCA) (17 September 2008). https://doi.org/10.1007/BF03361829

S v Kohler 1979 (1) SA 861 (T). https://doi.org/10.3917/cris.861.0001

S v Kruse 2018 (2) SACR 644 (WCC).

S v Pistorius (CC113/2013) [2014] ZAGPPHC 793 (12 September 2014). https://doi.org/10.1038/nrmicro3386

S v Mafunisa 1986 (3) SA 495 (V).

S v Makhubela 1981 (4) SA 210 (B).

S v Mavungu 2009 (1) SACR 425 (T).

S v Mbatha 2012 (2) SACR 302 (N).

S v Molefe 2012 (2) SACR 574 (GNP).

S v Motsepe 2015 (2) SACR 125 (GP).

S v Ngubane 1995 (1) SACR 384 (T). https://doi.org/10.1038/nm0495-384

S v Shaik 2007 (1) SA 240 (SCA) (6 November 2006).

S v Tshabalala 1999 (1) SACR 412 (C).

S v Van der Merwe 2011 (2) SACR 509 (FB).

S v Visagie 2009 (2) SACR 70 (W).

SASRIA v Slabbert Burger Transport (Pty) Ltd 2008 (5) SA 270 (SCA).

Smith v US 508 US 223 (1993).

South African Airways (Pty) Ltd v Aviation Union of South Africa 2011 (3) SA 148 (SCA).

South African Human Rights Commission v Qwulane (EQ44/2009) [2017] ZAGPJHC 2018.

South African Human Rights Commission v Khumalo 2019 (1) SA 289 (GJ).

South Durban Community Environmental Alliance v Minister of Forestry, Fisheries and the Environment (17554/2021) [2022] ZAGPPHC 741 (6 October 2022).

Starways Trading 21 CC v Pearl Island Trading 714 (Pty) Ltd [2017] 4 All SA 568 (WCC).

Starways Trading 21 CC v Pearl Island Trading (Pty) Ltd, 2019 (2) SA 650 (SCA) (3 December 2018).

Stellenbosch Wine Trust Ltd v Oude Meester Group Ltd 1974 (1) SA 729 (A).

Tau v Mashaba 2020 (5) SA 135 (SCA).

The Road Accident Fund v Mbele 2020 (6) SA 118 (SCA).

Universal Church of the Kingdom of God v Myeni (DA 3/14) 2015 ZALAC 31 (28 July 2015).

Wells v Atoll Media (Pty) Ltd [2010] 4 All SA 548 (WCC).

Index

E

F

G

H

I

J

K

L

M

N

T

U

V

W

www.ingramcontent.com/pod-product-compliance
Lightning Source LLC
LaVergne TN
LVHW060837170826
845678LV00007B/1788

* 9 7 8 1 7 7 6 4 3 8 8 8 4 *